*The Dying Self*

# The Dying Self

By CHARLES M. FAIR

WESLEYAN UNIVERSITY PRESS
Middletown, Connecticut

# CONTENTS

*The Dying Self*

# FOREWORD

THIS book concerns the structure and working principles of human nature, primarily as inferred from a study of the brain (or "physiological psychology"). That account mostly has to do with the relations between the conscious, reasoning self or "I" and the nonconscious instinctive self or Id. It shows, I believe, more clearly than has been possible up to now, the connection between man's religiousness and his higher forms of achievement. It "explains" history in the sense of disclosing an underlying logic in events which modern historians would have us believe are largely outgrowths of chance. This is not to deny the enormous role which chance, in fact, plays in human affairs. What I have argued is the remarkable ability of human intelligence to adapt to it—to flow around the random obstacles of everyday life which we call circumstance and continue on its own peculiar course to its own objectives. The brain itself has this odd tenacity—can sustain great accidental damage, and a daily loss of thousands of neurons,[1] and still conserve its coherence of function, which is to say most of its intelligence.

More than half of what follows has to do with history and the nature of the religious impulse and is addressed not to an audience of specialists, but to those who feel, as I do, that self-understanding is *the* problem, given that we have entered an age increasingly dominated by the politics of mass cruelty. Having just put himself within reach of an immensely freer and more secure existence, man is now evidently about to forfeit it, either turning the world, through his sheer numbers, into a vast concentration camp, or precluding any imaginable future by nuclear massacre.

Nor is this squalid denouement made inevitable, as many seem to suppose, by the fixity of human nature, that is to say by biological

---

1. On the basis of post-mortem studies many neurologists believe that past the third decade or so of life we lose gradually increasing numbers of neurons per day. Since neurons, in the mature nervous system, do not divide, these losses, unlike those occurring elsewhere in the body, are not made up, but the effect on brain function, over several decades, is apparently slight.

determinism alone. It may also, as I shall try to convince you, be the result of a general psychic regression. That phenomenon, as it amounts to the abandonment of ground won only yesterday from the instincts, gives dismaying strength to the belief that man's position is inherently hopeless. Now that the Id is returning in force, we say that it never left. Now that the soul is dying again, we say that it never existed. Now that the odds are bad, we resign ourselves and make them worse. This book takes a somewhat different view. It says that the odds are indeed bad—worse even than we imagine—but that our situation is in no final sense beyond repair.

Part I (Chapters II–IV) presents a model of the self derived from physiological evidence and concepts. In these chapters I have tried to simplify a rather formidably complex subject, using a minimum of the usual jargon;—the point not being to educate the reader in detail but rather to leave him in possession of certain clear essentials. Those with an aversion to scientific discourse, even in this relatively undemanding form, can probably skim through Part I and still come out with enough to follow the line of reasoning in the remainder of the book.

Part II (Chapters V–IX) chiefly concerns history—particularly that of the past several centuries, up through the disturbing present. Here, there should be almost no problem of "readability," given some understanding of what has gone before and a freshman's knowledge of history itself. Unfortunately, however, I can claim no scientific respectability for the ideas presented in this second section. Historical evidence is mostly of a kind one would never accept in the laboratory or even in law; and because almost no era is homogeneous or wholly in step with itself, one can interpret it according to one's bias by stressing the facts which are "significant" and underplaying or ignoring the rest.

Nevertheless, there are certain tests which can be applied to the theory which I have outlined. It says that given the brains we have, the human psyche works according to certain ultimately physiological principles. Experiment can therefore decide their tenability, if not now, soon. Should they prove untenable, the remainder of the argument fails also. If, on the other hand, they are substantially correct, the historical conclusions to which I have supposed they lead may have to be taken seriously. The most important of these is that the religious impulse is not the simple compound of animal fears and wishful imagining which most of us now think it, but the result of a real need rooted in the physiology of man's brain and reflected in his least animal aspirations.

In Part II I have relied on many examples drawn from the arts since these, I think, far more than most popular or official beliefs, reveal the real drift of their time. They are prophetic in the sense of showing us the actual present. This is not to deny the value of sociological evidence or statistics. But the fact is that statistics concerning many matters one urgently needs to know about are not to be had; or when available, are not to be trusted.[2]

The method used in this section is a discursive one. I have deliberately moved from one "discipline" or type of discourse to another— from history to ethology to literature to the physiology of stress and back again—with the object of suggesting a system of logical relations between sets of events we do not ordinarily see as closely connected. In all of this work I have acted from a sense of urgency best defined by George Steiner in the preface to his book *Language and Silence*:

> My own consciousness is possessed by the eruption of barbarism in modern Europe. . . . This is the crisis of rational humane expectation which has shaped my own life. . . . It did not spring up in the Gobi desert. . . . It rose from within, and from the core of European civilization. The cry of the murdered sounded in earshot of the universities; the sadism went on a street away from the theaters and museums.[3]

In the decades since World War II there has been little to suggest that the "crisis of rational humane expectation" ended with the Nazis. On the contrary, the Germans, with their usual odd mixture of literalness and virtuosity, may have anticipated us.

2. For example, statistics collected over the past hundred years which purport to show major differences in brain weight or structure among the races of man. Most of these, but not quite all, turn out to be exercises in corroborated prejudice. See the masterly review given by P. Bailey and G. von Bonin in *The Isocortex of Man* (University of Illinois Press, 1951).

3. Atheneum, 1967, p. viii.

*Chapter I*

---

## ARE THERE HISTORICAL CYCLES?

THE question of whether history is "cyclical" is really better put another way. Are civilizations in some sense definable entities? If so, and if, without exception, they "decay" after a certain period of sustained achievement, in what does that process consist and why does it invariably set in? Is one justified in describing history in these terms at all? The majority of professional historians would say not. Ved Mehta classes the latter as follows:

> Metaphysically inclined thinkers, like Marx, Spengler, and Toynbee (plum-cake historians), have had a large, all-embracing explanation of history—why things happen as they do—which they demonstrate with a nod now and again to examples. The professional academics (dry-biscuit historians), like R. H. Tawney and Sir Lewis Namier, respectively, detect causal connections between religion and capitalism, or between Parliament and the self-interest of the M.P.s, or, like A. J. P. Taylor, notice a discrepancy between an intention and an action, and then arrive at small theories—why particular things happen at a particular time—which they substantiate with analysis, illustrate with exhaustive examples, or prove, however obliquely or indirectly, by a sustained narrative of events.[1]

A third group comprises narrative (or "shortbread") historians like G. M. Trevelyan or Miss C. V. Wedgwood. At the moment it is probably safe to say that the dry-biscuit group are in the ascendant. In outlook and methods, they rather closely parallel the piecemeal-analytic approach of the sciences. They insist, with some justification, that Toynbee and Spengler worked from inadequate evidence or forced what evidence they had. For their part, the professional academics appear to be committed to the proposition that history cannot be expected to have a grand

---

1. *The New Yorker*, December 15, 1962, p. 47.

form, since any such expectation carries connotations which are unsound and lure one into further error. One may begin talking about Destiny (as Spengler did) or giving undue importance to ideas, as against economics or geography, as determinants of the larger course of events, and perhaps end up, like Toynbee, detecting some hint of *meaning* in human history. (Spengler found none.)

The dry-biscuit historians are, in fact, at only a slight remove from those whose view of man is biological, out and out—writers like Coon[2] or the converted playwright Robert Ardrey,[3] to whom history is simply a by-product of man's efforts at collective adaptation. On the part of such writers, there is always a tendency to reduce human behavior to its primitive essentials, to stress the role of innate mechanisms or "instinct," to see, as Freud did, the less interested forms of human aspiration as only primal motives in disguise. This inclination to simplify and, as it were, bestialize ourselves is widespread in modern thought and seems to have an increasing counterpart in modern behavior. It is believed to be "scientific": a sacrifice of illusions in favor of hard fact. Apart from whether that is really the case, it is apparent that we live in an age in which large-scale theoretical systems are out of favor, partly for good reason; and in the same period we have seemingly turned a negative asset—want of imagination—into a positive one, namely, extreme rigor.[4] It is only natural, given a mind which sees trees clearly and the woods hardly at all, to say that the woods really do not exist. Scientists put this theorem another way. They say the woods may exist, but that debate on the matter is a waste of time because the question is not "operational." Unlike trees, woods often have fuzzy boundaries and present other troublesome problems in definition. In this spirit, neobehaviorists and "physiological psychologists" tend to ignore the so-called mind-brain problem. Their view is that one can usefully study the brain or analyze the behavior "emitted" by the organism. Provided we amass enough information of this sort, the problem of mind may solve (obviate) itself. To talk about mind, on the other hand, is to talk about an entity which really is not one; it is to "reify" or give purely verbal unity to a bundle of miscellaneous functions: that is, the trees are real, but the woods illusory.

2. C. S. Coon, *The Origin of Races* (Knopf, 1962).
3. Robert Ardrey, *African Genesis* (Atheneum, 1961).
4. See J. L. Synge, *Science: Sense and Nonsense* (Jonathan Cape, 1951). p. 77.

Historians of the Lewis Namier–A. J. P. Taylor school seem to have adopted essentially the same stratagem. The concept of a "culture" or high civilization in the Spenglerian or Toynbeean sense appears to be as alien to them as is the concept of mind to physiological psychologists. The implication is that had we been clearheaded and scientific from the outset, notions such as mind or civilization (meaning particular civilizations, each with an outlook and art forms and customs in some degree peculiar to itself) would never have arisen. The question is, is this attitude justified? I happen to think it is not and will briefly try to explain why.

If one considers physical nature from the level of subatomic particles to that of astronomical systems, it is evident that we have been forced to devise very different theories to account for events occurring on these various scales. The assumption that electrons are tiny billiard balls cannot, it turns out, lead to a tenable theory of how electrons behave. The forces which hold the planets in their orbits are too small by many powers of ten to account for the cohesion of particles making up atomic nuclei.[5] Bodies of everyday size do not show frictionless recoil, whereas the particles making up a volume of gas must be supposed to do so. When atoms are brought together, they may interact according to the principles of chemistry to form compounds. When further aggregations of certain compounds occur, as is believed to have happened under conditions prevailing in early geologic time on earth, there results a variety of self-replicating systems, governed by still other principles, those of physiology. It is clear that all these realms are interlocked and that in time certain of them are anterior to others. The physical earth was present very probably long before the elements of life coalesced to become living things. Planetary and intergalactic matter may have been flung from the furnace of suns, whose primordial constituent may have been hydrogen, and whose primordial function, as it were, the manufacture of the heavier elements.

Regardless of the order in which nature, as we now find it, may have assembled itself, one principle seems clear. It is that the bringing together of large numbers of units having many properties in common may not result simply in a heap, whose properties are those of the units summed or multiplied. The properties of the chemical elements or their com-

---

5. John Cockcroft, in *Nature*, Vol. 168, No. 4286 (December 22, 1951), p. 1060.

pounds—that is, of everyday matter—are distinct from those of elementary particles, though the two are of course related, and quantum principles apply to both. Bohr devised his Correspondence Principle to reconcile the domains of particle and large-body physics, not so much, perhaps, because existing theories needed patching up, as because of the inhomogeneity of the real world. A famous chemist has said that, given the substances present and the physical conditions prevailing at the end of the Azoic period on earth, the appearance of living things was "virtually . . . inevitable."[6] Possibly so; the question is, could an observer standing at that point in time and familiar only with the properties of compounds up to the level of complexity, say, of proteinoids[7] have predicted that biological evolution would then occur—or later have inferred the "properties" of man from those of his much simpler forerunners? At the risk of contradicting a Nobel laureate, I rather doubt it.

The point is that nature appears to have what one might call a laminated structure. The aggregation of units of one "layer"—for instance, the subatomic—may give rise to a second, whose units or component systems have properties radically different from those characteristic of the first. A similar process of aggregation and transformation of properties may result in addition of a third "layer," a fourth, an $n$th. The sciences have with remarkable success defined many of the constituents of these various layers and have also, in certain cases, shown a kind of logical continuity between one layer and another (*vide* the Correspondence Principle, just mentioned). It is not surprising that they have been less successful in the latter attempt, since the problem is inherently more difficult. In my youth, there was keen interest in the question of what distinguishes living from nonliving matter. More recently, rapid progress in study of the brain has to a slight degree revived interest in the mind-brain problem. At bottom these are questions of the same kind. Both ask how, given building blocks of such and such characteristics, it is possible to end up with structures whose properties are, as it were, so unexpected. The pragmatic answer is simply that it occurs. The properties of the ultimate components of physical nature—protons, mesons, and the like—are such that they tend

6. Dr. Melvin Calvin, in New York *Sunday Times,* November 16, 1958.
7. See Chapter III, footnote 8.

to combine in certain configurations. The resulting second-order systems themselves tend to combine to generate a third order, and so on. What defines these metasystems as such is the new features they exhibit (new, if one regard their constituents as also their precursors in time, and the whole of reality as, in this sense, evolutionary. Under this view, biological evolution becomes a special case of a much more general phenomenon which one might call emergent nature).

If nature or "reality" does actually elaborate itself according to some such principle, it would seem unwise to set upper limits to the process. For purely practical reasons, scientists are obliged to disregard large classes of phenomena. It is one thing, however, to say that a given domain of nature cannot be explored with the methods at present available, and another to dismiss it as not really existent. One of the less attractive consequences of the prestige of science has been a kind of highhandedness, particularly on the part of those scientists whose success in the laboratory has caused them to live beyond their intellectual means outside of it.

Because "mind" or the rational conscious "I" of man presents great difficulties in definition or experimental manipulation, the tendency among scientists is to dismiss it as a verbalism. Freud was at some pains to show that the "ego" was no more than an arbiter between the machine-like Id and the almost equally mechanical superego. The current fashion is likewise to see no decisive transition between animal and human intelligence; that is, man has *more* intelligence than other species, but it is assumed that in us there has been no radical qualitative change in brain functions or psychic structure. A considerable body of evidence suggests that this idea is nonsense.

Like "mind," the concept of distinct cultures or civilizations presents great difficulties. Unless isolated and small, civilizations are apt to have fuzzy boundaries and to be inhomogeneous within their vague limits. Unlike organisms, they are not born at a precise place and time, nor do they die in any clear-cut way. Some disintegrate, like the late classical, under successive barbarian incursions. Alternatively, they may outlive their period of real growth by some centuries and in time be transformed or absorbed into others, as seems to be occurring in modern China and Japan. For all that, it may be incorrect to say that civilizations do not have distinct existence—that there is only "civilization," as there are societies of bees or chickens. While the latter are in some degree plastic—that is, responsive to the demands of the environment—there appear to be no animal societies which have religions or traditions. Julian Huxley has referred to tradition as "a second method of heredity based on the transmission of experience";[8] and it is worth noting that the process is cumulative, that traditions differ considerably from one another, and that more is transmitted by each than mere practical know-how.

The distinctive feature of human intelligence seems to be that it is self-acting to a degree not even approached in the animal world. It can work sustainedly in symbols and has, to that end, produced verbal and mathematical languages which have only the faintest equivalents in the dances of bees or the whistles of dolphins. It is difficult to escape the impression that with the appearance of Homo sapiens, a break or epochal change has occurred in the evolutionary process. Whereas up to man, only *more* intelligence of the same basic kind had been added, with man, a further expansion of the brain may suddenly have made possible a new mental "entity," the rational conscious self. Its potential degrees of freedom so far exceeded those of animal intelligence that they ultimately gave rise to the new and greatly accelerated form of evolution which we call history.

Some years ago, at a conference of neurophysiologists and similar scientists, one of the participants asked: "Is the element of subjectivity necessary to what the brain performs? In other words, is it necessary, say, in the morning, when I'm looking in the mirror and shaving? Couldn't the brain do all that by itself? Why do I have to be there?"[9] By implication, this question concedes the existence of the rational conscious self or "mind" (which in turn recalls Carlyle's reply to Margaret Fuller[10]). My own view, as is probably clear by now, is that with man two new "layers" may have been added to living nature: that of the more or less individuated waking conscious self of men severally and that of more or less distinct cultural realms, or civilizations, produced by men collectively.

If one grant this proposition—and many would not—the question

8. Julian Huxley, in *Perspectives in Biology and Medicine*, Vol. 8. No. 4 (1964), p. 410.

9. Paul MacLean, in *Transactions of the Second Conference on the Central Nervous System* (Josiah Macy, Jr. Foundation, 1959), p. 268.

10. Fuller: "I accept the universe." Carlyle: "By God she'd better."

arises as to whether civilizations do roughly have a certain life expectancy or probable span of true growth, as the historiographers have said. Neither Spengler nor Toynbee—and least of all Sorokin—showed *why* it was that civilizations tended to decline in late pragmatic middle age, or after a term of a thousand to fifteen hundred years. All one can say is that it seems to have occurred, and not once, but repeatedly. The vague unity of religious beliefs, art forms, and works of intellect and polity, which made up the civilizations of ancient Egypt, of Sumer and its successors, of India before the Moguls, of Achaemenid and Sassanid Persia, of Yucatan, of China before Shih Huang Ti, of the Classical and Byzantine worlds, all in time melted away. Those societies which, unlike the Classical, lived on side by side with younger contemporaries—for instance, Islam or colonial India or China of the Manchus—appear to have done so in a much enfeebled or fossilized state, in which corruption and inflexible custom had for centuries precluded further real advance and men tended, en masse, to take refuge in drugs or in religions of the "annihilation of consciousness."[11] In short, civilizations may not be superseded by conquest alone. The essential change which makes them vulnerable to alien arms or (like modern China) to alien example may depend on interior forces, which is to say, on psychological "laws" or principles not yet clearly understood. Almost by accident, my own work on the human brain[12] suggested what some of these principles might be. I believe, in other words, that history *is* in a rough way "cyclical" and that this phenomenon has its origins not in destiny but in man's given nature, which, to the degree that it is alterable, is not destiny but circumstance. The point is of more than academic interest, since the signs seem to be that our own civilization is well on into its pragmatic middle age and may already, as others before it have done, be losing those intangibles of character and intellect to which it owes its existence.

11. The phrase was used by Spengler to describe the disciplines of modern Yoga and Buddhism or that of the Stoics of late Classical times.

12. In part published under the title of *The Physical Foundations of the Psyche* (Wesleyan, 1963).

PART I *A Primer of Mind-Brain Relations*

*Chapter II*

---

## WHAT THE ORGANIZATION OF THE BRAIN TELLS US ABOUT THE "SELF"

IN vertebrates from the fishes up to man the basic plan of the brain is remarkably similar, as are the form and behavior of individual neurons.[1] Over the course of vertebrate evolution, the tendency has apparently been for the final controlling "centers" to move forward—or as anatomists say, rostrally—from the midbrain in fish and amphibians to the forebrain in mammals. With mammals, the principal new brain structure to appear is the so-called cortex, or outer mantle. This mantle spreads so as to cover most of the earlier evolved portions of the hemispheres, which are often therefore referred to as "subcortical." Some, but not all, comparative anatomists believe that the mammalian "cortex" (its correct name is neocortex) arose from the balloonlike expansion of a small portion of the reptilian hemisphere known as general pallium (pallium = mantle).

Most of us know, in a vague way, that the ultimate functional unit in nervous systems is the neuron, which can either be excited to "fire" by the firing of other neurons whose fibers reach it or inhibited by them and so made temporarily inactive. The actual mechanics of nervous activity is far more complex than this and still imperfectly understood. It is estimated that in human cortex alone there are some five to seven billions of neurons[2] and perhaps ten billions or $10^{10}$ neurons in the brain as a whole. The cortex is parceled out into fairly sharply defined regions, some evidently concerned in primary sense reception, some in the execution of actions, some in the recall (that is, the recording) of words, some in the organization of words into sentences, and so on.

1. To physiologists, the term *nerve* usually means a bundle of nerve-fibers; for instance, the optic nerve. The single nerve is usually called a neuron.
2. D. A. Sholl, *The Organization of the Cerebral Cortex* (Wiley, 1956), pp. 35–36.

The subcortical parts of the brain resolve into a bewildering assortment of subsystems (the neocortex is itself a subsystem, divisible into subsubsystems). The structure and connections of these have taken decades to work out, and the task is far from complete. We do, however, have enough evidence to form a fairly clear idea of the general plan on which central nervous functions are departmentalized in mammals, and from that plan certain important inferences about our given natures can, I think, be drawn.

The interrelations of subsystems of the brain are roughly like those of individual neurons. A given subsystem may activate another to which it "projects" (sends fibers); on other occasions, or when other parts of it are stimulated, it may inhibit the second system. Frequently the influence of one subsystem on another is a mixture of activation and inhibition. Frequently, also, such influence is reciprocal between subsystems. It is thought, on the basis of painstakingly accumulated data, that various subsystems or nuclei "represent" certain functions—for instance, that they control or initiate particular vegetative activities (digestion, circulation, and the like) or the activity of striped muscle, which is to say overt behavior. It would serve no purpose to go into the known details of these arrangements.

The essential points concerning brain organization appear to be these. First, as new structures have developed in the nervous system, they have in general supplemented but not supplanted those older structures in which corresponding functions are "represented." Second, the reciprocal connections or feed-back loops which are found throughout the nervous system may serve to do two things: to reconcile, or establish a kind of functional consistency between, the outputs of subsystems connected in this way, and to set limits to the control which any one subsystem can exert (for instance, by inhibition) over others. Third, as new systems have been added to the brain, they have not merely reduplicated or amplified functions represented elsewhere. A shift, as it were, in emphasis seems also to have occurred. The most striking of these shifts is the one which apparently followed upon the appearance of the cortex, or new mantle (neopallium), in mammals. In the analysis which follows, I shall deal mainly with the relations which seem to exist between the cortex and the remainder of the brain, called here simply the "subcortical" part (or "subcortical systems").

In everyday speech we distinguish "thinking" from "feeling" and learned parts of behavior from "instinctive" parts. What we mean by "feeling"[3] analyzes into "motives" or "drives" (some of which may be "instinctive" and some, apparently, acquired) and "emotions" or "moods." A mood is an emotional state often milder and more lingering than, say, a state of rage, which tends to preclude unrelated thoughts and come promptly to a head in action. In an earlier book I suggested that what we call emotion arises in general when a drive or motive is denied ready expression as behavior, emotion reinforcing the original drive and impelling the organism to acts which may in fact be quite dangerous and inappropriate.

A considerable body of experimental evidence implies that with the evolution of the mammalian brain, a gradual separation of cognitive and related memory functions from "instinctive" or "motivational-emotional" functions has occurred. This is the shift in emphasis referred to above, and it applies in particular to the cortex vis-à-vis subcortical systems. It means that in man, memory and cognitive activities are more highly developed in the cortex than elsewhere, whereas the "representation" of motives or basal drives, while not lacking in the cortex, is much more limited there than elsewhere. The converse applies to certain subcortical systems. These evidently play a major role in generating basic drive states or emotions and do not approach the cortex in their capacity for precise learning or the precise remolding of behavior.

The evidence for these statements is fairly good. By removing the cortex or temporarily inactivating it by application of a solution of potassium chloride, one can produce animals whose learning capacity or ability to perform learned actions is greatly reduced or abolished. With the exception of certain parts of the cortex—for instance, the so-called "strip" regions or the "pole" of the temporal lobe—stimulation of this system in man or animals does not produce marked "motivational" effects.

In subcortical parts of the brain, on the other hand, there are many sites at which electrical stimulation seems to be intensely pleasurable or intensely "punishing." Experiments of this kind have been carried out both in animals and in man. With animals, the procedure often used is to arrange the stimulating circuit so that the animal can trigger input to its own brain by pressing a lever. Using this arrangement, investiga-

---

3. In the sense of feelings, as distinct from sensation.

tors have found that animals will in general stimulate themselves at much higher rates in older, more posteriorly situated portions of the brain. Likewise, stimuli delivered to punishment sites there seem more violently unpleasant to the animal than is stimulation of such sites in systems lying further forward—that is, "newer" subcortical structures such as those comprising the so-called olfactory brain or rhinencephalon. The olfactory brain, which comprises the bulk of the cerebral hemisphere in the frog, is in mammals covered over and rolled under by the tremendous expansion of the cortex. Simultaneously with these changes, it seems to have undergone a kind of despecialization, so that many parts of it now concern "motivation" or emotion rather than olfaction proper.[4]

Certain parts of the cortex, notably the temporal lobe, are subject to important influxes from subcortical systems. In man, the temporal lobe is seemingly indispensable to the formation of lasting memories; for instance, of words. It is a matter of common knowledge that we most readily commit to memory things which are in some way connected with an intense drive state or emotion. When our motives for learning are relatively mild ones, learning itself may depend heavily on rehearsal or practice. It is easy to forget the face of someone met casually. The same face, seen when one is in a state of extreme terror or rage, may become engraved in one's memory for life, even though the whole "take" may have lasted no more than a few seconds and never have been repeated. Conversely, the tendency of lasting memories, when reactivated in the present, is to recreate something of the emotional climate in which they were originally formed. These facts of human experience appear to have clear parallels both in animal conditioning and in the mode of organization of the cortical memory systems.

Stimulating temporal cortex in epileptics, Penfield[5] evoked very vivid memories, including their emotional "auras." To date no comparable effects have been reported from stimulating elsewhere in the cortex (nor, it should be noted, have they been obtained from the temporal lobes of nonepileptics or from more than a few of Penfield's patients). A variety of other evidence suggests that the temporal lobes may be uniquely important in the formation of lasting recollections. This part

4. C. J. Herrick, *The Brain of the Tiger Salamander* (University of Chicago Press, 1948), p. 99.
5. Wilder Penfield, in *Science,* Vol. 129 (1959), pp. 1719–1725.

of the outer mantle receives a fiber system (or impulses) from, and sends fibers (or impulses) to, important subcortical structures comprising a part of the despecialized olfactory brain mentioned above. When one of these structures, called the hippocampus, is destroyed on both sides in man, he can no longer form memories lasting more than ten or twelve minutes, although most of those formed before operation are not affected. In other words, we may have, in the pathway just described, a major mechanism by which emotional or drive states give the cortex orders as to what to print. Similarly, what is already "printed," when "read out," may tend to revive the motives or emotions which caused it to be printed in the first place, inasmuch as the temporal lobe sends fibers *to* the same subcortical systems that it receives fibers from. (It also projects to others; for instance, in the midbrain.)

A recent study[6] seems to show that when a cat is learning a response to obtain food, subcortical electrical activity leads, or partially gives rise to, activity in the temporal lobe: whereas when the animal has learned the response, temporal-lobe activity leads that in the same subcortical systems. In other words, during conditioning, older brain structures may be determining what newer ones commit to memory. Conversely, when conditioning is complete, newer brain structures embodying memories may determine which older brain structures shall be most active or influential in that particular bit of learned behavior. In the first case, a drive state may be establishing certain memories; in the second, the memories now established may be reactivating or reinforcing the original drive.

The reason for describing these mechanisms at length is that in them we may have a model for certain basic psychological relationships. We ordinarily conceive of the self as divided into two principal parts: that which is conscious, which thinks and remembers and "wills" on the basis of reason, and that which is below and only indirectly accessible to "consciousness," generating feelings and adaptive drives and causing us to "will" in the prerational animal sense. The latter is roughly what Freud called the Id, and the former roughly the ego. It is clear that the former has only a qualified independence. Drives and feeling states may profoundly influence the course taken in the present by conscious thought; they also have a more profound or anterior influence in that they will

6. See W. R. Adey, *Brain Mechanisms and Learning,* ed. by A. Fessard, *et al.* (Oxford: Blackwell, 1961), pp. 577–588.

have determined, to a considerable extent, the materials *available* for thought in the present.

One need not labor the point that memory, quite possibly including memories not directly available to conscious inspection, plays an enormous part in deciding the directions taken by our thought, not to mention its comprehensiveness or validity. Whitehead remarked that "when memory and anticipation are completely absent, there is complete conformity to the average influence of the immediate past. . . . Such a situation produces the activity of mere matter. . . . Thus the universe is material in proportion to the restriction of memory and anticipation."[7] It is therefore of great importance that the Id, as both psychological and physiological evidence seems to show, is a major force in deciding *what* we shall lastingly recall.

From the biological standpoint, the meaning of this arrangement is clear enough. It is that as "higher" centers have been added to the brain, the connections between these and "lower" ones have been such as to guarantee that most of what the organism recalls or "thinks about" is related in some way to its basic needs. As a nineteenth-century writer might have put it, the course followed by the evolution of the vertebrate brain has been conservative, in that it has continued to guarantee "instinct" a measure of both direct and indirect control over the actions of "mind." The crucial question for man is not whether this statement applies to him. It clearly does apply, the question being how strictly? Is all that we do or think ultimately adaptive, and is our freedom (either internally in imagination or externally in daily fact) as limited in this sense as that of other living things? Is mind after all a captive faculty, like a bird which flies on an invisible tether? Are we at bottom animals, without the possibility of what Camus[8] calls transcendence? For more than seventy-five years, Western thought has tended toward that conclusion. It is implicit in Freud, in Watson and Loeb and the neobehaviorists, in the ideologies of the far Left and Right, in the hardrock businessman's view of human relations; even, by an oblique logic, in Carnap and Bridgman. For all its massive consequences in our daily life, the conclusion itself may be incorrect. The demonstration of this point turns on an analysis of the relations between the cortex and subcortical sys-

7. A. N. Whitehead, *Essays in Science and Philosophy* (Philosophical Library, 1948), p. 70.
8. Albert Camus, *The Rebel* (Vintage, 1956), pp. 135 and *passim*.

tems and the parallels which these may have in the structure of the human self, or psyche.

Physiologists, when speaking of the nervous system, often use the concept of functional dominance. Given certain signs, one infers that the sympathetic or parasympathetic branch of the autonomic system is "dominant"—that is, measurably more active than the other. Between brain structures, very complex dominance relations, sometimes one-way, sometimes reversible, have been shown experimentally. The basic drift of evolution has been toward centralization in the nervous system. The control of functions such as locomotion has migrated from semi-autonomous nuclei deployed in linear arrays (as in the spine of vertebrates or the ventral ganglionic chain of invertebrates) into a compact set of master ganglia, or brain. Thus in the mantis, a relatively primitive insect, cutting of the nerve cord just behind the head (which includes the "brain" and the subesophageal ganglion) abolishes spontaneous walking, though the insect can still right itself and walk a step or two if pushed. In the head proper, if only the "highest" structure—the brain or ganglion above the esophagus—is removed, the insect walks continuously, no matter what it runs into.[9] From these and other experiments, it seems that the "lower" part—the ganglion below the esophagus—generates a "forward command," while the "higher" part exerts an inhibitory control over this system, generating, for instance "turning commands," by slowing the legs on one side.

Very similar relationships are found between "old" and "new" (or "lower" and "higher") parts of the mammalian brain. In a rough way one can say that older, lower parts tend to generate forward commands or actions of a crude kind, while newer higher ones tend to inhibit these or else to carve more complex, appropriate actions out of them. Because higher brain structures *are* more complex in organization and apparently have fewer built-in response mechanisms, the processing of sensory information may often take longer in them than it does at lower levels. One purpose served by the highly developed inhibitory functions of such higher structures may therefore be to give the organism time to size up its situation and shape its actions accordingly. (Herrick and, before him, Coghill called this the "regarding reaction.") Provided the delay is not too long, the result may be behavior which is better "in-

9. K. D. Roeder, *Nerve Cells and Insect Behavior* (Harvard, 1963), pp. 150 ff.

formed" or more precisely suited to the occasion than might have been the case had the organism responded more promptly by reflex.

The foregoing means, then, that the mammalian cortex stands in a somewhat paradoxical relationship to the older subcortical systems. For the sake of argument, let us assume that in man the latter represent the Id, or instinctive self, whereas the cortex is the seat of those activities which are essential to, or largely constitute, the rational conscious self. As already noted, the stores of memory available to that self are vital in that they determine the kind and extent of our perspective on present experience. Given any set of sense data, we can act effectively in a rational sense in proportion as we can promptly infer what those data mean. Seeing "façade," we infer house; or tire tracks, we infer "car." Each time that we perceive our surround, a large percentage of what we seem directly to apprehend is in fact supplied by a process of automatic inference based upon prior experience, or memory. However, as noted above, subcortical systems, perhaps equivalent to the Id and therefore embodying a relatively primitive and inflexible logic, may from the outset of life play a major role in selecting *what* we store in memory. Similarly, since the cortex concerned has two-way connections with these subcortical systems, reactivation of any such memory in the present is apt to reinstate the drive or emotion which led to its formation in the first place. Such a drive or emotion may then give a direction to thought and behavior in the present which is not in fact rational or even suitable in purely adaptive terms. It is at this juncture that the power of the cortex to control older, lower systems becomes crucial. If its influence prevails and subcortical systems embodying the Id are held in check, flexible, rationally appropriate thought and action may result. If its influence does not prevail, the reverse may occur both behaviorally and in terms of brain events. That is, the cortex may be driven and disorganized or inhibited and functionally paralyzed from below and so play a minor role in determining behavior. In proportion as that occurs, thought may disintegrate and action become crude, violent, and unmindful of precedents or consequences.

In other words, the cortex and subcortical systems may compete for virtual control of the organism, the psychic parallel of this relationship in man being the perpetual contest between reason and impulse. How universal this contest is, how important, and how uncertain in its day-to-day outcome is shown by the variety of ways in which men have described it. In many of the great religions, achievement of a lasting victory over the Id or subrational adaptive self is seen as *the* problem.[10] What is at stake is not merely man's aptitude in practical self-management but something far subtler and more far-reaching. The issue at bottom is one of freedom. Given the adaptive necessities—that is, when relieved of the extreme pressure of circumstance—can man then go on to become free of the constraints automatically imposed on his thought, imagination, and feelings by the apparatus of "instinct" inside him? Most people to-day would say that he cannot. Why then has the question even come up in human thought? The very fact that it has, that man stands, in some way, apart from his adaptive-instinctive self, feels it as alien, and has devoted much effort to mastering it, suggests that such mastery is at least a dim possibility. So far as we can tell, nothing comparable to this struggle occurs even in our closest primate relatives, let alone in other mammals or in creatures belonging to other phyla. Such as it is, the evidence implies that animals have an interior unity that we do not. In them, the neocortex is an adjunct of subcortical systems in the sense that apparently its operations seldom run counter to those of the latter. To the extent that in man these two divisions of the brain have become functionally differentiated from each other through intense conflict (that is, competition for control of each other and hence of behavior), the higher one, the neocortex, may have come to "look" at the other, or to "represent" it, as a problem of the same order as those arising in the external environment. The psychological parallel is man's unique aware-ness not only of himself[11] but of parts of his own nature as *other* than himself.

To understand how this decisive inner change may have come about, it is necessary to consider further the organization of memory functions, since it may be through these that man cumulatively gains control not only over his surround but also over those primal interior forces which we traditionally regard as reason's most formidable competitor.

10. It is frequently *the* problem in psychotherapy as well.

11. And the less intelligent or socially privileged the man—that is, the less developed psychologically—the more he approaches the unself-consciousness of animals.

## Chapter III

---

## THE ORIGINS OF THE "I"

THE "interior unity" of animals, mentioned in the last chapter, might be attributed to the fact that in them the cortex (= neocortex) does not seriously compete with older brain structure for control of behavior. In mammals up to man, the cortex seems to be in the nature of an auxiliary, which contributes to the functioning of older subcortical systems by refining and further processing essentially the same sensory information. It remains under the control of these older systems, in that what it records in "permanent" memory may in effect be selected by them. Likewise, what it "attends to" may largely be determined from below (that is, subcortically). In general, in other words, an animal looks hardest at and is most apt to commit to memory the things which in some fairly direct way relate to its biological welfare.

However, the cortex is not a passive system, inactive unless called upon. Like the rest of the brain, it shows continuous electrical activity. The metabolic rate of its neurons is high. Moreover, it has its own command system, the pyramidal tract, by which it can send orders to the muscles responsible for overt actions.[1] From the platypus and opossum up to man, it shows a steady increase in both relative and absolute size. In man its total neuronal population is larger than in any other mammal, with a few exceptions such as the dolphin;[2] and both in numbers of neurons and in the degree of organization of these it may far exceed subcortical structures, with the possible exception of the cerebellum.[3]

1. It is important that only in primates does this system become what one might call a direct one. See H. G. J. M. Kuypers *et al.*, in *Science*, Vol. 132 (1960), pp. 38–40.

2. See John Lilly, in *The Central Nervous System and Behavior*, Trans., 2nd Conf. (Josiah Macy Jr. Foundation, 1959), p. 80.

3. Recent estimates by Braitenberg place the total of cerebellar "granule" cells alone at over $10^{10}$. However, the fine structure of the cerebellum is quite stereotyped. Its "old" and "new" divisions cannot be distinguished by their cellular

With the expansion of neocortex, one can imagine that two sorts of change in internal brain relations, and hence in behavior, occur. The first sort is gradual, consisting in a progressive refinement and amplification of adaptive actions as the neocortex comes to exert more and more influence on subcortical systems once solely responsible for such actions. This amounts to saying that if in the brain one of two subsystems which are reciprocally connected increases relative to the other in size and degree of internal organization, its probability of becoming the dominant system in the pair also increases. Here I should underscore a point made in the last chapter: namely, that in nervous systems one does not find the fixity of "dominance" relations or chains of command which exist in most machines. In the brain, as in the spinal cord, the tendency appears to be for various centers to "take turn about"[4] in the control of behavior and vegetative functions. All I am saying, then, is that the neocortex may be dominant more of the time, and possibly over more functions, the larger it becomes. This says nothing about the "interior unity" of the brain (hence of the "self") which may, and in fact apparently does, remain intact in most mammals under ordinary conditions. Though the cortex is new, as its full name (neocortex) implies, only marginal novelties appear in creature behavior until the arrival of man. With man, the second sort of change mentioned above may begin—a change in which the ancient unity or "functional unanimity" of the brain is at last radically disrupted. Not only is the balance of power shifted still further in favor of the neocortex but, as I will shortly try to show, a new functional system may take shape within the cortex itself—one whose logic and behavioral commands can be diametrically at odds with those typical of the subcortical systems.

One can see signs perhaps forecasting this change in the behavior of mammals whose brains approach ours in evolutionary development. While most of what most animals do relates in some way to their survival or procreation, the "higher" the animal, the more its behavior tends to deviate from this strict practicality; for instance, into play or

architecture—contrary to what one finds in forebrain cortex—and photomicrographs of, say, cat and human cerebellar tissue look much the same. V. Braitenberg and R. P. Atwood, in *Journal of Comparative Neurology*, Vol. 109 (1958), pp. 1–33.

4. The phrase was used by C. S. Sherrington, speaking of the tendency of one spinal reflex to be succeeded by another. See his *Integrative Action of the Nervous System* (Yale, 1961), p. 223.

into actions prompted by curiosity. Play has been interpreted as a preparation for adult life. The odd thing is that it often continues *into* adult
life. Wild otters and porpoises for instance, are evidently quite playful.
So far as I know, the same is not true of reptiles of any age, of relatively
intelligent invertebrates such as the octopus, or of most species of birds.
The usefulness of play to creatures which must learn much of their
hunting or mating behavior is obvious. To explain its persistence in
grown animals, one must conclude either that these need continual
refresher courses in the tactics of survival (which seems unlikely, life
in the wild being what it is) or else that play results from a combination
of free time and free central nervous energy (*free* here used in the sense
of *surplus, uncommitted*). That is, the improvements in brain function
which have made otters and porpoises highly efficient in the basic tasks
of life may likewise have given these animals an excess of organized
central nervous activity which manifests itself in playfulness or, under
other circumstances, in what we call curiosity. Conversely, it seems to be
roughly true that the less playful animals tend also to be the more incurious.

Granted that the foregoing may be facts and correctly interpreted, it
is still probable that no basic or decisive change in the workings of the
mammalian brain occurs prior to man. It would appear that behavior
on the "conditioning" model predominates in prehuman creatures. The
"unconditioned stimulus"—that is, an event to which the animal innately
responds—may act to fix an immediately preceding stimulus in its
memory. This last may then become the "conditioned stimulus" which,
when presented, will cause the animal to act as if it anticipated the unconditioned stimulus, or as if the latter had already been given.

There is much evidence to suggest that innate responses—responses
to unconditioned stimuli—are mainly subcortical, whereas the recording
of conditioned stimuli in memory, and the elaboration of behavior based,
say, on complex pattern discrimination, may depend more heavily on
the cortex. In terms of the simplified model given in the last chapter,
one might say that in animals, not only what the cortex records, but the
logical operations it performs on such data, remain closely tied to what
is going on subcortically. Put psychologically, this means that in animals,
"mental" activity is overwhelmingly determined by the Id or "instinct";
or, in still other language, that it is chiefly dependent on basic biologic

"motives" or the emotional states derived from these.[5] Only in the gradual appearance of playfulness and curiosity, and possibly of complex courting behavior, as in the bower bird, may one see the beginnings of a tendency of newer parts of the nervous system to break free from this tight primordial control.

With man, however, it is as if some sort of corner had been turned. To put it in the crudest way, man's brain is some hundreds of grams heavier and contains some thousands or millions more neurons than that, say, of a chimpanzee;[6] but the gain in manifest mental power or degrees of psychological freedom which occurs from the chimp to man is surely greater by several orders of magnitude. More precisely, the factor relating brain mass to mental power may be much the same over the range of mammals *up* to man, but becomes many times larger *with* man.

To a physicist, all this might suggest a state change. Whereas it takes one calorie to raise one gram of water one degree over the range from melting to boiling, it takes far more calories to convert one gram of water *at* boiling into steam of the same temperature. Characteristically, state changes (for example, liquid to gaseous) or critical points (such as boiling) involve the release or absorption of relatively large amounts of energy. (The outstanding characteristic of man is his relatively enormous mental energy, whose technological consequences have transformed the earth.)

This analogy is perhaps less far-fetched than it sounds. According to thermodynamics, the tendency of all known systems, at least on the everyday scale, is to "run down." Their energy tends to dissipate itself, to

5. The relation of emotion to basic drives is discussed in detail, and in reasonably untechnical language, in the Introduction to my earlier book *The Physical Foundations of the Psyche* (Wesleyan, 1963), pp. 3-12.

6. Human brains run 1,200-1,400 grams in weight, as compared to chimpanzee and gorilla brains, which are in the 350-450-gram range. However, mass alone is not the critical factor, since whale and elephant brains are much larger than ours (roughly by a factor of 4-6). The brain of the dolphin *Tursiops truncatus* may reach 1,700 grams; and a neuroanatomist friend who has examined one reports that the complexity of its cellular organization equals or exceeds that of human brain. Possibly this complexity is more involved in the refinement of muscular control than in the elaboration of intelligence, it being for this reason that Dr. Lilly's startling hopes for this animal have not so far been realized. See John C. Lilly, *Man and Dolphin* (Pyramid, 1962).

become unavailable, the measure of this condition being a quantity known as entropy. The more run down a system is, the more entropy it has, or conversely. Life is thought to represent an antientropic trend.[7] As the sun runs down, a part of its energy, radiated away, is trapped at the earth's surface, causing a local decrease in entropy. From this decrease there arises a small but finite probability that here systems will begin to organize themselves; that is, that here matter will begin to decrease its entropy. So, by a complex chain of fortuities involving lightning and methane gas and nitrogen,[8] the most elementary forms of living stuff may have come into existence toward the end of the Azoic period, thousands of millions of years ago. And as the sun has continued to pump energy into the earth's surface, life has continued to organize itself or, as we say, evolve. It is possibly not fanciful to regard the nervous system as a Maxwell's Demon,[9] or entropy-reducing device. It tends to focus the body's energies or make them available in more and more various and effective ways as evolution proceeds. The mind of man is almost literally a Maxwell's Demon in that it has become able to segregate or make available almost suicidally large amounts of energy; for instance by means of petroleum and fission techniques.

It is, in other words, by adding and combining systems, by going to successively higher levels of organization, that living things become increasingly able to make available, not only their own energies, but those latent in their environment. In proportion as it has these effects, the addition of any new system—for instance, to the brain—can be called a

7. "Open physical systems . . . are never in true equilibrium, but maintain themselves in steady states by continuous exchange of materials with the environment. The second law of the thermodynamics is a rather special case in that it applies only to closed systems. It does not define the steady state as this is exhibited in vital processes. Entropy may decrease in open systems. Therefore such systems may spontaneously develop toward states of greater heterogeneity and complexity." From C. J. Herrick, *The Evolution of Human Nature* (University of Texas Press, 1956), pp. 50–51.

8. See, for instance, S. W. Fox, "How Did Life Begin?", *Science,* Vol. 132 (1960), pp. 200–208; also Fox and Harada, in *Science,* Vol. 133 (1961), pp. 1923–1924.

9. For those who have forgotten their elementary physics, Maxwell's Demon was a hypothetical gnome who operated a valve connecting two volumes of the same gas at the same temperature. By letting only high-speed molecules through in one direction and only low-speed in the other, he gradually raised the gas temperature in one compartment and lowered it in the other, thereby reversing the normal course of events.

state change. Considering man's unique possession of language and mathematics and music, his unprecedented command of the material world, one is almost driven to conclude that with the appearance of human intelligence, a state change or sudden shift to a far higher level of organization has occurred in the mammalian brain. Granting that such a shift may have taken place (and many at present would not), one would naturally like to know in what it consists. One thing is certain. Although the human brain is much larger than that of other primates, its basic plan of organization is nearly the same. So far as we can tell by either anatomical or physiological methods, no new structures or organs of mentation have been added. In human neocortex (or cortex), the so-called association areas, for instance, are enormously expanded, but their fine structure—the appearance of the cells, their arrangement into layers, the distribution of cortical input and output fibers—are very like those found in other primates or even in the mouse.

The key to the problem of man's peculiar psychic endowment is evidently not to be found in the comparative morphology or the gross physiology of the brain. Nor is it correct to imagine, as some do, that the use of symbols, or the performance of logical operations such as abstraction and generalization, is uniquely human. A conditioned stimulus is in a sense a symbol of the event it "predicts." Animals can also be shown to make certain types of generalization, or to respond to significant patterns (for instance, of tones) after these have been subjected to certain logical transforms (such as a shift in pitch, which leaves the high-low relations between tones unchanged). The last implies abstraction of a particular relation which can then be recognized as the relevant stimulus in other contexts, or regardless of changes in irrelevant variables. There is even experimental evidence of economic thinking in chimpanzees and cats.[10] It is next to impossible, in short, to characterize the difference between human and animal intelligence by any *single* class of mental operation which the one can perform and the other cannot. The

10. It was shown some years ago that chimpanzees would work for tokens which they could then "cash in" for food, some being misers who would amass fortunes in tokens.

If pairs of cats are placed together in a cage with a food-delivery box on one side and a lever releasing food into the box on the other, one may become the "parasite" cat, staying close to the box, while the other becomes the "worker" who presses the lever and races over for what is left. See J. H. Masserman, in *The Scientific American Reader* (Simon and Schuster, 1953), pp. 444–445.

unique feature of human intelligence is perhaps that it can build trains or *systems* of such operations. Still more important is the fact that this process is more continuous than episodic. It develops a kind of momentum and, with it, an unpredictability or potential novelty in outcome which have few parallels in animal "thinking."

For instance, there are evidently ants which can learn;[11] but even among those which herd aphids or practice agriculture, there is little to suggest the existence of ant traditions or ant history. In the three hundred and fifty million years or so in which insects are said to have been in existence, there has certainly been evolutionary improvement, but the pace of such changes has been biological rather than historic. If it were not so, the competition between men and insects would now be far more intense than it is or possibly long since have gone decisively in favor of the latter.

By biological changes, I mean those resulting from mutation and natural selection. Historical changes occur over epochs so much shorter that it is highly unlikely that genetic changes play a major part in them.[12] They depend rather on the way in which customs and traditional beliefs are reshaped from generation to generation under the pressure of new circumstances (which include new ideas, and not necessarily those having immediate practical application). The history of a given era is, in other words, the outcome not merely of adaptive imperatives peculiar to the time but also of the *Geist* or general outlook, which carries over much from the past and adds much in the present that is only obliquely related to problems of brute survival.

Animal societies do not seem capable of this type of rapid cumulative development, this pyramiding of intangibles. They show what one might call greater inertia, paralleling the difference in inertia between behavior dependent on conditioning and behavior which arises from rational conscious decision. The latter (to quote myself)

> is apt to have a fluidity or capacity for moment to moment change . . . which the former does not. Conditioned behavior, by contrast, persists as habit so long as it results in terminal "reward" states; is succeeded by periods of behavioral incoherence or "variability"[13] when it begins to fail;

11. D. W. Morley, *The Ant World* (Penguin, 1953), pp. 161–165.

12. That is, old-fashioned theories which attributed the decadence of nations to a deterioration of "the stock," "coddling of the unfit," and so on are probably untenable, since human gene pools may not change that fast.

13. See R. J. Hernstein, in *Science*, Vol. 133 (1961), pp. 2068–2069.

and at last . . . becomes reorganized [e.g., by trial-and-error] into some more reliably rewarding form. As compared to many of the actions arising directly out of conscious reasoning, it shows a high degree of inertia or a greater tendency to recur in situations to which it is, in fact, not suited.[14]

Freud defined "pleasure principle" processes as those arising out of the Id, or "instinct." One might equally define them as activities—perhaps mainly of the subcortical core of the brain—touched off by "unconditioned stimuli." These last include not only signals from the surround but also many originating within the organism itself; for instance, hunger pangs. What Freud called "reality principle" processes have to do with observed or inferred relations between events, things, and so on in the outside world. Much evidence suggests that the neocortex, more than any other part of the brain, is concerned with these. (And in man the "outside world" may include much of his own physical and psychic being which he feels to be other than his "real" self and treats as a kind of external problem or instrumentality, as the case may be.)

In animals, it is as though "reality principle" processes had little momentum of their own, but rather were called into action only as the "pleasure principle" or particular drive states dictated. Speaking in terms of brain events, one might guess that in animal neocortex, learning occurs only when the subcortical conditions (equivalent to a certain minimal drive strength) are favorable. Similarly what the neocortex does with immediate or stored (recalled) information is limited by the duration and intensity of such subcortical states. This amounts to saying that animals "think" episodically and that *what* they "think" is far more determined by what they are concurrently feeling or "wishing" than the other way round.

With man, these fundamental relationships seem to have become partially reversed. There is no question but that, like animals, we can frequently learn very rapidly under the stress of primitive drives or motivation and that, like theirs, a good deal of our behavior is conditioned or habitual rather than spontaneous or rationally improvised. However, it is also true that man, by thinking, can manipulate his own emotional life, can produce moods or drive states in himself almost arbitrarily. There is something of the theatrical in all of us, and one

14. Fair, *Physical Foundations,* p. 50 .

cannot say that our contrived feelings are wholly false. It is probable also that we use the same technique, in less flamboyant form, whenever we concentrate on a particular task—the more so the more it demands of us. Here, a part of what we mean by "concentration" consists in the deliberate conscious effort to maintain the type and intensity of basic motivational state needed to get the job done. Often, what is required is not one such state, but several in a particular order. At one stage, perhaps, one must "let oneself go"—forget nuances and work oneself up to a massive outpouring of energy; at another coolness, restraint, and close attention to detail may be necessary; at still another one must ignore (not act on) ordinary cues, but look only for certain key things and, failing to find these, move on with all possible speed. Each of these mental "sets" has its corresponding motivational or emotional one and related physiological signs.[15]

The plans men devise in this way may reach anywhere from minutes to decades ahead in time. Their common feature is that they primarily involve "reality principle" processes, or our understanding of the world and ourselves, such as it may be. This says nothing about the objectives of such plans, which may be "instinctive"—to win the girl, to make a fortune or become famous and so rise in the peck-order, and so forth. Whatever its objective, a plan, particularly if complex and extended in time, may require that we suppress or hold in check many ordinarily tyrannical drives or feelings and only permit ourselves those which are appropriate to the stage of the plan we happen to have reached.

There is no evidence that animals can manage themselves in any such sustained way as this. Much of the complex sequencing of animal behavior seems to be a matter of the entrainment of innate patterns of response, so that completion of one action in the train automatically sets up conditions likely to initiate the next. Particularly in higher forms, there is some room left for "choice" or unexpected alterations in behavior,[16] but seldom very much. It is logical, on the other hand, to see

15. There is clinical evidence which suggests that this management of basic drives or emotional states depends critically on parts of our frontal lobes. See, for instance, J. F. Fulton, *Frontal Lobotomy and Affective Behavior* (Norton, 1951), *passim.*

16. For example, the behavior of hawks while cruising in search of prey may be much more flexible or less "preprogramed" than it is during the final stages of the kill. See N. Tinbergen, *The Study of Instinct* (Oxford, 1951), p. 105.

our peculiarly human capacity to conceive highly complex plans, and our ability to manipulate the Id sufficiently to permit carrying some of them out, as aspects of the same phenomenon; namely, a "state change" equivalent to the appearance of a new system in the mammalian brain.

The important feature of this system is that it is apparently a functional one; that is, it does not result from the addition of any known new organ to the central nervous system. In man's brain, the nuclei, the main fiber tracts, the arrangement of cortical receptor and motor areas, all are the same as those found in other primates. But whereas in animals the operations performed by neocortex may in general be episodic (or disjunct in time) as well as disjunct in space (involving scattered cortical sites, with relatively poor co-ordination of the whole), in man a kind of coalescence of neocortical activities may have occurred. The result is that human "reality principle" processes or thought do not wait upon instinct, but have become more or less continuous in time and may involve a much higher degree of co-ordination between cortical areas.

The foregoing does not mean that instinct, in the shape of subcortical influence, may not greatly affect the course of our thought, in the shape of neocortical activity. It only means that thought can now bridge the temporal gap between one such occasion of "instinctive" intervention and the next. In so doing, thought itself may develop a logical trend or momentum which is increasingly at odds with that of instinct. Finally, since neocortex projects (sends fibers) to subcortical parts of the brain,[17] thought may play upon instinct or profoundly alter the intensity and even the sequence of appearance of our basic drives. In part its ability to do so may derive from the fact that in man thought shows unique temporal continuity, or persists as such between periods of acute adaptive need. Its greatest triumphs may be won, as it were, on the downslope from violent crises of feeling—in those long quiet intervals of preparation for the next series of exigencies which our realistic knowledge of the world tells us to expect. Begun early enough, such preparations may in effect bring about a gradual reshaping of the Id, enabling some men[18] finally to act in defiance of the strongest of instinctive drives, the fear of death, or to control states of ferocity or sexual arousal which less disciplined, less "conscious" human beings readily give way to.

17. For instance, to the rhinencephalon; it is perhaps also significant that reciprocal connections (from rhinencephalon to neocortex) are less massive.

18. Not including the author.

It would be a mistake, however, to exaggerate the numbers in whom this change occurs, or to see man's emergence into rational self-possession as in any sense given or automatic. While the basic theorem of animal psychic life seems to be *I think because I feel,* and of human life, *I feel because I think,* it is also true that most of us are all too readily overwhelmed by the feelings that our thoughts stir up in us. As a result we spend our lives not merely in coping with external circumstance but (as Freud said of neurotics) in manipulating circumstances, even including our own thoughts, so as not too powerfully to arouse the Id. A great deal of our "practical" behavior is really directed to this end—to keeping the beast inside of us appeased and quiet, which in turn permits us the illusion of sane self-mastery. The deepest psychological difference between the truly religious man and the "realist" lies just here. The former *contests* the Id and would make it an adjunct of reason—would establish "free will" at whatever cost to himself in deprivation or mental turmoil. The realist regards the Id as given, as a kind of biological absolute; and instead of striving for the freedom in mind that its conquest might entail, allows that freedom to be restricted to whatever degree he feels may be necessary to his peace of mind. (Hence modern agnostic man might be described simply as a functioning neurotic. Likewise "realism" as the habit of mind of aging civilizations may amount to a gradual surrender of the powers of creation and change.)

Our problem, in short, is to prevent our relatively great capacity for thought and anticipation from merely inflaming the Id to the point that thought itself is kept to its self-serving animal function and hobbled accordingly. It is not enough that we feel because we think. Indeed that condition is often our undoing, ensuring as it does a kind of bestiality aggravated by reflection. Threatened as no other species is by our combination of appetites and brains, incapable of the innocent serenity of animals, we are almost driven to the next stage of development latent within us—the stage at which emotion becomes to some extent altruistic, and the imperatives of the Id cease to dominate our conscious lives.[19]

19. To the Hindus, *maya* is simply the world as seen by unregenerate "instinctive" man, and *avidya* the state of sin or blindness—that is, the condition of mind in subservience to the "pleasure principle." The Puritans distinguished Natural Reason from Right Reason—meaning, by the former, mind preoccupied with matters of use and advantage, and by the latter, mind preoccupied with truth, regardless of use or advantage. See C. P. Smith, *Yankees and God* (Hermitage

The history of the rise of great civilizations is in part the history of such small progress as we have made in that direction; and at bottom the yearning for freedom comes to the same thing—to a longing not merely for the necessary goods of life but for the freedom in spirit, the *possession* of our own powers of imagination and feeling, which will permit us really to embrace the world for as long as we may be in it.

The arts, one might say, begin this process of freeing the emotions from their prehuman adaptive role; and it hardly matters that they often do so by a kind of trick—by playing upon the very habits of mind they would have us go beyond.[20] Appearing earlier in man's history than

House, 1954). Much epistemological argument over the question of truth may have been beside the point. The real question is not how precisely or deeply we may come to know reality, but to what extent we can free ourselves from the pervasive influence of the Id—from avidya, or subtler forms of wishful thinking. The question raised by Kant in *The Critique of Pure Reason* is a different one. It has to do with the extent to which our understanding of reality is dependent on a priori "intuitions." These seem to correspond to the given (inherited) categories into which we tend to analyze our primary sense data. Such categories evidently exist, but it may be mistaken to assume reason cannot go beyond them.

20. The painter's use of the human figure, for instance, is like the author's of plot and main characters. Much music is sensuous from the outset, presenting abstract figures in a meshwork of sounds and rhythms which have strong sexual overtones or suggest tumult, danger, violent conflict, and the like. The novelist lures us into identifying with one or another of his main characters—the self's surrogate, the Hero. He *must* then lead us from one event to another, till we learn how we finally come out. Only if he meets this requirement—has sufficient action or plot—will he maintain our interest and so convey to us, painlessly and almost on the sly, his own ideas and feelings about existence. This is, so to speak, the "pleasure principle" way of doing things: a paradigm of the mode of life in which reason and curiosity remain closely tied to basic biological necessity, to emotion and impulse and the struggle with living competitors or inanimate circumstance.

Most of us, in fact, live that sort of life most of the time. Our main business is to adapt to the tribe and to our physical environment; and only a vanishingly small part of our energies is devoted to reflection in the full philosophic sense: to understanding for its own sake. Nevertheless our delight in primitive story telling, or in later art forms like the novel, betrays this impulse to know, this urge of mind or the I to begin seeking its own objects. It is not merely that stories often make a moral point. Some of the best do so only by indirection; their power lies in the fact that they reveal us to ourselves. They enlist our interest by an appeal to the "pleasure principle," but then go on to show us how our lives look "under the aspect of eternity," a phrase implying essentially a suspension of the usual rules of practical self-concern. One feels with others for a change, sees the world with their eyes, accepts events as they occur, not without emotion, certainly, but also with less subjectivity or gross partisanship than usual. In this context, emo-

philosophy and science, they make more concessions to the "pleasure principle," but in the end have the same objective, the apprehension of truth—which is to say, the world dispassionately viewed, rather than as it habitually appears to us through the distorting lens of creature interest.

That a functional system such as the I of man can at last appear as a result of the continued enlargement of an existing system such as neo-cortex suggests the principle given in the first chapter here; namely, that in nature "the bringing together of large numbers of units having many properties in common may not result simply in a heap, whose properties are those of the units summed or multiplied," but in the emergence of new properties and a new class of phenomena. Neurons, in fact, occur in a few standard varieties; and their architectural organization in neo-cortex follows much the same plan in all higher mammals. But when a certain critical size is reached in neocortex, a "metasystem" may begin to take shape. A state change occurs in which old orders of functional dominance are partially reversed and still further reversals may be latent. The key to this occurrence—granted for the moment that it may really be one—must lie in an understanding of the way in which intrinsic activi-ties of the cortex organize themselves. In psychological terms, one wants to know how the rational conscious self puts itself together and some of the processes which make what we call thinking possible. Because memory is one of the more important means by which both behavior and thought can arrive at and persist in new forms, it seems reasonable

tion is to some extent taken out of its primal role. It is no longer entirely *for me,* a manifestation of the Id favoring the Id's purposes, but is now for others, or sim-ply for things as they are. To this degree it becomes an adjunct of reason, repre-senting perhaps a reversal of ancient dominance relations between neocortex and the subcortical core of the brain.

In contrast to imagination, what we call fantasy is a far more primitive phe-nomenon. Like the sort of rambling recollection we sometimes slip into at the end of a day, or of life, fantasy has the self as its central object, and takes the form of interior dramas in which the "wishes" of the Id are acted out with only the crud-est and most perfunctory concessions to external reality. It is, in short, a form of Id-thinking, like rationalization; and the crudity of both, the violence that they do to the truth, are the parallel, perhaps, of the primitivization of neocortical functions that results when control of neocortex remains with the subcortical core-systems. The girls whom we ravish or the enemies whom we undo in our day-dreams are without real identity, just as our rationalizations defy the usual rules of reasoning. The fact that we do not clearly distinguish fantasy from imagination, or that some of our arts now have the facelessness and crudity of daydreams, sug-gests that Id-thinking may be on the increase among us.

to suppose that in the organization of memory-functions, one may find much to explain those cumulative gains which reason can make over instinct in the course of individual human lives, or has made, with some irregularity, in the longer course of human history.

*Chapter IV*

---

## OPERATION BOOTSTRAP

A FILING system is a kind of memory, and commonly the material on file is alphabetized by proper name or by subject. To improve our chances of finding what we want, we also cross-file, so that any one of several "descriptor" words may lead us to the same item. A file depends essentially on classification, and classification depends essentially on features held in common, or "invariances" among the things classified. So long as the system is consistent, it hardly matters whether the invariances used to classify its contents are "real" ones or purely arbitrary. All authors whose surnames begin with A comprise a class based on an invariance which is arbitrary in the sense that it is man-made and conveys no further information about members of the class. Material filed under Geography or Biochemistry represents classification according to real invariances in the sense that these rubrics imply considerable information about members of the classes involved. To retrieve an item filed in this way, we often use a method of progressive specification or run the original process in reverse. Filing systems, in other words, are memories whose contents are relatively resistant to erosion by time; and an important part of what they "remember" is what one might call the logic of their contents, it being this logic which makes the contents accessible.

In neocortex, I believe, a quite similar system for the retrieval (recall) of information or for the filing (committing to memory) of new material may begin to take shape as we emerge from infancy. This retrieval system is distinct from—and logically somewhat at variance with—that responsible for emotional or primally motivated recall. The latter, though it involves neocortex, may be essentially subcortical (Chapters II and IV, above), reflecting processes in older parts of the nervous system which come to full efficiency much earlier in life, and themselves involve much less learning, than do activities of the neocortex proper.[1] By contrast, the processes *within* neocortex which tend to direct retrieval or further memory formation may be quite late-maturing, as is our capacity to think for ourselves. This amounts to saying that our earliest memories, neocortical included, are essentially emotional in origin, representing simply a miscellany of things that happen to have happened to us.

As such memories accumulate, the neocortex may begin to organize them further, according to principles we would be more apt to call logical. In effect, the neocortex, given the miscellany of recalled information forced upon it by experience and subcortical influence combined, gradually orders it or reduces its miscellaneity. To just that degree its outputs may become more highly articulated, so that as the neocortex orders its store of information in this way, it shows a proportional gain in control of subcortical motivational systems, including those responsible for memory formation in the neocortex itself. As this occurs, we no longer accumulate memories only or largely as the accidents of experience dictate, but also "voluntarily"; that is, we can now study or systematically commit to memory facts which our knowledge of external reality tells us are apt to be relevant. We also become able to "think," which means, among other things, to call up facts from memory as they are logically required.

To think effectively, we often have to resist the subrational wishes or convictions which immediate circumstances tend to force upon us through the agency of the instinctive self or Id. The fact that we *can* resist them and see them as subrational sets us apart from other species. Our ability to work to distant ends—on occasion ends having no clear adaptive value—implies a unique ability to hold the Id in check, or rather to shape its workings in appropriate ways. In terms of brain events, the equivalent statement is that human neocortex shows a unique capacity to gain control over subcortical systems and, to that degree, over its own operations which include the formation of new memories or the retrieval of old ones. The result is that man begins life as merely conditionable, like his animal relatives, but in time also becomes able to learn in a planned, logical, self-directed way seen in no other creature. This dualism, perhaps, is his predicament, since it

1. That is, the logic of drives—of desire or aversion—is given, whereas much of the logic of external events may be acquired as the brain matures.

means that two often highly divergent modes of psychological being compete within him for dominance. For the fact seems to be that the same memories which are the prime materials of thought are also to a considerable extent emotional in origin and hence capable of reactivating the basal drives or motives in which they originated. This means that to think in a rational sense may, as it involves memory, incidentally and quite irrelevantly arouse the Id, or subrational processes which cut across the lines of rational thought, tending to fragment it or send it off in other directions. In a sense, then, all human thinking involves some degree of active struggle between the conscious I and the prehuman instinctive self—between the learned and the conditioned. It is this situation which, I believe, barely exists in animals and distinguishes man from them. In proportion as the struggle goes consistently in favor of the I (as represented in neocortex), man achieves the insight, the capacity to plan, and the self-possession which we regard as uniquely human. In proportion as the battle goes the other way, man succumbs to an interior disunity also not normally seen in animals (in which the subcortical systems are more automatic or independent of controls imposed by learning, and the neocortex remains a more strict subcortical dependency). The consequence is that man, under conditions of his own making, is liable to mental disorders, many of which have no known equivalents in the animal world. In short, while a potential for radical increase in control over the rest of the nervous system exists in human neocortex, it is only that: a potential. There is no guarantee that at maturity the individual will have realized enough of it to think clearly or reliably control himself, more particularly in a complex urban world which plays upon his dreads and inflames his hatred or his desires with an intensity seldom approached in tribal societies. My object in this chapter is to show, as clearly as may be, certain of the fundamental processes by which that potential is realized—that is to say, the processes by which the self-aware self comes into being. Because these, once started, increasingly depend on the insight and the active decisions of man himself, one can say that man pulls himself out of the condition of animality by his own bootstraps. From shreds of reason, he builds reason proper; from primal fantasy, imagination; from the bestial, the human. This is not the same as saying that all men do so, or even that those given every opportunity avail themselves of it. If anything, the contrary; and from this fact, perhaps more than any other, arises the peril in which we find ourselves today.

From the outset of life—to stress a familiar point—memory formation in neocortex may depend on subcortical inputs which "decide" what is to be lastingly recorded there. Such "decisions" may chiefly result from emotional or drive states of more than a certain minimal intensity; and such emotions or drives reflect (at the outset) chiefly the immediate physiological state of the organism. This means in effect that at the beginning of life what we commit to memory is largely decided for us by the joint action of external circumstances and the internal machinery of instinct.

As the raw data of memory accumulate in this way, I believe that they are processed in neocortex, this being a major function of the continuous electrical activity one can record there. The primary operation performed on them may be taxonomic; that is, the cortex does something one might describe as sifting these data for the principal formal elements they hold in common.[2] By "formal" I mean to suggest objective structural features, as contrasted to the miscellaneous emotional or adaptive meanings of the same memories. This process may result in formation of second-order memories and from there go to several higher levels of abstraction, giving rise finally to a layered organization of recall. The layering of memories may be pyramidal in the sense that the raw data or particulars form the bottom of the pyramid, while the memories, so to speak, at the top—those last to form—represent generalizations from generalizations, or a very small group of key rules which give access to virtually everything in the system.[3]

It seems quite probable that the formation of primary, and subse-

2. For a detailed discussion of the cortical structures and pathways possibly involved in this process, see C. M. Fair, *The Physical Foundations of the Psyche* (Wesleyan, 1963), Chapters III–V. The beginnings of abstract memory formation may be seen in Vygotsky's study, for instance, of methods of block sorting in preschool children.

3. An essentially similar hypothesis of memory organization was suggested by Heinz von Foerster at the Bionics Symposium, Dayton, Ohio, May 3–5, 1966. It seems to me that further work on such a scheme of organization of memory might show it to account for the relation between "deep" and surface sentence-structure and possibly lead to a logical model for a machine to interpret language roughly in the way the human brain does. The model itself (mine) is still too primitive, and I know too little about linguistics, to permit taking these thoughts any further.

quently of derived or "abstract" memories depends heavily on the cortical association areas. To these, the sensory "analyzer" areas may stand in the relation of a feeder system.[4] The best evidence at present is that the cortical analyzers come into action very soon after birth and thereafter do little that could be called learning.[5] This means that the elements of perception—the bits and pieces from which we put together our mental picture of the world around—may to a considerable extent be given. This arrangement does not, I think, imply the fixed limits to understanding or imaginative insight which one might suppose. It merely means that our primary memories are formed from certain standard ultimate components, equivalent to the standard ultimate components into which we resolve our sensory inputs. There are perhaps far fewer limits set on the ways in which primary memories of this type can become organized through elaboration of the superstructure of abstract memories I have just described.

The remarkable ability of human intellect to penetrate natural phenomena argues that our understanding can in fact go far beyond the limitations of sense or primary perception. In science, some of our most successful theories have involved "pictures" of reality so remote from everyday experience that we cannot easily represent them by constructs derived from that experience. Nonetheless, the human brain

---

4. Not, however, primarily via the transcortical fiber systems. Evidence on this point is reviewed in my earlier book.

5. The cortex, I should explain, is roughly divided into primary projection ("specific"; "analyzer") areas, which receive sense-data, and association areas, which do not have direct sensory inputs, via the thalamus. The analyzer areas are relatively new in evolution, appearing only in the mammalian brain. The work of Mountcastle and of Hubel and Wiesel suggests that their operations are largely preprogramed or "wired in". (See C. M. Fair, in *Neurosciences Research Program Bulletin* Vol. 3, No. 1 [April, 1965] pp. 27–62. Jung *et al.*, and more recently Morrell, have presented evidence suggesting greater functional plasticity in this type of cortex. See for instance, F. Morrell, *Informal Proceedings, Fourth Interdisciplinary Sciences Symposium,* Office of Naval Research, Pasadena, California, 1966, pp. 77–92.)

The association areas, which have homologues in the reptilian and amphibian brains, and have become hugely expanded in man, appear to be concerned in the further or "higher" processing of the primary data of sense. They perhaps represent an elaboration of a relatively old unspecialized system subserving learning in lower vertebrates. Recent Russian studies have in fact shown that the hemisphere is apparently necessary to visual conditioning in the frog, even though the frog's primary visual cortex lies elsewhere (in the midbrain).

evolved them, and experiment seems to say that something roughly like them may lie behind the real as we commonly apprehend it. In physics, we have inferred the existence of particles having properties radically unlike those of any directly perceptible body. The indirect evidence is that such particles indeed exist and have many of the odd properties predicted for them (*vide* the neutrino, or various anti-particles).

The success of science implies an epistemological conclusion; namely, that we are not bound by the relatively few and fixed categories into which our senses resolve the flux of daily events. An essential function of intellect—more particularly of the faculty we call imagination—may be to add an indefinite number of other categories to those which, from infancy, are given, in the sense of being integral to the apparatus of primary perception. The more or less automatic formation of "abstract" memories perhaps represents the start of this process. To the extent that through it the neocortex becomes more decisively dominant or a more truly "self-acting" system, the same process may cease to be wholly automatic and itself become subject to rational direction. It is at this stage that man comes into his own as a fully grown representative of a unique species. The feature of that condition—ideally, the human—which sets it apart from that of most animals (or of most men, for that matter) is the inner freedom which it appears to confer. The essence of that freedom is that it involves a minimum of subservience to mental habit, which is to say a maximum of potential creativity, defined as a capacity for imaginative innovation. It is, in short, to the machinery of primary perception that we owe our Kantian "intuitions"; whereas to intellect or the rational conscious I arising out of abstract memory we owe our deeper insights, our imagination or capacity for the new, such as they may be. One might add that men or eras of little imagination naturally incline to philosophic pessimism, since they are by definition quite closely tied to the primal categories of sense and therefore quite convinced of the ultimate unknowability of the real.[6]

6. Likewise, in such eras the notion gets abroad that human knowledge is reaching some sort of completion—that nothing beyond a few corroborating details needs to be learned; that is, there is a domain which man's intelligence cannot penetrate and another which it has completely mastered, leaving little for the heirs to do but annotate the works of the past, as generations of Alexandrians and mandarins did and many modern scholars are beginning to do.

These relations have interesting parallels in the evolution and present structures of the brain. In premammals, there are no primary sensory analyzers in the hemisphere. From primitive mammals up to the primate level, the analyzer areas account for a considerable percentage of the whole cortical mantle. With the primates, a reverse trend develops. The phylogenetically older association cortex now begins an enormous expansion. By comparison the analyzers are now dwarfed and, in man, become folded into fissures so that a surface map of cortical areas hardly shows them.

In this expanded older cortex—notably of the temporal lobe—our earliest lasting memories may be laid down, thanks to the influence of the subcortical motivational systems discussed in the preceding three chapters. There is probably some parceling of such memories according to the sense modality primarily involved,[7] but that does not mean that we remember in only one modality at a time—merely that a particular memory may involve activity at widely separated cortical sites. In fact, the evidence is that most cortical memories do not have point location and cannot be deleted piecemeal by the removal of small bits of gray matter. It is probable also that many cortical memories have cruder subcortical equivalents; that is, that memory formation occurs on several levels of the nervous system more or less simultaneously.

The fact that from the start of life, lasting memory formation may depend on the subcortical motivational systems means that the contents of lasting memory are apt to be in a logical sense somewhat arbitrary. In a frightening situation I may notice and never afterward forget some absolutely trivial detail. By extension of this principle, it is easy to see how our memories might quickly fill up with irrelevant particulars, with the result that any given drive or emotion would tend to flood our minds with useless information. To produce an efficiently functioning brain, what is wanted is a second system of control which can do two things: restrict retrieval of memory data to probably useful

7. For instance, Charles Gross and Peter Schiller made a study (unpublished) at M.I.T. several years ago of unit responses in the temporal lobe of the monkey. In inferotemporal cortex, they found units responsive to light but not to sound; and in lateral cortex, homologous to Area 22 in man, they found units responsive to sound but not to light. The first of these findings is in agreement with earlier studies of Pribram suggesting the indispensability of inferotemporal cortex to complex learned visual discriminations in the monkey. K. Pribram, in *Behavioral Science*, Vol. 4, No. 4 (1959), pp. 274 ff.

items and direct the process of memory formation itself so that the *accumulation* of recalled information also begins to follow some more rational plan.

Imagine a neocortical memory stocked with $n$ miscellaneous items —$n$ being quite a large number, perhaps on the order of $10^6$ or larger. Early in life, the only organizing feature of these data is that they fall into groups according to common emotional or drive states of origin. Obviously this is a very primitive type of ordering. The number of our possible drives or emotions is small—on the order of tens, if one includes socialized or "sublimated" drives and nuances of feeling. Moreover, the items of memory lumped together under this scheme may have no other logical connection with one another. A state of fear or anger or sensual warmth may therefore bring to mind a wild assortment of recollections, few of which have any immediate use or any relation to each other besides the one mentioned. At most they may tell us what an animal's conditioning seems to tell it: that given A in the present, resembling a recalled A, we should expect B, like the B which followed A in the past. This last amounts to rerunning a memory like a bit of movie film, and then acting accordingly—that is, as if the scene on film were about to be re-enacted in the real world more or less exactly. This simple scheme, which evidently underlies much learned behavior in animals, may be dependable or efficient only so long as memory itself is not too capacious and well stocked; that is, so long as given A, too many possible B's ($B_1, B_2, \ldots B_n$) do not automatically suggest themselves. For in this case, how is the animal to decide promptly which B is most probable and so which is the most promising course of action? The very fact, in other words, that human memory is so large may have made conditioning an inadequate mode of learning for man and required that he develop another, so to speak, on top of it.

In the second chapter I mentioned that neocortex, like most other parts of the nervous system, shows continuous, more or less rhythmic electrical activity. Presumably the latter accomplishes something, since the energy expenditure involved is quite large.[8] It has been vaguely suggested that the electrical activity of the cortex represents a scanning

8. According to Warren McCulloch, the human brain is a 20-watt device drawing about as much power as a more than adequate monoaural amplifier or a less than adequate light bulb.

process.[9] Possibly so; but the idea is of little use unless one specifies what is being scanned for what. My own view is that, among other things, the contents of memory are being scanned for their most prominent (widely distributed) common features, or invariances. Such invariances may then become memories and as such may themselves be scanned, giving rise to invariances of a second order, which likewise become items of recall, and so on. In this way, one arrives at the "pyramid of generalizations" (or categories) described at the beginning of this chapter. The latter forms the basis of filing systems by which one can retrieve a particular item by first specifying its most general characters and then adding further specifications, until one arrives at the final subclass containing only the item itself.[10]

A filing system of this kind, invented by man, is perhaps simply a replica of the system embodied in his own cortex. The function of that system is essentially to consolidate and thereby control the contents of memory. To clarify what is meant by this statement, let me give a rough model or metaphor suggesting what one might call the structure of waking mental activity. At its base (and perhaps literally at the base of neocortex[11]) lies an assortment of memories (acquired neuronal "firing patterns"), some active and some quiescent at any given moment. In the middle ground (and perhaps literally in layers IV–lower III of six-layered cortex) occur those usually more vivid and transitory events equivalent to our moment-to-moment sensory experience. Both sensory experience and activated memories give impulsion or direction to what we call thinking or "consciousness" (the given or spontaneous activity of neocortex). In the system just described they *are* thinking or consciousness; the waking self is no more than an epiphenomenon jostled into being by the combined pressures of the senses and the (subcortical) motivational or instinctive systems. This is, in fact, the view of consciousness adopted by neobehaviorists and to a degree by Freudians. It involves, I believe, a serious error, and I would like for that reason to discuss it briefly.

9. By W. G. Walter, *The Living Brain* (Norton, 1951).

10. Not necessarily only *one* of the item.

11. On the possible localization of "memory" units at the base of neocortex, or more generally, on the output side of any neuronal system which "remembers," see C. M. Fair in *Neurosciences Research Program Bulletin*, Vol. 3, No. 1 (April, 1965), pp. 27–62.

The prime feature of living things is that they are self-organizing; and the higher one looks in evolution, the more one seems to see forms of self-organization which depend not directly on inheritance or the unfolding of innate characters during growth, but rather on the shaping of relatively unspecialized systems by day-to-day circumstance. That is, the key feature of higher organisms—the feature which defines them as that—is that they include systems which through aeons of natural selection have become minimally preprogramed or restricted in the number of things they may do. Compared to a cat's paw, the human hand is a generalized limb. The rhinencephalon of mammals is homologous to structures in lower forms which appear to be primarily olfactory; in mammals, this "smell-brain" has evidently become generalized so as to represent feeling states—drives or emotions not necessarily tied to any particular sensory modality, but capable of attachment to any, as experience may dictate.[12]

In the transition from a specialized or highly "committed" mode of organization to a more generalized or "uncommitted" one, what is lost are highly specific automatic forms of response, and what is retained or enlarged is a plasticity equivalent to a greater repertoire of *potential* actions. The basis of this plasticity is something one might call a latent logic: a set of quite generalized theorems embodied in neurons, just as systems of theorems are embodied in computer hardware. The difference is that brains so far seem to have more logical degrees of freedom, including a remarkable ability to variegate the logic they start out with. This statement probably applies more in the collective than the individual case. At seventeen any one of us may become any number of things; but by thirty-five most of us are relatively specialized or "set," and only rare individuals, given the chance, can basically change by that time—go on to develop the other selves once potential in them.

The neocortex of man, particularly perhaps those parts of it (the association areas) derived from the "general pallium" of premammals, may be par excellence a despecialized system in that the range of things it may do is enormous. What this means, in terms of the model proposed above, is that consciousness is an activity equivalent to those

12. Regarding this generalization of function, see C. J. Herrick, *The Brain of the Tiger Salamander* (University of Chicago Press, 1948), p. 99. The well-known mixed, or polysensory, responses of the hippocampus and amygdala (major structures of the rhinencephalon) are consistent with this account.

processes and to that logic by which the neocortex organizes the data either "presented" to it by the senses or already stored in it as memories. In other words, consciousness is not passive and epiphenomenal, but one of the most complex and, in its consequences, the most unpredictable, of those self-organizing processes which characterize all living things. It is *the* agency of innovation, as shown by the enormous acceleration in the rate of ecological change which has occurred with man. It represents, essentially, a form of central nervous organization in which rigid early-achieved efficiency of response is sacrificed to later-acquired improvised modes of action. Biologically, it amounts to a considerable risk. Man, of all creatures, is the longest and most helpless in infancy, and, through his very plasticity, the most subject to functional central nervous disorders at maturity. His only guarantee of survival, let alone of eventual victory over other species, lay in having a cortex whose "latent logic" sufficiently mimicked that of the real world to permit him to improvise his way in the latter successfully. Added to that, he needed the raw energy to drive his self-organizing processes forward night and day, with or without the prompting of instinct, since only in that way might his relatively despecialized brain become adequately forearmed against those occasions which other creatures meet more or less automatically. This, I think, is the biological meaning of the fact that we are conscious or mentally active even when there is no obvious need to be—or, as the physiologist Paul MacLean put it, no apparent need to be conscious at all.[13]

The "latent logic" of neocortex and its inherent activity or free energy between them may give rise to the structure of abstract memories described above. Inasmuch as our original store of primary (particular) memories is simply given through the combined influence of experience and the motivational systems, our brains resemble filing systems in which the contents begin to accumulate first and the rules for filing or retrieval develop later. At the start of the latter process, there is perhaps a definite repertoire of rules (= the latent logic of the

---

13. This same relentless activity, this restlessness of the spirit, as we once would have called it, makes us liable as few other creatures seem to be to boredom. One might define boredom as a purely psychic form of frustration, since one is attacked by it often when all one's adaptive needs are satisfied, the only thing lacking being something to engage intelligent interest, something for "consciousness" to work on.

cortex) to draw upon, those which are actually called into action depending on the type of memory data first introduced into the file. Later on, the system as a whole may generate an indefinite number of other rules for filing and retrieval, this process being equivalent to the diversification or subtilizing of thought as a cumulative consequence of thought itself (thought being here conceived of as a manifestation of the "given activity" or free energy of the system as a whole). These new rules, the residues of thought, like those inherent in the system from the outset, take the form of what I have called abstract memories.[14]

So far I have spoken of memory formation or learning, but said nothing about forgetting or more active forms of unlearning. Both of the latter occur, as we know from everyday experience and from studies of animal behavior. Both may also be necessary, given that the nervous system is finite and that conservation of some capacity for change is vital if biological competence is to be maintained over the life of the individual or his generation. Several very important principles seem to be involved in forgetting. One is that it may never be quite complete; when an animal "extinguishes" a conditioned response which no longer serves, it can in general relearn the response more easily than it acquired it in the first place. A second principle is that the memories or conditioned responses established earliest in life are in general those most resistant to extinction. A third, perhaps inferrable from our own experience, is that what I have called abstract memories may generally be more alterable than the particulate specific recollections from which they derive[15]—with the qualification that earliest-established abstract memories or principles of thought may, as in the case of specific recollections, be the most enduring.

In stability, then, abstract memories may range from the near "permanence" of early-established specific memories proper to the almost complete fugitiveness of "thought." A great many of what we call our ideas fall into the latter category, enduring for a few seconds or minutes as part of the logical structure of thought itself and then recur-

14. For a detailed analysis aimed at suggesting how such a memory system could take shape in neocortex, see Fair, *Physical Foundations,* Chapters II–V.

15. A feature relating to their possible mode of cortical representation. See Fair, *Physical Foundations,* Chapters IV–V.

ring, under a variety of transforms, in other contexts as often unrecognizable descendants of themselves.

All this amounts to saying that the pyramid of memories described earlier is most stable at the bottom and most fluid at the top. But since it may be the upper or abstract organization of memory data which gives the rational conscious self its coherence or (in physiological terms) the neocortex its control over subcortical systems representative of the Id, it follows that man is peculiarly vulnerable in the realm of ideas or concepts. Anything which seems extensively to invalidate his notions of reality, anything representing a sharp inexplicable break with his previous experience, tends to disrupt thought and damage his control of himself, often releasing quantities of "arousal" and primitive emotion.[16] This peculiarity is inherent, I believe, in the way our brains are organized, and it has certain clear parallels in the behavior of animals.

When an animal is learning a new way of coping with its environment, it is apt to show widespread and electrical signs of activation in the neocortex. This corresponds to a situation in which a subcortical system (the midbrain reticular formation and related structures[17]) has greatly increased its input *to* the neocortex. In the excitement arising from extreme pain or fear or frustration, the cortex may simply be flooded with gross energy, one function of which is to break down a variety of memories or acquired action patterns, thereby clearing the way for a new learning.[18] Essentially this can be regarded as a "release"

16. "For whatever reason . . . the more or less sudden realization that an enduring plan must be changed at a strategic level is accompanied by a great deal of emotional excitation. When this excitation can find no focus . . . the person experiences 'anxiety.' " G. A. Miller *et al., Plans and the Structure of Behavior* (Holt, 1960), p. 116.

17. See H. H. Jasper *et al.,* eds., *The Reticular Formation of the Brain* (Little, Brown, 1958), *passim.*

18. As mentioned earlier, gross "activation" of the cortex, presumably reticular in origin, accompanies "extinction" of a now inappropriate conditioned response in animals. The technique of brainwashing apparently tries to make use of the same principle. See William Sargant, *Battle for the Mind* (Doubleday, 1958). The difficulty here is that the memories the indoctrinator most needs to expunge correspond to ideas and principles of behavior established very early in the subject, or victim, and therefore those most resistant to "extinction." I know of no follow-up studies, for instance, of repatriated Korean war prisoners which give information as to how deep or lasting the effects of brainwashing are. Such studies should certainly be made.

phenomenon. Experience new to the organism is experience which finds few or no matching patterns in neocortical memory. The neocortex cannot, in consequence, efficiently handle such inputs—that is, convert them promptly into well-organized outputs. As a result, control of subcortical systems by the neocortex begins to falter,[19] release of the reticular arousal apparatus follows, the cortex is deluged with "activation," and disorganization of its processes is carried a step further. At this stage, we are being brainwashed by violent emotion,[20] which as it subsides will leave the neocortex like a partially erased blackboard on which new messages will presently be written. Unpleasant as it is as a private experience, and disastrous as it has been in its social consequences—witness the savage persecution which heretics "radicals" or other innovators have so often brought upon themselves—this mode of functioning may be a principal means by which the brain remains in part an "open" system. Without some such capacity for periodic disorganization and re-formation of ourselves, we would probably be much more habit-ridden than we are or become dogmatic and tiresome and incapable of further growth even sooner in life than we do. The whole mechanism I have just described reflects another principle which is part, one might say, of the basic logic of instinct. Note that the new tends to release *fearlike* activation—something between anxiety and outright terror—which may then precipitate retreat or a rebound into rage, as does fear arising from more familiar causes. The basic theorem is that it is wisest (has proved on the whole adaptive) for the organism to respond to the new as though it were a threat. The "orienting reflex" in animals is a mild form of that response, human persecution of the novel or unorthodox being a more extreme form of it.

One may view our psychological life as a continuous struggle between activities internal to mind itself, which tend to overconsolidate or rigidify its functions, and activities derived from without and below (from the external world and the Id), which tend to disorganize it

19. Witness the devastating effects of intense fear or anger on both reason and self-control.

20. The important feature of this process being that it chiefly affects the more unstable "abstract" memory system, with the consequence that rational (= neocortical) control is diminished, pending reorganization of retrieval processes within the neocortex proper.

to the point of amorphousness, thereby dissolving its control over feeling states and behavior. The intelligent but unoriginal man is perhaps one gifted with a mechanically efficient neocortex in which consolidative processes have too decisively prevailed. Such a man may brilliantly handle the already known, but neither in daily life nor in mind have any capacity for innovation, being too "well adjusted." The creative, or original, man is by contrast one almost chronically vulnerable to circumstance—partly perhaps as result of an inherited violence of temperament, partly because of early painful conditioning, predisposing him to react with anxiety and arousal in later life to situations which for others have no such residual emotional meanings. Willy-nilly, such a man lives dangerously in that in him the consolidative powers of mind are continually threatened with dissolution from too intense or too prolonged arousal, it being in just this sense that great wits are allied to madness. In the extreme, such people *must* exercise their creative powers—must write or paint or think or play an instrument to the top of their bent—to stay sane.[21] Provided they do so, they have the enormous advantage that their very instability leaves them uniquely open, enabling them to arrive at new ideas or insights or ways of doing of which most men, however endowed in intelligence alone, are simply incapable. It is more a symptom of our time than a statement of the whole truth to say that those who have what we call genius are often if not invariably psychologically damaged people—cripples who have "overcompensated" in some way. The evidence is that we produce large numbers of such people.[22] Most of them achieve nothing at all, and not a few are apparently driven over the edge into neurotic sterility or psychosis. It might be more correct to say that a certain combination of native intelligence and turbulence tends to produce creativity. The turbulence may result from an inherited tendency to strong passions, or still more from the impact of unfortunate early experience on such a nature. The *combination* of intelligence and turbulence may be more

21. In her diary, Virginia Woolf spoke of "something very profound about the synthesis of my being: how only writing composes it: how nothing makes a whole unless I am writing." Quoted by Stuart Hampshire in the *New York Review of Books,* September 22, 1966, p. 3.

22. Several estimates have placed our rate of mental disturbance at about 10 per cent of the population, meaning that this percentage will at some time in their lives have an acute episode requiring psychiatric care, including drug therapy, and possibly hospitalization.

important than either one alone. This conclusion is suggested by recent studies of creativity ratings as compared to intelligence test scores among college students. The creative group did not simply overlap the highest I.Q. groups but took in students at lower levels as well, down to what might be judged the level of mediocrity. The inference is that one can afford to be considerably stupider if one has that other intangible, creativity—in essence, perhaps, a kind of fruitful instability, an exaggeration of the capacity, built into all of our brains, to raze and reconstruct whole worlds in memory. This is the faculty we call imagination—a faculty of continual progression in the realm of ideas. One can regard it as a vastly heightened form of the power which animals have to arrive at new states of central nervous order following each of the crises of arousal forced upon them by inner or outer circumstance. Because it has these origins—because to be creative means to live in a state in which the consolidative forces in neocortex, as represented by abstract memory formation, never decisively win out over the forces of primal arousal and erasure—there is perhaps always in men of genius something of the feral and the mad, something which makes them awesome and sets them apart and unfits them, as more normal men correctly sense, for the practical conduct of affairs. It is an understandable paradox that while such men can enormously benefit their fellows by the disinterested unfolding of their abilities in art or science or literature or by their detached appraisal of events, they are nonetheless apt to make disastrous leaders. To its credit, the Anglo-Saxon world seems always to have understood this principle, for the most part entrusting the control of its politics, its universities, and its large corporate business to men of very little distinction.[23]

23. Not all the motives for this policy being, perhaps, quite so straightforward as the one given.

In *The House of Intellect* (Harper, 1959), p. 33, Jacques Barzun remarks: "One detects a kind of revenge, a turning of the tables on Intellect, in the common desire to disregard what evidence of mental powers [in a man] there may be, and prefer the duffers."

PART II *The Self as the Origin of Cultures*

---

## Chapter V

## RELIGION AND THE TEMPORAL FORM
## OF CULTURES

To the enlightened of this century, religion is in principle unacceptable because ultimately superstitious. Superstition might be defined as a form of supernaturalist thinking based on fear—chiefly the fear of death, but also the fear of the unfamiliar or unfathomable. As such it resembles the thinking I defined earlier as rationalization, in that both represent a situation in which neocortical activity is being forced along by inputs from subcortical systems. By "forced along" I mean that neocortical processes which, of themselves, incline to be logical or internally consistent are, in this situation, repeatedly disrupted or made to reflect theorems embodied elsewhere in the brain. Whereas neocortical processes proper may mimic the logic of external events, subcortical activity probably follows a logic of innate wishes with far fewer concessions to reality in the larger sense. In other words, the same subcortical inputs which overactivate the cortex in fear or anger also tend to falsify its workings as an organ of insight.

The more primitive the condition of man, the less he can cope with handily or really understand. To the same degree, the more vulnerable he is to fear. The furnishings of his mind are scanty; in physiological terms, the memory systems of his neocortex are poorly developed, and control of the Id by the rational conscious self is correspondingly uncertain. Primitive religions perfectly reflect this condition, being fantasy-ridden and magical. Their gods are frequently ferocious and amoral, requiring to be placated rather than pleased.

By *awe,* we mean wonder tinged with fear; and the stronger the tinge, the feebler the influence of reason. Witness the effects on us of fright, or terror, or of powerful or famed personages. So long as awe has not progressed to the stage of wonder, the religions of man are apt to remain dark and placatory and superstitious. Not that even the "highest" religions are lacking in those elements. It is simply that they include others which, being grounded in real insight, contain the seeds of real progress, as the history of higher civilizations seems to show. One might say that the history of man's self-improvement is that of his slow and uneven conquest of dread; more precisely of his gradual escape from the vicious circle created by the action of ignorance on his fears and of fear on his reason.

Our escape would perhaps have been less gradual and would now be more complete, were it not for the fact that fear—which is to say the subcortical emergency system—is aroused not merely by events which our conditioning or innate releasers[1] "recognize" as threatening. As mentioned in the last chapter, it is also stirred up by the unfamiliar. That this is so we know both from daily experience and from physiological studies of the brain. I should like briefly to restate the principle involved, since it is an important one.

Present evidence suggests that the nervous system is organized in such a way as particularly to take note of changes in the surround reported to it by the senses. One manifestation of this principle is shown in what Russian physiologists call the "orienting reflex." Imagine a cat with recording electrodes affixed to its neocortex, sitting in a cage in a quiet room. The experimenter suddenly exposes it to a loud beeping sound. The recording electrodes will very probably report a widespread increase in "fast" electrical activity in the cortex. That this is often a response of an emergency or fearlike sort is indicated by other physiological signs typical of fear-inspired alertness; for instance, increases in heart rate, changes in pupillary size reflecting increased activity in the sympathetic nervous system, or steep rises in the blood levels of hormones associated with stress reactions.

After the beeping has continued a while, however, the fast activity tends to subside, suggesting that alertness or fear is passing. In time the animal may even fall asleep. If the rhythmic beeping is now stopped, the same sequence of events is apt to repeat itself. Fast activity again appears in the cortex, and the animal, if asleep, may abruptly wake up.

If this whole sequence is repeated a number of times, the animal may cease to show the orienting reflex just described, at least to the

1. See N. Tinbergen, *The Study of Instinct* (Oxford, 1951), Index and *passim*.

same degree that it did in the beginning. What is happening is possibly something like this: after several "ons" and "offs" of the sound, the animal learns in effect that this intermittent noise is simply a part of this particular environment. It forms, that is, a set of memories whose effect is to minimize the arousal produced by that stimulus. (Besides getting used to the tone being on, it also learns that periodic "offs" are to be expected or includes this additional feature in its memory image of the situation.) More generally, a basic function of memory is to improve the channeling of inputs to the brain and so to restrict the amount of gross excitation caused by the impingement of external events on the senses. It is the agency by which higher forms, in particular, progressively reduce the outlay of central nervous energy needed to cope with the world. The same mechanism is involved whether the familiar stimulus is irrelevant, as here, or *is* relevant and so becomes part of an overt learned response.

In the case of neocortex, one can see that the more fully stocked neocortical memory becomes, and the more widely these materials become organized by the mechanism of abstract memory described in the last chapter, the less is the neocortex apt to be "driven," or propelled into diffuse ill-organized activity from without or below. To the same extent, its dominance over subcortical systems will be extended or made the more secure. Translated into terms of human psychology, this means that the more one knows and the better organized is one's knowledge, the less one is at the mercy of the orienting reflex: the less one is apt to be propelled into fright or confabulation[2] by the unfamiliar. It is thanks to this principle that man, as he progresses from the primitive tribal to the civilized state becomes less subject to awe or terror[3] and more liable to the benign response we call wonder. In step with this change, the purely superstitious fear-inspired elements

2. For instance, the sort of babbling often done by those who have seen "flying saucers."

3. Malinowski had the interesting idea that magic represents eleventh-hour behavior in which men, at a loss for real recourses, resort to a kind of desperate pseudo thinking. If the crisis then passes, it follows that the pseudo thoughts and their consequent actions were effective, which may lead to their becoming standard practice. See Edward Norbeck, *Religion in Primitive Society* (Harper and Row, 1961), pp. 46-47. Playing the numbers by dreambook (as in Harlem) and attacking enemies by voodoo (as in Haiti) perhaps represent the recourses of minorities socially too frustrated to act otherwise.

in his religion come to be overlaid with psychological and moral intuitions which are much more humane and truthlike in that they represent insights much less contaminated by primal wishes and much more based on observation. In this progression we are, perhaps, watching the human neocortex and its corresponding psychic system, the waking I, in the process of freeing themselves from the subcortical self or Id.

It follows from this analysis that what we call the religious impulse in man is exceedingly mixed. His sense of the unseen—of the possible or the soon-to-be—has two roots and so two forms, often coexistent. One is primal, restrictive (in the sense that all projections of the Id into conscious thought tend to limit it), and grounded in dread. Its dominant emotion is awe; and it eventuates in moral systems of the totem and taboo type often as rigidly prescriptive and as resistant to reasoned change as the dictates of fear itself. No religion, even the highest, is free of these features. The second, and necessarily later-appearing, form of the religious impulse is grounded more in reflection and wonder than in fear and forced thinking.[4] Its moral systems stress

4. A particularly clear example is Zoroastrianism, which was the faith of the Persia of the Achaemenides, supplanting earlier Aryan gods (Indra, Varuna, Nasatya, or others of the Indian pantheon) with a God-devil system of a more abstract kind. Under this system, the older gods became personifications of evil, apparently in the sense of error or delusion (as in maya, and its consequence, avidya). In old Persian, the word for these discredited gods was *daeva* (in later Persian, *div*). Thus the word *devil* comes from the same root which in other Aryan languages survived in its nonperjorative sense—for instance, in pantheistic Rome, as *Divus* (used for the god-emperors, pursuant to a Senate resolution of 42 B.C. creating Divus Julius, such deification evidently being a routine funerary procedure in later times. See Edward Gibbon, *The History of the Decline and Fall of the Roman Empire*, I, 304–305). "The essence of Ormuzd is Truth and Law. . . . The essence of the wicked spirit (ahriman) is falsehood. . . . Zoroaster says of himself he had received from God a commission to purify religion. . . . He purified it from the grossly sensual elements of *daeva* worship." K. F. Geldner, in *Encyclopaedia Brittanica* (11th ed.): "Zoroaster."

Zoroastrianism evidently retained for some centuries a kind of Unitarian simplicity, only becoming a state religion in the full sense in Sassanid times. As Ortega y Gasset said of liberalism, this commentator (Geldner) said of Zoroaster's doctrine: that it was too difficult for the majority, and so "the old gods received honor again"—the faith survived by debasement or, more accurately, died of prematurity. It did, however, stress works of a more or less Christian kind and "purity" (that is, of the soul vis-à-vis the unregenerate animal self); and it conceived of life as following a strict moral economy of the debit-credit type, such that at death the soul, to reach heaven, had to pass over the "accountant's bridge."

mild permissive emotion, tolerance, and forgiveness—in short, expansion both of affection and of the understanding, which are conceived as the complements of each other. As such it is perhaps more nearly allied to the sexual side of man than to his impulse toward self-preservation. One should not conclude from this, however, that religion or the arts and sciences are simply "sublimations." It might be more correct to say that sexuality and creativity are closely related in that (unlike emergency or fear states) both involve a tendency toward expressiveness or freedom in imagination. As the cortex becomes sufficiently organized, it can perhaps selectively play upon the subcortical sexual-ferocity system and in this way favor its own activity. This does not mean that creative pursuits represent diverted sexuality. It means that in man, the sexual divisions of the nervous system have come to serve nonsexual purposes,[5] just as the olfactory brain of submammals came to subserve emotion in mammals.

The coming to ascendancy of the neocortex—or of the corresponding psychic system, the waking conscious I—may then in effect increase a shift in the tenor of man's emotional life which began when his life as a whole became less nomadic and violent, more centered around agriculture than the hunt. It is essentially a movement away from the constrictive state of fear and toward the more expansive states associated with courting and love-making and the happy confidence with which, in the ideal, we "attack" the problems of daily life.

This shift is paralleled by the difference in tenor between primitive

5. In my previous book, I reviewed evidence suggesting that the subcortical motivational system is roughly a dual one, embodying emergency functions in one division and sexual, feeding, and ferocity (e.g. hunting) functions in another. The trend of that evidence was also that intrinsic activity of the neocortex may be more favored by inputs from the sexual-ferocity than from the emergency system. Part of the argument rested on evidence from the converse case. When neocortical dominance fails decisively in man—in psychological terms, when the Id prevails and man succumbs to mental disorder—it is most often the emergency system which appears to have become dominant. Certain organic mental illnesses aside, there are few neuroses or psychoses in which the prevailing mood is euphoric. Even the manic phase in manic-depressive disease is tinged, as one observer noted, with fear and melancholy. As a matter of everyday experience, we know that of all emotions intense fear is perhaps the most paralyzing to thought. Even rage can scarcely compete with it; and in fact it is only as our fear rebounds into rage that we usually become able to act or think at all. See L. D. Campbell, *Manic-Depressive Disease* (Lippincott, 1953). See also G. G. Haydu, in *Annals of the New York Academy of Sciences*, Vol. 98, Article 4 (1962), pp. 1126–1138.

tribal and some higher religions, most notably Brahmanism, Buddhism, and Christianity. The gods of the ancients were plural and cruel. Of the classical pantheon, only a few stood for what we would regard as enlightened ideals or hopes. Others represented the Id simply accepted as such. They personified eternal objects of the inner world, malign forces to which man must bow as he bows to external necessity. The same seems to have been true of the gods of Egypt, of Akkad and Sumer, and of pre-Columbian America.

With Brahmanism, there appears the revolutionary idea that the world seen through the eyes of instinct or everyday self-interest is an illusion. This remarkable notion makes explicit and sets up as an ideal an intuition which in other religions never finds expression at all; namely, the intuition that consciousness or the rational I, usually enslaved to the adaptive and the animal in ourselves, is not properly an auxiliary of this sort. To the extent that it remains so in daily fact, man is stunted and lives in a state of animal darkness, neither really master of himself nor capable of real insight into the world around him.

To judge from Yoga and other forms of the holy life in India, the prime means of achieving grace under Brahmanism was by suppression or near suspension of ordinary adaptive behavior. By its very negativism, this approach concedes the formidable power of normal life to diminish mankind—that is, to keep reason from doing more than subserving gratification and preservation of the physical self. That such ascetic disciplines can in fact increase man's conscious control over his own nervous system is shown by the ability of some Yogis to regulate activity of the lower gut and by a recent study[6] of the EEG during the state of samadhi. The defect of this approach is that in the end it tends to impoverish even the waking conscious life of the holy man. It neglects the processes of in-forming (*sic*) by which the neocortex comes to predominate. Instead of enlarging reason and imagination directly, it apparently attempts to starve the Id into submission,[7] thereby permitting reason and imagination to prevail by default. In the nature of the

6. In this study, it was shown that four Yogis could, in the trance state, block the normal cortical EEG effects of sudden loud noises, intense light, or touching of the skin with a hot glass rod. See B. K. Anand *et al.*, in *EEG and Clinical Neurophysiology*, Vol. 3 (1961), pp. 452–456.

7. For example, by withdrawal from active life into a meditative asceticism.

case, this process can only go so far. Yoga and Zen Buddhism, for this essential reason, perhaps, appear sterile and "subjective" to us and may, in fact, represent a kind of Pyrrhic victory of the soul. They purge consciousness of the chimera of instinct, but at such a cost to consciousness itself that adepts of these religions resemble somnambulists, whose state of grace is incommunicable and whose visions, like a drug addict's, eventuate in nothing. Hence Spengler's somewhat overdramatic description of them as "religions of the annihilation of consciousness."

The ascetic's approach to grace, the anchoritic solution to the problem of sin, is certainly not missing from Christianity. One finds here, however, a new insight and the beginnings of a new stratagem of salvation. In the doctrine of Christian love, it is as though man had come to realize that to conquer the Id he must turn one part of it against another, rather than trying to suppress it *in toto*. This comes down to the physiological principle mentioned earlier; namely, that the subcortical systems embodying sexual functions (including affection) may be less disruptive of intrinsic neocortical processes than are subcortical systems embodying the functions of self-preservation. In urging us to cultivate affection for one another, Christ is in effect saying that if by rational effort we habitually substitute this emotion for others, then understanding and forgiveness, enlargement of ourselves—in short, grace—may follow.[8] *This* is the proper state of man:

8. Whereas Christ and St. Francis meant an affection generalized or detached from its instinctively prescribed objects (wife, child, husband, tribe), Christianity in fact retained a strong admixture of the primitive, in the sense that the divisions of the Id having to do with ferocity and sex were never wholly subjugated by it and put to other uses, except in a saintly few. Karl Jaspers remarked that "a strange atmosphere of arrogant humility, of sensual asceticism of perpetual veiling and reversal, runs through Christianity more than any other faith." *The Great Philosophers* (Harcourt, Brace, and World, 1957), p. 229.

Speaking of the period roughly from the twelfth to the mid-fourteenth century, Henry Adams said: "Perhaps the passion of love was more serious than that of religion, and gave to religion its deepest emotion, and the most complicated one which society knew. Love was certainly a passion; and even more certainly it was, as seen in poets like Dante and Petrarch—in romans like 'Lancelot' and 'Aucassin'—in ideals like the Virgin—complicated beyond modern conception." *Mont St. Michel and Chartres* (Houghton Mifflin, 1933), p. 216.

In the same era, ecclesiastical ferocity "puts forth its strength" (to borrow a phrase of Freud's) not only in the Crusades, which were attended by pogroms and a notable massacre in Jerusalem (in 1099), but also, and more enduringly, in the torture and extermination of heretics. St. Francis was hardly in his grave before the perversion of his order began.

a humanness not bought by isolation and denial, but won in everyday life, under direct fire of the instincts ("temptation"), and manifesting itself in works, that is, in active help and forgiveness, in the love of others and of beauty or knowledge, for their own sakes—to no other end. In the ideal, Christianity viewed practical life as merely a platform upon which men could stand and at last be men. The ideal Christian therefore shares what goods he has, sets no store by goods as such, and will compromise on any practical issue to a degree which un-redeemed men of instinct can only regard as absurd and take contemptuous or spiteful advantage of.

The final paradox is that grace or illumination must not be striven for as such, as a *reward,* for in that case self-interest will vitiate the whole undertaking. If one tries to love others only to the degree that one expects to be loved or otherwise repaid oneself, if goodness is put on this strict economic basis, then by definition the effort at it is conditional, not wholehearted. One must rather, by conscious resolve, adhere to a program which will either go unrewarded or possibly expose one to punishment or exploitation by the unredeemed. If a majority does not agree to this moral economy—and no majority ever has—virtue may in time succumb to uncertainty[9] and disillusionment; and with this the conquest of the animal self will cease, as is in fact happening in

"If Satan existed, the future of the [Franciscan] order . . . would afford him the most exquisite gratification. The saint's immediate successor . . . Brother Elias, wallowed in luxury. . . . The chief work of the Franciscans in the years immediately following the death of their founder [in 1226] was as recruiting sergeants in the bitter and bloody wars of the Guelphs and Ghibellines. The Inquisition . . . was in several countries, chiefly conducted by Franciscans. A small minority, called the Spirituals, remained true to his teaching; many of these were burnt by the Inquisition for heresy." Bertrand Russell in *A History of Western Philosophy* (Simon and Schuster, 1945), p. 450.

"Action ranks higher than contemplation," Innocent III wrote to his deputy in the South of France in 1205. This type of mind, while it must eventually cede to the inherently stronger secular power as represented by Philippe le Bel, was still to preserve the Church, at the eventual cost of the faith, for centuries.

9. Including the metaphysical uncertainty which has come to haunt us in this century. If God does not exist; if life is blind in the sense of being a phenomenon with no more point or further purpose than any other, our efforts at moral self-improvement must seem absurd if not, to a hardrock behaviorist, impossible. The only true improvements are *ethical* (according to the present view); but history, including our own, suggests that enlightened selfishness is a contradiction. To the extent that it *is* selfishness, it sooner or later ceases to be enlightened.

the modern world. It is not surprising that (in Ortega y Gasset's phrase) a doctrine so difficult took so little root. What is surprising, and what modern scepticism too easily dismisses, is the real effect Christianity has had, despite the innumerable ways in which it has been misunderstood and innocently or otherwise perverted.

I am here speaking of the ideal aspect of our religion. The important point is that it represents a body of insights perhaps far closer to the truth, more faithful to the principles on which our brains and our natures may actually be organized, than most today would concede.[10] It is to such insights, disseminated as traditional precepts or ideals, that Christianity or its forebears may have owed their remarkable power to bring surpassing cultures in their train—this despite the grossest forms of superstition and institutional frightfulness which have invariably persisted along with them. It is a fortunate paradox that the same clerics who would order the most bloodthirsty suppression of dissent or lend "moral" support to devastating wars continued to teach traditional principles of conduct diametrically opposed to such actions. In many cases unregenerate men of the Id, they nonetheless handed on a legacy enabling a few to develop inwardly as they had been unable or unwilling to do themselves. It is these few, the real heirs of the Word, who, despite often violent persecution, become the leaven of their society: men in whom human character and intellect reach something like full stature, whose example at last gives reality to the truths rattled off daily by the hacks of religion, and whose unique freedom in mind produces that body of moral and intellectual achievement we call culture.

In this line of historical development one sees as it were, acted out, the duality which lies at the root of the religious impulse—a duality built into man's brain and therefore reflected in his psychic constitution. This is not exactly the duality of good and evil, of Ormuzd and Ahriman, of grace versus the darkness of sin, though in outcome it can often be described that way.

The duality consists in the fact that the I of man, corresponding perhaps to a new functional system of the neocortex, may exist in

10. The basic principle being that man does not live by adaptation alone, because the proper development of his intellect requires more in-forming than practical concerns or an animal ("wholesome realistic") existence can provide.

increasing opposition to the Id or subcortical instinctive self. In the process of achieving a degree of autonomy, this new neocortical system extends its control over subcortical systems, in part, I have supposed, by favoring activity of the sexual-ferocity over that of the emergency system: that is, it has tended to turn the dual organization of instinctive or motivational functions to its own advantage.[11] This, in turn, has had a peculiarly disadvantageous result in that as man has become more civilized, it has increasingly protected him perhaps from primary fear but made him increasingly liable to primary ferocity.[12] The result has been yet another paradox: that as human civilizations have reached quite high, apparently stable, levels of development, they have tended to plunge into prolonged wars of annihilation. Historiographers have called these Times of Troubles,[13] and such periods seem to have occurred late in the history of all great cultures, including at the present time our own. This liability to primary ferocity is, one might say, the exposed flank of the developed self. It has figured, no doubt, in the odd readiness of many genuinely pious Christians to massacre the heterodox. And at a later stage in the growth of cultures, it may—as I shall try to demonstrate in Chapters VII and VIII—play a part in their decline, their permanent loss of what Walter Bagehot called the "secret of progression."

Considering only the higher forms of the religious impulse and ignoring its more superstitious or fear-inspired forms, one might surmise that religion represents man's sense of his own as yet unrealized self. This is the self capable of achieving clarity and "grace," the self which inclines to true disinterestedness. In the brain, it corresponds, I have supposed, to the new functional system or I which tends to take

11. C. M. Fair, *The Physical Foundations of the Psyche* (Wesleyan, 1963), pp. 176–177.

12. Of the several examples given in Konrad Lorenz' *On Aggression* (Harcourt, Brace, and World, 1966), perhaps the best is that of unorganized versus organized groups of rats (*ibid.,* p. 158). The unorganized rat is anxious and on the run. No sooner has he settled down and begun to breed a clan than he becomes violently aggressive toward outsiders. By analogy, in human societies the safe stay-at-home tends to be quite a ferocious patriot and fomenter of opinion, whereas the infantryman is simply a man doing a dirty job and trying to control his fear and revulsion in the process.

13. In fact, in human Times of Troubles, the dominant emotion (except among a protected influential few) comes to be fear. See Chapters VIII–IX, below.

shape in the neocortex. The gift of the greatest religious visionaries has been to see the potential in all of us for radical enlargement of that self, together with some of the moral principles which, if adhered to, would make such enlargement possible. Thanks to their teaching, the great religions came to include precepts very different from, if not radically at odds with, those derived from purely practical experience. The result was to give the most favored inheritors of such traditions a perspective on experience and a degree of psychic development scarcely approached even by the best of their tribal forebears.

This amounts to saying that the neocortex of man can perhaps never achieve full functional development if man himself is concerned only with practical success and uses his mental powers only in the interests of what biologists call adaptation. At first glance it would seem that religions such as Christianity teach principles of belief and conduct which are hopelessly unrealistic. And as proof one can point to the scarcity of model Christians. In fact, the matter is not so easily disposed of. For, as has been the case in other civilizations, the major artistic and intellectual, and even practical, achievements of this one came *after* their parent religion—long after the coalescence of tribal Europe into medieval Christendom. If the view of man's psychic nature which I have outlined here is approximately correct, it is only logical that events should have followed this course, or more generally, that great cultures have of necessity been the children of great faiths. For it was precisely the "unrealistic" precepts of Christianity which permitted west European man gradually to enlarge the waking conscious I, to the point that it finally became capable of far more than mere day-to-day practical problem-solving.

In physiological terms, one can perhaps infer that the teaching of moral principles acts to increase man's repertoire of abstract memories on a scale which no purely practical tradition is likely to approximate.[14]

14. Vide late sceptical Rome vis-à-vis Greece of the 5th century B.C. See also the relative poverty of Russian achievements in basic science since the beginning of the Marxist era. Today, the USSR has many "workers" in physiology and chemistry, but as yet no Mendeleevs or Sechenovs. That lack is certainly not due to a want of "facilities" or official encouragement. In most cases it is not even traceable to ideological restrictions. The real explanation, I believe, may lie in Marxian pragmatism, after all a late Western import and ironically enough a more destructive one than the Petrinism that the Pan-Slavs of Dostoevski's day so feared and distrusted.

Furthermore, the world viewed from the standpoint of moral ideality is more objectively seen in the sense that one's creature interests are less directly involved in one's judgment. The result, in short, of "unrealistic" moral teaching is apt to be far greater realism in the long run, since it tends to expand the limited perspective of self-interest and to act as a continual counterargument to those rationalizations which spring so readily from the pressure of the Id on the intelligence. At the bottom of all great religions is an awareness that what man needs is greater *clarity,* and to this end their greatest prophets have urged systematically impractical or antipractical modes of thought and being. A remarkable outcome, in our own civilization, has been the emergence of science— that is, of experiment or the study of the real for its own sake, without regard to use or profit.

In comparision to advances made during earlier centuries, when man approached nature chiefly for what benefit he could directly wring from her, the success of science has been astronomically great; and its most momentous practical results have in general flowed from work which was least practically motivated. Essentially what the success of science demonstrates is the enormous power of the neocortex or its corresponding system, the rational I, when these have become freed, in some departments at least, of the ancient tyranny of the subcortical Id. Though the Christian Establishment has more often than not been the enemy of reason, it may nevertheless be to the teachings of that Establishment that reason owes its present triumphs.[15] The same may be said of such small moral progress as we have made since Charlemagne's time. In most West Christian countries, violent or extreme punishments are no longer meted out for trivial offences; and in several, it is no longer legal to take a man's life for any reason[16] except unfortunately in war. Today we regard dueling as barbaric, but in its day it represented a moral advance in that it apparently developed as a substitute for the

---

15. Had the church fully understood the dangers of even rote instruction in Christian morality, it would doubtless have "reformed" its doctrines centuries ago and thereby precluded much later progress. At that, Catholicism has evidently managed to block much that occurred in the neighboring Protestant world in the centuries since the Renaissance; witness the status of modern Italy, Spain, and South America versus that of England, Scandinavia, and the United States.

16. For example, in England, Scandinavia, and some states in the United States.

"killing affray."[17] Democracy rests ultimately on a concept which, like Christian morality, is anti-Darwinian and in that sense impractical. To be sure, it favored the practical interests of some, but even those have made substantial concessions in its behalf, which probably would not have been the case had the only motive for the establishment of democracy been practical in the first place; that is, if the morality of liberalism had not had real social effect.

> Liberal democracy [Ortega y Gasset said] carries to the extreme the determination to have consideration for one's neighbor and is the prototype of "indirect action." . . . Liberalism—it is well to recall this today—is the supreme form of generosity; it is the right which the majority concedes to minorities, and hence it is the noblest cry which has ever resounded on this planet. It announces the determination to share existence with the enemy; more than that, with an enemy which is weak. It was incredible that the human species should have arrived at so noble an attitude, so paradoxical, so refined, so acrobatic, so anti-natural. Hence it is not to be wondered at that this same humanity should soon appear anxious to be rid of it. It is a discipline too difficult and complex to take firm root on earth.[18]

A major effect of democracy, in other words, has been to impose a system of checks on man's urge to dominate, exploit, or otherwise abuse his tribal inferiors—his urge to *make* inferiors of others. The urge is still inextinguishably there. The democratic world, heaven knows, is full of peck-orders, usually with the most coldhearted Darwinian types at the top. But liberal custom has decreed, and liberal law helps to insure, that all such victories shall be limited or temporary or both. Less and less does one have privilege merely by right of birth; one is increasingly forced to earn or merit it. While we still have the problem of entrenched wealth, the entrenchment of power and status, the use of power purely to suppress competition and insure the powerful a large "take" is far

17. See G. M. Trevelyan, *English Social History* (Longmans, Green, 1944), p. 159.
18. José Ortega y Gasset, *The Revolt of the Masses* (Norton, 1932), p. 88. J. S. Mill, speaking of the moral foundations of liberalism, remarks: "It would . . . be easy to show that whatever steadiness or consistency these moral beliefs have attained, has been mainly due to the tacit influence of a standard not recognized." *Utilitarianism, Liberty and Representative Government* (Everyman's, 1900), p. 3.

less of a problem in our world than it is, say, in Spain or Latin America. We have so far escaped the near paralysis which afflicts those countries —have tended much more to diversify our society and have in general remained more fluid and capable of advance.

It is as though in democracies unredeemed practical men had come to see that there really are long-run benefits to be gained from not bearing down too hard on the less able or less fortunate. On the contrary, the greatest benefits may result from improving the condition of all: providing general education at public expense, awarding social promotions on the basis of merit, alleviating extremes of poverty by welfare or "made work," and so on. We regard these changes today as the result of enlightened self-interest, but the fact is that before they were made, most practical men would have opposed them as unworkable; witness the fact that no matter how far liberalism has gone or how successful its innovations have proved, there is always a considerable minority which wants it to go no further. A good part of the initiative which overrode this reluctance is almost certainly moral and derives, in our case, from Christian ideals. To the extent that liberalism has worked—that is, has given rise to societies which are more productive and less confining or oppressive to the individual than are their authoritarian contemporaries —the morality in which it originated can be described as conducive to a higher order of objectivity. What appeared to be unadaptive at first glance turns out to have been a superior form of adaptation in the longer course.

It is in the several senses just described that the moral intuitions which make up the core of religions such as Christianity are parental to great civilizations. The essential reason may be that man is born with a mind which is a *tabula rasa* in a far more qualified and complex sense than Locke could have known. Unlike the brains of even his nearest evolutionary relatives, man's brain is inadequately used simply in the perfection of the day-to-day tactics of survival and procreation.[19] While many higher forms may have a considerable potential which remains unused after the demands of adaptation have been met, man's predicament seems to be that adaptation may not exact the necessary *minimum* of functional development of his intelligence. In

19. Or even in the strategic mastery of his environment, a form of adaptation of which no other species is really capable.

psychological terms, man the primitive is not then fully human; in physiological terms, the dominance relations within his central nervous system have not come into proper balance—the same applying to men of higher civilizations who live by hard-rock practicality or Darwinian survival ethics or to those who come to maturity as pampered amorphs. In religious language, man the primitive or man the civilized sinner suffers from avidya, an inner darkening, an inchoate, never quite sane or stable mental life, in which he is continually a prey to fear or hubris, to emotionally inspired nonsensical beliefs, and to a wanton nonsensical ferocity. Such is the condition of many who achieve control of vast institutions—the wizards of *Realpolitik,* or warfare, or finance, or mechanical invention—of those, in short, with the gift of adapting on a grand scale. The singing of Nero, the *pensées* of Ford and Edison,[20] the public utterances of Eisenhower, the prose and political thinking in *Mein Kampf,* the *mots* of the Sun King or George III, are mystifying only to the extent that one fails to understand the structure of man's nature. The Puritans of the seventeenth century distinguished "Right Reason" from "Natural Reason."[21] The former is the reason which (to quote Whitehead) "Plato shares with God"; the latter, or "pragmatic reason," is that which "Ulysses shares with the foxes."[22] It is likewise the reason which the great succeeders often share with the least suc-

20. For a brief review of Edison's rather odd theories of the psyche and of spirit phenomena, see Martin Gardner, *Fads and Fallacies in the Name of Science* (Dover, 1957), p. 311.

Entertaining and probably accurate appraisals of Mussolini's opera *Cesare* and Hitler's conversation are to be found in *The Ciano Diaries,* by Count Galeazzo Ciano (Doubleday, 1946), pp. 71 and 478.

Some years ago, there circulated an anonymous version of Lincoln's Gettysburg Address, as Eisenhower might have phrased it ("I haven't checked these figures but eighty-seven years ago I think it was, a number of individuals organized a governmental setup here in this country. . . ."). It is also interesting to compare General George Patton's speech, delivered when he took over command of the Third Army in 1944 ("Men, this stuff some sources sling around about America . . . not wanting to fight is a lot of baloney . . . etc."), with, for instance, the exchange of notes between Generals Sherman and Hood regarding the evacuation of Atlanta in 1864 (W. T. Sherman, *Memoirs* [Appleton, 1875], II, 118 ff.). The significance of the deterioration of language in this century is discussed below in Chapter X.

21. See the opening chapters of C. P. Smith's *Yankees and God* (Hermitage, 1954).

22. See Reinhold Niebuhr, *The Nature and Destiny of Man* (Scribner's, 1941), p. 113.

cessful in their society, the submerged, unstable, perennially stunted poor.

Translated into the language of physiological psychology, these distinctions can be restated as follows. "Natural" or "pragmatic" reason represents a degree of functional development of human neocortex sufficient to make it a highly effective servant of the Id. Men of much native ability, developed only to this degree, tend to dominate the tribe and to perform with brilliance so long as the pressure of circumstance upon the Id, or the Id itself, propels them into action. When these pressures are lacking or are suddenly relieved, such men tend to show little further growth, and some spectacularly deteriorate. They can be defined as adaptive or pure "response" types, in that most of the time, the waking I, as embodied in neocortex, lacks sufficient momentum of its own to produce understanding or origination, in the fullest sense of those words. They lack the spontaneity which eventuates in great works of art or intellect—works often arising from no clear practical motive, but rather from a kind of unspecifiable inner need.[23] It has been said that disinterested work of this kind is in reality done for deferred or intangible gain: that it results from a diverted biological drive and represents no more than a subtilized and often misguided form of adaptation. One might equally say that it is done from non-adaptive need first, the hope of fame or money being the sop which this type of man then throws to his adaptive self—a means of placating the always restive Id.[24] Not a few have known they would never be recognized during their own lifetimes (Stendhal was one); and to the intelligent sceptic, there can be little real comfort in the prospect of

23. Because unspecifiable and not shared by all, it is not perhaps seen for what it is: namely, the higher mammalian impulse of curiosity or idle investigation become in (some) men a true drive—the drive of mind, fully formed, to seek its own satisfactions. As such, it is added to our older repertoire of drives, all of which are to a degree competitive with one another. Freud's error may have been that he failed to see that this new category of purely mental impulsions—the drive to know—might have to be recognized as such and might also have clear equivalents in the internal relations of the brain.

24. The technique of putting off the Id with imagined or anticipated gratifications is something like the mechanism of rationalization run in reverse, a case of reason, for once, bemusing the animal self, rather than conversely. It is a technique which all men use in some degree in working to distant ends. What distinguishes basic human types—for instance, the "instinctive" from the "creative"—is the ends toward which they work.

posthumous acclaim, even supposing one has, for a certainty, earned it.

The fact that men do such impractical work, often at great cost to themselves, argues in favor of the principle I have suggested here: namely, that with sufficient in-formation—a sufficient base in recalled fact and a sufficiently articulated superstructure of abstract memories— the neocortex of man produces a new system, the I, which has a clear momentum and clear objectives of its own. This is the state change described earlier, the stage in psychic evolution forecast by the appearance of curiosity in higher animals. Its purest expression is in the drive to know or to create, to no other end, and if need be at some sacrifice in creature rewards, including those of power and status. Such sacrifice is an acting out of a basic tenet of many higher religions: that adaptive success is only a means toward a more human end and should be treated accordingly. Finally, it is significant that men so dedicated to nonpractical pursuits rarely arise in tribal societies[25] and appear in ever-diminishing numbers in the late "realistic" eras of high civilizations.[26] The reason may be that, to appear at all, they require a tradition

25. Except as the (usually anonymous) artist—cave painter, carver of figureheads, engraver of intricate designs on weapons.

26. A good case, I think, can be made for the assertion that the rate of fundamental achievement in the sciences has progressively decreased since the last decade of the nineteenth century (see footnote 34 below)—this at a time when the application of scientific knowledge has increased to the point of revolutionizing the economy of the world. The underlying assumption here is that modern "realism" encourages technological thinking and academic careerism, but discourages the breadth and disinterestedness of mind needed for really important work. This is similar to the point made by the physicist John Synge: "We can never understand what science is if we think of it only as logical and Greek. The mystical religious theme is very often there, buried and despised in ages not sympathetic to it, outcropping strangely from time to time with words hard to understand in terms of ... logic, but nearer to the secrets of nature than logic alone can ever hope to come." J. L. Synge, *Science: Sense and Nonsense* (Jonathan Cape, 1951), p. 97.

M. K. Hubbert, a geophysicist, whom I have cited later in another connection, believes that we may in fact be retrogressing in science. He points out that the present practical demands of career might have been the undoing of Darwin or Newton, who took upwards of two decades before publishing *On the Origin of Species* and the *Principia*. He is concerned also about what he calls a "reversion to authoritarianism" in the sciences "whereby statements, if made by proper 'authorities' are to be accepted as valid" whereas "if a contrary statement is made by one who is not an 'authority' ... little credence can be given to it." *Science*, Vol. 139 (1963), pp. 884–890. What Hubbert is describing is the sort of system which grows up in the world of learning when the ideals and the corresponding powers of intellect on which learning depends begin to die out. The result is a corporate

which bequeaths to each generation an increasing store of more than pragmatic intangibles which are capable of expanding the mature civilized mind far beyond the limits likely to be imposed on it by a purely practical tradition. When this process—essentially an accumulation of thinking or evaluating devices—has reached a certain point in the history of a given civilization, a virtually new species of man begins to emerge. Always few in numbers but enormous in effect, these are the spontaneous ones—men who in certain directions, at least, have become radically free inside their own heads and whose particular nonadaptive interests are matched by an equally nonadaptive drive to self-expression. Their appearance coincides with, or rather produces, those eras of concentrated achievement which our own and earlier civilizations have experienced: the astonishing, if brief Athenian age; Egypt of the Twelfth Dynasty; the Renaissance; the subsequent explosions of accomplishment in Western music and philosophy and more latterly in literature and science. Viewed from this standpoint, the history of all major civilizations seems to have followed much the same course. Each apparently starts with the coalescence of diverse state or tribelike communities, themselves often fragments of preceding cultures, into a larger, more nebulous community of faith (the middle east of Achaemenid times; Egypt *circa* 2800 B.C.; Greece and parts of Asia Minor after the invasions and the fall of Minos; Christendom of Charlemagne's and Erigena's day). Such periods are, in Spengler's phrase, the springtime of cultures— the time of mass conversions in which there begins that slow accumulation of principles, generally agreed on and variously inculcated, which are to make up the tradition. In the sense that many of their root ideas

---

enterprise modeled after big business or government bureaucracy, with hundreds of millions of dollars in "plant," a huge payroll, and a very poor record in gains achieved per dollar or per man-hour. One might apply the same method of analysis to the modern arts, philosophy, or mathematics. Given the numbers and "facilities" now available, the results have not been impressive.

Nor have the audiences for art grown as one might have expected. A quite similar change seems to have occurred in the classical world between the time of Periclean Athens and that of Augustan Rome. Even in literature the Romans were scarcely equal to the greatest of the Greek poets and dramatists and produced no thinkers at all of the caliber of Democritus, Archimedes, Aristotle, Zeno, Pythagoras, and so on. In the same way, the arts of the Egyptian Twelfth Dynasty were never equaled in the later centuries of the Empire, and many learned papyri, such as the Edwin Smith, appear to date from the same period. See J. H. Breasted, *The Conquest of Civilization* (Literary Guild, 1938), pp. 88 ff.

are highly mutable, differentiating out, over some centuries, into clear, often purely secular systems of thought, the growth of traditions is in a rough way like that of organisms. An organism takes final shape as a result of the interaction between circumstance and the logic, or pattern of unfolding, incorporated in its germinal cells. Traditions, one might say, represent the unfolding of certain basic, widely held notions, a process clearly including the interaction of belief with circumstance or, if you prefer, the impact of a people's history upon their ideas. It is probable, but not at all certain, that traditions have more degrees of freedom than does organic growth dependent on DNA–RNA. It may also be true, though not perhaps to the degree that Spengler thought, that all traditions tend to retain a certain primal stock of ideas, capable of only so many logical transforms before the stock is, so to speak, logically exhausted and its parent culture forced into stagnation and decline.[27]

The relevant point here is that because many of the transmitted principles comprising traditions such as our own are religious in origin and therefore not constrained by the requirements of immediate utility, they tend to confer an increasingly large and more variegated repertoire of abstract memories on succeeding generations. Moreover, a good share of these are abstract memories of a particular type; namely, devices for thinking or apprehending reality in other than purely pragmatic ways. With this the probability grows that at least a few—usually the more gifted and otherwise fortunate of their era—will undergo the psychic state change mentioned above. When that probability has reached the point of near-certainty, there occur those sudden Golden Ages of achievement which all great cultures have experienced and which mark their emergence, as it were, from the anonymous centuries of preparation, the period when all was vague striving and potential, and life itself had barely risen above the tribal.

Whereas the art of those early centuries may reach a prophetic force and perfection, as in the case of the Gothic, or of primitive Greek vase painting and sculpture, it is apt to be collective and unsigned, as though men individually were not yet sufficiently developed in mind to make a clear break with custom or to distinguish themselves from their social surround.[28] There are no *masters,* only slow perfection of the art-form

27. See Chapter IX, below.
28. The anonymity of tribal man results from a kind of mutuality in unaware-

itself, by a piling up of anonymous contributions to what is essentially a common enterprise. The emergence from this period of the preindividual occurs in waves as clusters of men of a radically new sort appear, now in one sphere of life, now in another. Such men represent maturation of the probability just mentioned. In them, the I—as distinct from mere animal ego or drive, which is the common birthright—decisively takes shape. Freed to seek its own ends and vigorous in proportion as it is free, mind transforms the world. In one field after another, in the realm of character itself at some periods, great masters appear, bringing in their wake rapid, often revolutionary changes in taste and outlook and ways of doing. Such was the world of fifteenth-century Italy, which Burckhardt describes:

> An acute and practised eye might be able to trace, step by step, the increase in the number of complete men during the fifteenth century. Whether they had before them as a conscious object the harmonious development of their spiritual and material existence is hard to say; but several of them attained it so far as is consistent with the imperfection of all that is earthly. . . . When this impulse to the highest individual development was combined with a powerful and varied nature, which had mastered all the elements of the culture of the age, then arose the "all-sided man" —"*l'uomo universale*"—who belonged to Italy alone. . . . In Italy at the time of the Renaissance, we find artists who in every branch created new and perfect works, and who also made the greatest impression as men. . . . There is no biography which does not, besides the chief work of its hero, speak of other pursuits, all passing beyond the limits of dilettantism. The Florentine merchant and statesman was often learned in both classical languages; the most famous humanists read the ethics and politics of Aristotle to him and his sons; even the daughters of the house were highly educated. It is in these circles that private education was first treated seriously.[29]

As the center of gravity of West Christian culture shifted northward, similar periods occurred elsewhere. Of Elizabeth's England, Trevelyan says:

ness. In *Coming of Age in Samoa* (Morrow, 1928), p. 221, Margaret Mead noted that the islanders did not seem clearly to perceive others' identity. From the romaunt to the modern novel, one can trace the emergence of perceived identity, if not of identity itself (that is, in social fact).

29. Jacob Burckhardt, *The Civilization of the Renaissance in Italy* (Phaidon, 1944), p. 84.

It was no accident that Shakespeare's plays were more poetry than prose, for the audience he addressed, as indeed the common English in town and country alike, were accustomed to poetry as the vehicle of story-telling, entertainment, history, and news of contemporary incidents. . . . Ballads were multiplied and sold, many thousand of them, each with a story from the Bible, or classical myths and histories, medieval legend or happenings of the day. . . . And lyrics and lovesongs, of which the words survive as masterpieces of literature in our modern anthologies, were sung as the common music and sentiment of the people.[30]

Of the England of the mid-seventeenth century he writes:

Not all the year round could maids "sit in the shade singing of ballads." . . . There was much hardship, poverty and cold in those pleasant villages; but the simplicity and beauty of the life with nature was an historical reality, not a poet's dream.

The great generation of men who between them produced the high English tragedy of Roundhead and Cavalier, were not brought up on the Bible and on the influences of the country life alone. . . . The age of Milton, Marvell and Herrick was an age of poetry and learning often in close alliance. Not only were simple and beautiful songs being written and set to music and sung by all classes, but in cultivated households more elaborate and scholarly poems circulated in manuscript before they found their way into print or passed into oblivion. When the music of Lawes was married to the immortal verse of Milton's *Comus* for the private theatricals of Lord Bridgewater's family (1634), English domestic culture touched perhaps the highest mark to which it ever attained. And the learning of the time, classical as well as Christian, was very widely spread.[31]

To judge from the history of classical times and from our own, the realization of a tradition in the shape of great individuals and great works occurs first in the realm of the nonexplicit arts (architecture, painting, sculpture, music). It then goes on to include literature (beginning with the ballad and poetry), philosophy, mathematics, and, in the West, science. In its final phase all the virtuosity and accumulated knowledge of the culture tend to be concentrated on *things*. The social and material worlds are organized as never before, and engineering in one form or another—as bridge building, military technics, statecraft,

30. Trevelyan, *English Social History,* p. 202.
31. Loc. cit., p. 238.

or finance—predominates. With enlightenment and the spread of scepticism, life reverts to the purely adaptive once more. The mentality of the age is increasingly pragmatic; and thanks largely to the fundamental achievements of former times, it is a pragmatism hugely successful, resulting in decisive conquests of man and nature and in a proportioned indifference to the poetic and the ideal, which are seen as foibles of the less sophisticated past. These are the periods which Sorokin,[32] in his peculiar terminology, called "sensate"; or which Spengler[33] more usefully defined as stages of transition from the state of culture to that of civilization. Under that definition, a culture is a society whose boundaries are determined by a common religion and whose accomplishments are as much in the realm of the intangible and the not yet as in that of the practical and the here and now. A civilization is the same religious community in dissolution. Its accomplishments are more and more exclusively in the realm of the practical as though its ideas or spirit were taking final form in things. And to the extent that it is cashing in on the intangible achievements of the past while doing less and less to renew them,[34] it is in effect living on its

32. Pitirim Sorokin, *Social and Cultural Dynamics* (American Book, 1937, 4 vols.).

33. Oswald Spengler, *The Decline of the West* (Knopf, 1932).

34. According to a report in *Science*, Vol. 133 (1961), pp. 1463–1466, patenting in the United States has shown a per capita decline, not only in relation to the population as a whole but also relative to the numbers engaged in science and engineering. Its sharpest decline is in relation to the per annum outlay for research and development. "Does the decline in patenting," the writer asks, "indicate a similar decline in the relative number of inventions?"

An answer to this question is suggested by some figures compiled by Sorokin, in his *Social and Cultural Dynamics*, Vol. II, Chapter III. These include a table, after Darmstaedter, covering the number of major scientific and technological discoveries or inventions made in successive ten-year periods from 1401 to 1900. These data, Sorokin says, "indicate an unmistakable retardation in the *rate* of increase during the last years of the nineteenth century. . . . Not only has the rate evidenced retardation, but even the absolute number of discoveries has been less in some [recent] decades than in those immediately preceding."

Concerning British and American patent statistics (up to the mid-1930's), he adds: "These data well agree . . . with the movement of discoveries and inventions derived from Darmstaedter. . . . They all, as far as sheer number of discoveries is concerned, show 'increasing fatigue' . . . in scientific and technological progress at the end of the nineteenth and in the twentieth century."

One might add that it is now more than half a century since the major work of Planck, Einstein, and Bohr. During that time there has been an enormous pro-

capital, however prosperous for the time it may appear. This last is
the stage which the classical world was reaching during the Scipionic
age[35] and which our own seems to have entered since the time of Grant
and Bismarck. (In Egypt it evidently began in the Hyksos period or the
later empire of Thutmose III; in China, in the century or so before
Shih Huang Ti; in Central America, somewhere between the collapse
of the Mayan and the rise of the Aztec civilization.)

The whole cycle from the Spenglerian springtime to the late stage of
civilization and "cashing in" takes approximately fifteen hundred
years.[36] Of these the first five to eight hundred are gestatory—"eras
of the imagination," as Brooks Adams called them—in which the
promise of human life is more felt than actualized, but in which men
seem propelled toward future attainment by an inner momentum
amounting to fatality. There is about such ages an almost brutish optimism. However ferociously the church may abuse its trust or give the
lie to its own teachings, men continue to believe. Provided only that
its saints and visionaries have sufficient insight, a great religion in its
youth is like a spring that cannot be poisoned. It cannot because the
impulses which are its source are deep and real, arising in a kind of
physiological necessity.

The same optimism which drives men on to become what they
intuitively feel they must be—that is to say, creatures distinctively
"human" and so unique on earth—apparently enables them, in such
ages, to tolerate all manner of civic frightfulness without serious loss
of faith.[37] One senses this spirit in Chaucer and Boccaccio, in the

liferation of experimental findings in particle physics, to the point that many
physicists believe some fundamental revision of existing theory, or some new and
better theory, is desperately needed. None has been offered; a fact all the more
remarkable when one considers the numbers and "facilities" involved in particle
research since the start of the Nuclear age.

35. From approximately 150 B.C. onwards.

36. That is, if one dates Classical civilization roughly from Mycenean times,
the Egyptian from 2800 B.C. (accepting 2781 as the most probable date of institution
of the Egyptian calendar, computed from the "Sothic cycle"), or our own from the
time of Clovis I in the latter half of the fifth century.

37. The failure of the medieval "synthesis" is not surprising, given men like
Innocent III and Henry Dandolo. What is surprising is that Christianity itself
outlasted such horrors as the slaughter of the Albigensians; the Inquisition (formally instituted in 1233, under Gregory IX); the corruption of the Franciscan
order, directly upon the death of its founder (in 1226); the later extermination

exuberant violence of the Crusades, in the sheer fortitude with which medieval Europe accepted its rulers and its plagues.[38]

If one regards the history of a culture as a record of the gradual conversion of ideas into works—which is to say, classes, institutions, and brilliant individuals—the notion of cultures as organisms becomes less fanciful than it once seemed. At the base of this phenomenon, granted that it may be one, lie the processes of individuation of the human psyche

of the Templars, conducted publicly and with much gratuitous cruelty by Philip the Fair; the shameless betrayal of John Hus; and so on and so on.

In the early fourteenth century parts of the Rhineland and southwest Germany were stripped of their pastors because of "the resistance of the towns to the exactions of the Papal Curia. . . . The Empire was in ruins, its vast churches empty. But the void was not left tenantless. Numerous small groups sprang up whose aim was to lead a common life of devotion, secure in the peace of soul conferred by an inward and personal apprehension of God. . . . The great majority of these brothers and sisters in piety had no thought of separation from the Church; it was a combination of circumstances—the lack of pastoral care, the animosity of the higher clergy . . . the constant denunciations at Rome and Avignon—that drove them into precarious positions on the margins of orthodoxy, and finally over the brink, to be swallowed up in successive waves of persecution." Friedrich Heer, *The Medieval World* (World, 1962), p. 309.

Such are the processes by which great religions, through the agency of their Darwinian masters, uproot and destroy their finest exemplars and, after centuries more, faith itself. The fact that it takes so long—that so many, like the Templars, die bravely and unshaken, or like the German mystics live uncorrupted by the overwhelming example of others' corruption—is a tribute to the remarkable force of man's aspiration to be more than the animal science now insists he is.

That aspiration is perhaps strongest not merely when conditions have become most favorable to its appearance, as in Europe of the eleventh to fourteenth centuries, but also when its realization as intellect and imagination and sensibility has only begun. In such eras the relative ignorance of the majority protects them from the sort of scientism or philosophic practicality which in later ages undermines all ideals of self-transcendence, returning men at last to an animality which they feel they *must* accept. In this sense, the last Puritans are those of reason, who bow to what they feel the evidence forces upon them. What violence this submission does to their natures can be judged from the atmosphere of profound uneasiness and gathering despair characteristic of "modern" epochs like our own, even among classes like the present American middle, which by purely practical standards have little cause for dismay. This uneasiness or revolutionary discontent is simply an *étape*, since the Puritanism of reason ultimately destroys reason itself. The revolutionaries who follow no longer suffer; they *act,* and all that remains of the old idealism and its social institutions is swept away.

38. Or refused to accept, witness for instance the fierce defiance which the burghers of Flanders showed the French in the fourteenth century even after the massacre of their army at Cassel in 1328 and the unbridled vengeance then visited upon them by Louis of Nevers.

which I have tried to describe here. An essential feature of them is that as the individual's stock of usable abstract memories increases, his powers of reason or of creativity, the degrees of freedom of the conscious I vis-à-vis external necessity and the Id, may grow exponentially or as a permutative function of the available devices for thinking.[39] Translated into collective terms, this may mean that the history of cultures tends to follow an accelerative course, starting with a period of very gradual rise lasting nearly one-half of the whole cycle and going into steep ascent during the second half.

In Europe, from 500 to 1000 A.D., there were few thinkers of the caliber of Erigena and only poorly defined artistic or business classes. By the time of François Villon and the Wars of the Roses, such classes had long since taken shape. Patronage of painting and literature was well established. The great ages of the madrigal and the verse drama were soon to come, and after them the era of enormous overseas expansion and world trade, as personified by the East India Company (which was incorporated, under Elizabeth, by royal charter in December of 1600).

From Elizabeth's time until just recently, the slope of the curve has become ever steeper. The diversification of art and learning, of society itself, including both the producer and the means of production, have proceeded at a rate which, if measurable, would probably be best fitted by a third-order differential; that is, by a mathematical expression for rate of rate of change.[40] In the classical world, roughly from 600 B.C. to the time of Archimedes, a similar period of growth evidently occurred. These and their parallels in other cultures perhaps represent a collective or statistical phenomenon in principle quite like the explosive growth which occurs in the human individual from puberty until such time as he reaches the peak of his powers—often by the early or middle twenties, but sometimes much later, depending upon his temperament and his métier. In either case what we may be seeing is the maturation of certain probabilities into near certainties, the ap-

---

39. Which are likewise devices for controlling the Id: in physiological terms, the means by which neocortex extends its dominance over the rest of the nervous system.

40. For an interesting analytic approach to the problem of the growth rates involved in "cultural evolution," see H. Blum, in *Annals of the New York Academy of Sciences*, Vol. 138, Article 2 (1967), pp. 489–502.

pearance of the distinctive human self as a cumulative consequence of the structuring of memory, not merely through the incorporation of facts but also, and most essentially, through the incorporation of ideas imposing order and meaning upon facts. It follows that (as Julian Huxley has said) tradition rather than mutation or natural selection has become the prime instrument of evolution, since it is through tradition that the human individual acquires the necessary store of in-formation (*sic*) to become what we regard as fully human; that is, to realize his inherited potential. And it is only as man realizes that potential, or brings into being at least a part of the self called by mystics the soul, that he becomes able to understand and manipulate nature in radically new ways. And with that, paradoxically, has come his complete— perhaps too complete—biological victory over all other species. Few practical men—for that matter, few mystics—could have foreseen that development of the Higher Self would have that result.

The question I have not yet gone into is why, when a culture reaches the level of growth described above, it does not continue to progress indefinitely. It is fairly easy to understand why the history of human accomplishment has gone in spurts. What is less obvious is why such fertile periods should be self-limiting—why all cultures should pass into civilization, go sterile, suffer long Times of Troubles, and at last become what Toynbee calls living fossils. There are, I think, clear reasons why events tend to follow this course; and in the next chapter I shall try to show what some of them may be.

*Chapter VI*

---

## THE IDEA OF THE SOUL AND THE
## REVOLUTIONS OF THE
## TWENTIETH CENTURY

THE unfolding of a culture—in essence, the differentiation of a certain core of ideas into divers new forms and of a society into multitudinous smaller worlds, each with its own special ideals and powers and relations to the rest—involves certain paradoxes. Latent in his nature from the beginning, these paradoxes come back to haunt man in his civilized middle age. Because of them, one might guess, all cultures, as they pass into the later stages of growth and reach their apogee of practical virtuosity, become revolutionary in the profound, almost metaphysical sense that our own is.

The fundamental paradox is that while a culture such as the classical or West Christian affects nearly every phase of the communal life, nevertheless, in any era only a very few out of the whole population are its true beneficiaries. Through some combination of native endowment, early training, energy, and luck, they manage to realize themselves or become fully human in the sense I have tried to define here. Depending on their special gifts, their society then may or may not grant them honors, respect, and the right to lead lives reasonably free of want and distraction. If society does not grant them these things, as has often happened, they may suffer greatly, but it is still a suffering different in kind and quite different in meaning from that of the perennially poor. For the latter are not merely the victims of economic circumstance; they are deprived from childhood of their most essential selves as well, condemned to an animal amorphousness, to the point of seeming to the educated almost members of another race. They are. Even those who succeed in rising from the ranks of the anonymous carry for life the scars, or rather the withered limbs, which betray their beginnings. It is not only that to rise from the bottom to the top of human society exacts such penalties in itself; for instance, in the over-development of aggression and ruthlessness. The real penalty is to have been born at the bottom in the first place; to have grown up in a world of people themselves trapped in an almost precultural crudity of mind, and so unable to give their children that necessary minimum of intangibles to grow on.

There is much evidence, from the study of both man and animals, that the earliest-established memories are the most enduring. It has been suggested[1] that man, like lower forms, passes through certain critical learning periods in the years up to and just beyond sexual maturity. Every teacher knows from experience that young people's minds do not glide smoothly toward adulthood. Instead, they seem to mature in jumps, with long discouraging fallow periods in between. The greatest jumps forward may correspond to critical learning periods.[2]

Conversely, what is not taught young people either explicitly at school or more or less implicitly at home, during the early years critical for functional development of the brain, may never later be learnt at all. A crude analogy is that of learning to play a musical instrument; unless one starts on it very young, one will never have the technique, and possibly never the mental facility either, to play it really well. Among the processes which go to form the psyche as a whole, the seeding of young minds with a variety of ready-made abstract memories may be crucial, since it is these which bring the contents of memory under rational control and with them the Id. It is thus perhaps not enough

1. See, for instance, J. P. Scott, "Critical Periods in Behavioral Development," *Science,* Vol. 138 (1962), p. 949.

2. These have parallels among the higher mammals. For example, young Greenland Eskimo dogs up to sexual maturity do not appear to have learned the territory of their pack and so continually stray and get into trouble. However, "within a week" of coming of age "their trespassing adventures are over." (N. Tinbergen, *The Study of Instinct* [Oxford, 1951], p. 150.) This may be an instance of what psychologists call "latent learning." Some of the abilities or talents which suddenly show themselves in young people at around puberty may result from new and greatly intensified, "motivation" which acts to draw together into working wholes a vast assortment of recalled facts and ideas, many of which were until then "latent" in the sense of being too unorganized to be readily retrievable. In fact much of what we call the unconscious may not be repressed memory-data, but rather information which was randomly acquired and which has remained, in a logical sense, inaccessible.

for a child to acquire a set of principles enabling it to cope with day-to-day problems of life in the neighborhood. Later on, such a child may have great difficulty in learning anything else and in addition may remain emotionally unstable, in or out of his home environment: a creature perennially superstitious and parochial, fantasy-ridden rather than imaginative, and correspondingly unable to tell his own pseudo-thoughts from real ones, to distinguish logical necessity from the pressure of instinct, wishes from facts. Quite frequently, this seems to be the mentality of the "underprivileged" who even today make up the vast majority of mankind.[3]

What makes the poor man's lot terrible is not simply that he hasn't enough to eat or must work too hard for what he gets. It is that he is doomed to live in a kind of psychological twilight halfway between the state of Australopithecus and that of man proper. The more natively intelligent he is, the more terrible must his condition seem to him, the more keenly must he sense the self he has been thwarted of, the gulf that lies between him and those who have become inwardly as well as outwardly free, who *are* imaginative and can think for themselves. The upper levels of society, often including otherwise quite sensitive and gentle men, tend to be repelled by the stuntedness and violence they see in him and so deny him real fellow feeling or consideration, as they have frequently done the insane. The *nouveau riche* is a stock comic figure. He has capability and power, but is still not quite all there, not a *person*—though his children may be, or theirs.

Marxism, with its emphasis on the external and the mechanical, even nineteenth-century Liberalism, with its faith in the power of education, underestimated the enormity, in every sense, of this problem. Rousseau was responsible for a gross and still widespread misunderstanding of it. The poor represent those who, since Neolithic times, have occupied the lowest ranks in the human peck-order. In the tribal world of prehistory, during the reign of primal religions, the difference in psychic development between them and the remainder of the tribe was perhaps not very great. As a result, surviving "Neolithic" societies such as those of the American Indian have no class problem of the kind that forever threatens high civilizations. There is not yet such a

---

3. On the question of to what degree this mentality may be created rather than inherited, see D. D. Jackson, in *Science,* Vol. 134 (1961), p. 1910.

difference between upper and lower orders in inward formation of the
self as to make each almost a separate species.[4] In parallel with the
increasing difference in wealth and power which develops between
upper and lower ranks as tribal societies become "civilized," there appears this deeper split, representing an ever-increasing divergence in
psychic type, until at last, in eras such as the Victorian, the upper classes
can with verisimilitude describe the poor as their inferiors in mind
and character as well as in material success.[5]

4. However, among the Polynesians the principle of mana, which was believed
to be concentrated in the head and (like intellect) was both suprapractical and the
key to practical success, was chiefly an attribute of the upper classes. (The same
holds for the principle of *kami* in ancient Japan.) It is interesting also that the
Polynesians regarded this principle as *dangerous,* perhaps because the productions
of intellect, while often useful and powerful, are likewise, if only from their un-
expectedness, rather frightening. A similar power principle, but one not regarded
as dangerous or as confined to certain classes, was believed in by the Melanesians
and the American Plains Indians. Cf. Edward Norbeck, *Religion in Primitive
Society* (Harper and Row, 1961), pp. 38–43.

5. The Victorians found in Darwinian selection a convenient mechanism to
explain these class differences. Racism provides a means by which both high and
low castes in a given society can look down on aliens, especially colonial peoples,
either abroad or imported. Considering the sentimental popularity of the Irish in
America today, one is amused to read this review of Johnston's *Notes on North
America*, in the *Edinburgh Review* for July, 1851 (p. 29): "The author's observa-
tions . . . show that he has hit upon the real explanation of the frequent energy and
success displayed by many of the emigrants from the sister island, on being trans-
planted to the New World, in comparison with their listlessness and helpless misery
at home. . . . Where the Irish settled *singly,* and among a population of different
origin and habit, he generally found them doing well, though rarely *so* well as
either English or Scotch emigrants. Where they settled *en masse"* the results reportedly were terrible, a duplication of conditions at home: " 'wretched looking
houses . . . much dirt about themselves and their holdings, nasty-looking pigs
running about . . .' " Mrs. Trollope describes the dreadful mistreatment of Irish
immigrant labor on the Potomac two decades earlier, and the low esteem in which
the Irish in this country were generally held. Frances Trollope, *Domestic Manners
of the Americans* (Vintage, 1949), 287–290.

It might be more just to say that the Irish in the New World continued to
show the effects of the psychic stunting inflicted upon them by centuries of British
misrule. In the same period—the 1820's—when the Irish in the Old Country were
beginning to turn revolutionary (see Alexis De Tocqueville, *Journeys to England
and Ireland,* Faber and Faber, 1958, p. 118 ff), the great Irish fighting gangs were
beginning to spring up in New York. The Five Points district, where before 1820
one watchman or "Leatherhead" (so-called from his helmet) had been able to
maintain order, became a perennial battleground, as did other parts of the city in
such memorable explosions as the Abolition Riot of 1834, the Dead Rabbit Riot
of 1857, and the so-called Draft Riots which occurred ten days or so after Gettys-

One paradox lying at the root of all cultures or high civilizations is, then, that the same processes of growth which bring a few men to superb fulfillment, and small classes of men to great power and comfort, divide the culture as a whole into psychological castes and thereby prepare it for devastating upheavals. The lowest of these castes comprises a large number of men so inwardly impoverished as perhaps to be irretrievable, in the sense that if substantial opportunity were suddenly made available to them, they would almost certainly misuse it.[6] What the Liberals of the nineteenth century failed to see was that many children of the poor, by the time they reach school age, may already be half ineducable. Marx appears to have thought that a change in material fortune would directly result in an improvement in man's psychic lot—that workers needed only to be schooled in the techniques of acquiring power and taught to respect themselves as future citizens of substance, to become wise and capable administrators and good all-round human beings when the time came. The course actually followed by the Russian Revolution from 1917 to the present, or by the Chinese since World War II, argues that such optimism, no less than Rousseau's, was ill-grounded. To dismiss as "idealist" all concern with man's inner life as such, to see the self as a by-product of external conditions rather than as a major source of them, is an attitude which Marx—after all a Victorian materialist à la Comte and Dalton—shares with most of his capitalist adversaries of today. Both sides are wrong, and the revolution which neither succeeded in understanding has now spread over most of the world, including many societies[7] incapable either of democracy on the American plan or state socialism on the Russian.

burgh and Vicksburg, in 1863. The Draft Riots were in reality a spontaneous rebellion of the amorphous Irish poor against their step-parent society. By comparison with modern riots, the casualties were staggering, "conservative estimates" (according to Herbert Asbury) being 2000 killed and 8000 wounded. (See Herbert Asbury, *The Gangs of New York*, Knopf, 1928, *passim*).

6. Retrospective newspaper stories have I believe shown that winners of the Irish Sweepstakes seldom invest their winnings intelligently or hold on to them for long. A similar reckless improvidence, an inability to contain themselves or parlay their good fortune, was shown by the winners of the French Revolution, who soon gave way to Napoleon, as the old revolutionists in Russia soon gave way to Stalin.

7. For instance much of the Arab world or that of the new African Negro nations.

To form an idea of some of the principles which have determined the course of human history, one must, I believe, view it simultaneously from the standpoint of an ethologist and of a social historian. The study of animal and insect societies makes it clear that man's group behavior has much more in common with that of other forms than we might have preferred to think. Like animals, we are committed to pecking- or butting-orders, are driven by powerful reflexes to compete with or dominate our fellows, and derive from our victories, however senseless or sterile, an equally senseless satisfaction. Such triumphs owe both their appeal and their frequent absurdity to the fact that the appetite for them is simply built into us as one among many instinctive needs, whose fulfillment we feel as a mixture of pleasure and relief. In contrast to the "appetites" of reason—the love of knowing or creating for its own sake—the appetites of the Id require some learning, but not very much, to eventuate in suitable behavior;[8] whereas in the same individual the appetites of reason, along with higher forms of reason itself, may never develop at all. All of this merely illustrates the conservative organization of human nature. In the interests of survival, we adapt first, and with luck realize our full potential as men later on. The same theorem seems to apply to human societies. They begin as associations on the animal pattern: essentially herds, each arranged in a certain butting-order; clusters of families, having their scouts and forage leaders as do troops of baboons. As with jackdaws, when a man high in the peck-order marries a woman of lower rank, she is promoted to his level and may then bully and lord it over those who once bullied and lorded it over her. As with rats forced to live in an enclosure too small really to accommodate all, the dominant males in human societies, especially crowded ones, tend to live at the expense of the bottommost members of the community, never doubting their right to do so, any more than they doubt the right of a strong arm to prevail over a weak one, or of the crafty to outwit the less cunning. These are not rights but facts, and facts furthermore produced and

8. For instance, much of primate sexual behavior, including our own, is learned, as is our hunting behavior or that, say, of cats. The principle, in all cases, is the same. The organism inherits an assortment of disjunct motor mechanisms related to mating or hunting (or both) and at maturity learns to put these together in appropriate ways, meaning ways which lead to a maximum of "reward." For a further discussion and references, see C. M. Fair, *The Physical Foundations of the Psyche* (Wesleyan, 1963), Introductory.

sanctioned by the Id. That is to say, they are automatically brought into being by the acting out of innate drives and rewarded by an equally automatic state of pleasure when, having set out to master others, one succeeds. The same Id logic applies to love-making as to conquest, success with a woman often being called a conquest.

Throughout most of recorded time, both in high civilizations and in more static tribal communities, this has been the basic pattern of life and with minor modifications continues to be. It is then upon this ancient structure, with its adaptive compromises such as near monogamy or the near prohibition of incest, murder, gross theft, and cannibalism—one might say its instinctive morality—that the insights of the higher religions come to be imposed. Their essential appeal is perhaps to the incomplete in all of us—our sense of being far less than we might be, our *boredom,* when adaptively successful, with that sort of success. Besides the reassurances offered by all religions, primitive or advanced, the advanced give clear voice to what the majority only dimly glimpses: the fact that in man there is something beyond his sheer animal competence, his adaptive superiority over other forms— namely, a principle of transcendence, another self struggling to take shape. If I am correct in my appraisal of the relations which in man make for dominance of the neocortex, and so for the emergence of its psychic equivalent, the disinterested rational conscious I, it follows that these intuitions—essentially the Christian concept of grace, or the Hindu concept of Brahman—may have real foundations in physiological fact. Of the immortality of the soul one can say nothing, except that this idea may be one of the many sops we throw to the Id. It represents a survival from the days of more primitive magical forms of belief, its function being, as of old, to allay the fear and gloom and demoralization which come with the certainty that we must die. It has been suggested[9] that the Puritans of the seventeenth century no longer felt the need to believe in an afterlife, but regarded heaven and hell as metaphors for present states of being and grace as a condition to

9. By C. P. Smith, in *Yankees and God* (Hermitage, 1954), pp. 81, 208: "The old ministers—Cotton, Shepard, Eliot, Richard (the first), Mather and the rest— rarely talked about the fiery pit of hell. The problem was to get into cosmic equipoise here, and the punishment for failing to do so was an unhappy existence now. The 'rewards' and 'punishments' to be distributed at the Last Judgment were a dramatization, a metaphor, of the actual psychic present."

be achieved, if ever, now. I do not know if that was true, in the sense of being a generally held idea. However, it does seem to be the case that men who have most deeply realized themselves are apt to be those who least need magical protection against fear, which is only another way of saying that to become conscious and free in mind to near the limits of one's potential is by definition to deliver oneself from the Id by coming into control of those same engines of feeling by which the Id, in the less inwardly developed, controls and manipulates the actions of conscious intelligence.

It is not accidental, I think, that great religions often seize, like an epidemic, upon populations which are just emerging from a warlike nomadic existence into a more settled one. The classical gods and their temples spring up after the successive invasions of Greece and Asia Minor, in particular perhaps after the fall of Cnossus and the Cretan sea kings to the Dorians, *circa* 1400 B.C.[10] In early medieval Europe, Christianity takes root after the last remnants of the Roman system have been swept away and the several waves of Gothic and Hunnish invaders have begun to be absorbed into the pre-existing community. Something similar seems to have happened in the Near East of Achaemenid times (*circa* 500 B.C.), where, after long centuries of Hittite, Egyptian, and Assyrian incursions, a new religion, Zoroastrianism, and with it a new vehicular language, Aramaic, became widespread.[11]

I mentioned earlier that the instinctive apparatus or Id seems to be roughly a dual system, embodying emergency functions (including states of fear or anxious alertness) in one branch and feeding, sexual, and ferocity functions in the other. Like all systems within the brain —like the cortex vis-à-vis subcortical systems—these tend to take turn about in control. The dominance of one sets up the conditions for dominance presently to pass to the other, and conversely. This principle, which I called the answering effect,[12] guarantees the continual flux of our emotions and drives to the point that external circumstances

10. See J. H. Breasted, *The Conquest of Civilization* (Literary Guild, 1938), pp. 257 ff.

11. See Chapter V, footnote 4; see also Breasted, *op. cit.* Spengler mentions the spread of Aramaic as indicative of the rise of a new culture and uses it to illustrate his thesis that "religion is race." *The Decline of the West* (Knopf, 1932), II, 168. In fact, it may be so in a more complex sense than he thought, since religion has much to do with the appearance of radically different psychic types *within* a society.

12. Fair, *Physical Foundations,* Chapter I and *passim.*

cannot too long arrest them or freeze us into fixed attitudes of feeling and desire. (Such fixity, in fact, amounts to mental disorder and is often approached in the insane.) If we are forced to wait too long before coming to grips with an adversary or making love to a woman, it often happens that the impulse to do so passes—a principle to which delaying tactics owe their frequent effectiveness.

So far as the neocortex—and therefore the conscious I—are concerned, states of fear, or dominance of the emergency system, may be the more crippling (though *any* drive or feeling, if strong enough, disrupts thought and conscious control). The evolutionary logic behind this fact is, as I have also mentioned, that emergencies may take *any* form, so the best guard against them is likely to be a type of response that abruptly precludes deliberation (which may take too long and be futile in any case) and sets certain primitive all-purpose mechanisms in motion in its place. Our first impulse in fear is not to think; it is to run. It is then on the rebound from fear, or as dominance passes from the emergency to the sexual-ferocity system, that we may pass from fear to anger and instead of fleeing fight back. Only as these changes occur, does our ability to think coherently at last return. Conversely the extinction of thought in intense sudden fear is often so complete as to reduce us to automatism.

So long as men remain nomadic, warlike, and uncertain of what the morrow will bring, it is probable they live more on the rebound from continual dread than in the comparatively relaxed "spontaneous" state which goes with dominance of the second instinctive system. Their ferocity, even their sexuality, is of a kind constantly whetted by fear, which also deforms their conscious mental lives, filling their minds with ghosts and monsters. The Kwakiutls, the Iroquois, and much of the Arab[13] world are surviving examples of that mode of life. It is one capable of producing little in the way of real progress. In physiological terms, the state of fear, when habitual, is perhaps *the* most destructive of those influences which the (subcortical) Id can exert upon the (neocortical) rational self or I; witness the intense fear and the destruction of self which occur in many psychoses. More than anything else, it may be the chronic anxiety of neurotics which arrests their development (that is, the functional maturation of the neocortex),

13. See Paul Bowles, "The Incredible Arab," *Holiday* (August, 1956), pp. 48 ff.

thereby precluding not only real thought but real control of the rational over the irrational self, which in turn condemns the neurotic to a life of endless, Id-inspired, ineffectual ritual.[14] The same may be said of many primitive societies, and of higher civilizations in very early and very late periods of their history.

In general, before religions of the more advanced type can spring up, the societies which produce them must perhaps have begun making the transition from a dynamic, fear-inspired type of existence to one more orderly, secure, and conducive to the expansion of mind and the affections. What is needed is something like the peace of rural life and the moderate excitement and bustle of towns before they have reached the ruthless, overdriven, neobarbaric stage—the megalopolitan "jungle" (as their inhabitants half-proudly call it) represented by modern cities like New York and Chicago. As anyone who has lived it knows, the agricultural life is a hard one even today. Nonetheless the peace and poetic joy of which Trevelyan writes, in the England of Elizabeth and Cromwell and Queen Anne, were probably real and have faint equivalents still in the mechanized countryside of this century. One can imagine that the conditions eventually making for that state of mind were established long ago, in Europe of the eighth to eleventh centuries, with the turning back of the Moors and the absorption of what had once been barbarian raiders into the society of the Christian Middle Ages. The life of Christ himself may have owed much, besides his martyrdom, to the Roman presence, since for better or worse, that presence meant a kind of order and therewith a potential flowering of human warmth and insight. Such is the springtime of prophets, of men who come to understand more of man's nature and of his possibilities than there are yet words to tell. Unencumbered by the later-developed apparatus of conscious formal thought and by the peculiar prejudices and lacunae in understanding which these inevitably bring, the seers of early cultural time, who are the source of much that is to come, apprehend before all else what man *might* be. And in a populace itself slowly coming over to a more secure, more inwardly expansive way of life, their words take profound effect, for collectively such a populace is like a youth emerging from the fiat rule and mental dependence of his

14. The "defences" described by Freud, whose object is not to cope with external events so much as to ward off inner crises by a system of tactics which manipulates external events to this purely subjective end.

childhood. It is ready to shed or rather to regrasp much of the past, to recognize the possibility of transcendence in itself, to approach the uncertainties of existence not with awe and fright, but at last with hope and wonder. It is ready, in a word, to be "saved," and the era of mass conversions begins. With these there gradually comes into being, through the spread of religious teaching and so of new moral ways of viewing the world, an enormous counterforce to more ancient modes of thought. The latter, grounded less in hope or *élan* than in fear and a forced alertness, reduced always to the adaptive. The Id, one way or another, always won. Even supposedly disinterested virtues such as courage merely submerged the interest of the individual in that of the flock and were more enforced by awe of the Others than generated out of any conviction rationally arrived at by the courageous.

The essence of the religious view is that man's behavior need *not* always reduce to the adaptive—had better not, in fact, if he is to be truly saved. From this basic conviction there flows a kind of hope for the future which purely adaptive tribal man can never have.[15] Whether

---

15. This is the hope symbolized by Augustine's concept of the *Civitas Dei,* whose late secular form is liberal democracy. Such also was the moral impetus for the abolition of slavery. It reflected man's conviction that he could improve, if need be denying himself substantial practical advantages to that end. Apropos of the suggested analogy between Augustine's *Civitas* and democracy, see the "equations" which Bertrand Russell gives in *A History of Western Philosophy* (Simon and Schuster, 1945), p. 364, relating the elements of Augustine's system to Marx's. They are:

Yahweh = Dialectical Materialism
The Messiah = Marx
The Elect = The Proletariat
The Church = The Communist Party
The Second Coming = The Revolution
Hell = Punishment of Capitalists
The Millennium = The Communist Commonwealth

With appropriate substitutions—for example, Yahweh = the U.S. Constitution; the Messiah = Tom Paine; the Elect = the Common Man; the Second Coming = Global Victory of the American Way—you have the analogy I mentioned. Russell adds: "The terms on the left give the emotional content of the terms on the right, and it is this emotional content, familiar to those who have had a Christian or a Jewish upbringing, that makes Marx's eschatology credible." One might put this another way by saying that the wish of the saints becomes the father to late secular institutions which they are often fortunate in not living to see. For all its imperfections, however, democracy, I think, can be shown to be an improvement over Absolutism as generally practiced.

primitive or late-civilized, the latter always knows that the life of instinct is all there is. He is a "realist", accepting the self-evident boundaries of existence as fixed and all-inclusive, seeing no essential difference between himself and other species or other men. No amount of evidence to the contrary is likely to sway him because experience has taught him his own limits, and from these, often with a certain egalitarian jealousy, he infers the limits of his peers, or of life. Consequently, apart from material promise—the power and ease and *réclame* he may win—there *is* no future for him—only the same endless animal round, no matter how we all work to disguise and glamorize it. This is the "weariness" which overtakes late civilized worlds such as our own. Its tribal form is the stoicism and gloom of the American Indian or the flaccidity and boredom and early aging which some anthropologists have reported among Polynesian Islanders.

Once a new higher faith has spread, in particular perhaps among newly settled peoples ripe by that fact for decisive inner change, it evidently takes centuries for the basic optimism released by their conversion to wear out. This phenomenon is the more remarkable since the

It should be added that the Icelandic Althing, or assembly of all free men, which was the earliest of European parliaments, was founded in 930, seventy years before it voted to accept the introduction of Christianity into Iceland (see Friedrich Heer, *The Medieval World* [World, 1962], p. 300). The social system of pre-Christian Iceland seems to have been remarkably advanced, the franklin or free-holder having the right to change his chieftain, or overlord, at will and also the right of judgment by his peers. The Constitution of Ulfliot was adopted in 930 to settle existing disputes between chiefs and clients, and it was then that the Althing came into being, along with a law-speaker for the land as a whole. In 964 the Reforms of Thord Gellir divided the island into four quarters, with a court for each and a fifth court of final appeal. While grand in concept, this judiciary apparently never worked very well, for want of the power to enforce its decisions.

While there were certainly some Christians in Iceland (for example, among the Irish who preceded the Norse and among the later Irish immigrants), Christianity before or after its formal adoption may not have had much effect on the life of the commonwealth. As one writer puts it: "The . . . church system brought little change. The great families put their members into orders, and so continued to enjoy the profits of the land which they had given to the church; the priests married and otherwise behaved like the franklins around them in everyday matters." And it was as a result of a dispute over church jurisdiction that the country fell into civil war in the thirteenth century, incurring a series of misfortunes in the shape of foreign interference from which it never really recovered. One might say of this land that it could perhaps have got on quite well without the Word, whereas institutional Christianity was its undoing.

societies in which it arises are essentially Neolithic. Men of the baronial or strong-arm type head the peck-order, and as soon as conversion to the new faith has gone far enough, a new sort of careerist arises to institutionalize and pervert it, producing yet another power bloc, the church. Whether in league with secular authority or its active competitor, the church is an institution in principle like any other, which is to say a vehicle by which unregenerate adaptive man can come to power over his fellows.[16] There can be no question but that in the Christian church, Protestant as well as Catholic, he has habitually done so, outranking the more truly pious, if not actively persecuting them. The difference be-

16. In fact, for some time in the early Middle Ages, church and state were literally fused in the persons of the so-called secular clergy. In these sword-swinging prelates who attended to the spiritual needs of their people with one hand and kept them physically subdued with the other, there is an unabashedness that is almost appealing. As Darwinian realists, they faced up to the threat of the spiritual and did the most direct logical thing: appropriated it.

Later, when Gregory VII and his successors had established the church as an institution commanding considerable secular respect, the situation was not materially improved. Innocent III, himself a formidable realist, wrote: "It often happens that bishops, by reason of their manifold preoccupations, fleshly pleasures and bellicose leanings, and from other causes . . . are unfitted to proclaim the word of God." Quoted in Heer, *The Medieval World,* p. 178.

In the centuries following the Gregorian reforms, it was still not unusual for high-ranking clerics to take to the field, and that in purely secular wars. Thomas à Becket, for instance, led a private contingent of seven hundred knights in Henry II's campaign against Toulouse (1159), and seems moreover to have been a commander of some ability. The Bishop of Durham commanded one of the three English divisions (or "battles") at Falkirk (1298) during the reign of Edward I.

A certain spirit of violence evidently persisted also among the lower clergy. The great Abélard, in effect exiled from Paris to an abbey in Brittany, in 1125, lived in terror of his monks and solicited help from the Pope, who sent a special legate to cow them into submission.

"Even then" Abélard wrote "they would not keep quiet . . . It was no longer a question of poison; it was the dagger they now sharpened against my breast. I had great difficulty in escaping from them under the guidance of one of the neighboring lords." (Quoted in Henry Adams' Mont Saint-Michel and Chartres, Houghton Mifflin, 1905, p. 307).

In the fourteenth century, Oxford, although already divided between "regular" and "secular" clergy, was still essentially a training ground for future clerics. They and the townspeople were a vigorously combative lot. "Town and gown used daggers, swords and even bows in their pitched battles in High Street. In 1355 the townsmen made a regular massacre of clerks and students: the survivors fled in terror . . . and the University closed down until the King intervened to protect and avenge the scholars" (G. M. Trevelyan, English Social History, Longmans Green, 1942, p. 53).

tween the church and other institutions is that it is more explicitly educative than most; and some of what it teaches is not cant and nonsense, but saving psychological truth. To just that extent the church teaches its own undoing. It helps men to think for themselves, and think, moreover, in ways which are certain at last to show it in a bad light, thereby threatening it with drastic reforms or dissolution. In fact, over the centuries, the Christian clergy has looked with disfavor and on occasion visited savage reprisals upon those who took the doctrines of our Lord too literally. The paradox of its position is that, dangerous as the ideas of Christ have always been to it, it could not afford to pervert or overlook them entirely, since what in them most deeply appealed to men was their truth, and without that appeal, the church's power would have been gravely weakened. Given any leisure and means to think for themselves, many men know that the life of adaptation is not enough. They sense their own incompleteness and can guess, even if they mostly cannot experience, the diabolic boredom of a life of perfect creature satisfaction. It is chiefly the hungry and frustrated who dream of lifetimes of eating or making love, or those at some time starved of respect and affection who want the acclaim of vast multitudes. Notwithstanding the relentless, almost machinelike efforts to which they drive us, the adaptive rewards are still not all of life—in a sense not even the best of it. What we complain of as a lack of *meaning* in existence is really a lack of interior freedom and substance, a lack which reduces our keenest pleasures to an enigmatic triviality. Doctrines of transcendence appeal to this profound unease in us—our need to be what we are not. Thus, in addition to its run-of-the-mill nonsense, the church found itself obliged to teach certain revolutionary moral ideas whose consequences it then had to develop a special *Staatspolizei* to keep in check.

"Thou hast no right to add anything to what Thou hadst said of old [the Grand Inquisitor tells Him]; "Why then art Thou come to hinder us? . . . Tomorrow I shall condemn Thee and burn Thee at the stake as the worst of heretics. And the very people who have today kissed Thy feet, tomorrow at the faintest sign from me will rush to heap up the embers of Thy fire. . . . Thou wouldst go into the world . . . with some promise of freedom which men in their simplicity and natural unruliness, cannot even understand, which they fear and dread. . . . Thou didst choose what was utterly beyond the strength of men, acting as though Thou didst not love them at all."[17]

Because the teachings of a religion in its early stages are addressed to people still illiterate and not far removed from savagery—addressed to them, moreover, by men often of the same type—there is much primitivism and naïve Id-thinking in the acts of faith of such periods. An outstanding example of this muddle of good and bad, in all senses of those words, was the Christian Crusades, which began as armed wanderings and later became a kind of disheveled commercial venture (notably the Fourth which, under the doge Enrico Dandolo, began with the sack of a Christian town, Zara, in Dalmatia, and ended by enormously expanding Venetian power at the expense of Byzantium). And throughout, so far as the ineptitude of the campaigners permitted, the Crusades served as vehicles for baronial aggrandizement.[18] Their less tainted motives seem, to modern minds, childlike and magical: to possess the Sepulchre and the True Cross,[19] the holiest of relics; to realize somehow, in *things,* aspirations which were essentially intangible and barely expressible in words, let alone in objects. Whatever their other motives or their practical results, it is probable that the enormous energy which produced the Crusades was, as Brooks Adams said,[20] that of the imagination. More specifically, they perhaps represented an inchoate, almost insane[21] optimism released in men by the new faith—an optimism springing from the intimation that human life might after all come to more than mere ani-

17. Fëdor Dostoevski, *The Brothers Karamazov* (Modern Library), pp. 307, 313.

18. Not that the eastern fiefs were worse off under their new masters. "If we may trust the evidence of a Mohammedan traveler, Ibn Jubair, the lot of the Mohammedan who lived on Frankish manors was better than it had been under their native lords" (Encyclopedia Brittanica, 11th Edition, Vol. 7, p. 535).

19. The loss of which to Saladin's army at the Battle of Hattin, in 1187, was quite naturally a devestating blow to Christian morale.

20. In *The Law of Civilization and Decay* (Knopf, 1943).

21. Insane partly because tainted oftentimes, with a frightful ferocity. The relationship between the two becomes more understandable when one considers that the emotions underlying optimism are related to the sexual side of our nature, and sexuality and ferocity form subdepartments of the same branch of instinct. In men still emerging from a primitive tribal existence, as the Europeans then were, the lack of differentiation of the self perhaps includes a lack of differentiation of the Id proper—the result being that great and genuine Christian zeal often led to hideously unchristian acts.

mal drudgery and animal satisfactions, that there lay in all of us a further self, ready to be saved, dragged up by stern effort out of the perennial dark: in short, a soul. It is the periodic rebirth of this idea, of the sense of soul, which, more than anything else, I believe, underlies the rise of great civilizations. For it corresponds to something potential in all of us —which is to say, potential ultimately in the structure and working principles of the human brain. It owes its hold, as an idea, to the fact that it releases new energies in us; not fancied powers, but real ones, even though in fact only a few ever came into full possession of them.[22]

Likewise, it is the transforms through which this idea of the soul passes, as cultures (to use Spengler's distinction) move on toward the stage of civilization, which determine the form of many of their accomplishments—their arts and statecraft and jurisprudence, the motivation for many of their wars, their moral ideals and triumphs of intellect, finally even their decline. For it is always at the end of civilizations that notions of the soul begin to disintegrate, and with them whole systems of ideals and precepts on which, without anyone's having understood quite why, the psychic completion (not to say the self-control and the practical competence) of future generations depends. From want of conviction in its preceptors, the tradition starts, in effect, to shrink, and civilization becomes, by degrees, a burden and an enigma to those who inherit it. The balance of early training shifts back toward the purely adaptive, and in the process much of the benefit of that training is unwittingly lost. As more of practical principles or know-how and fewer and fewer of those disinterested intangibles which men vitally need to become psychically whole or "delivered" are instilled in the young, the likelihood of further explosions of achievement, new Golden Ages of the mind, gradually diminishes. The tide of probability, which formerly flowed in the direction of real innovation and even of slight improvement in the lives of all, now begins to set the other way, though it may take centuries more to run out. When it has run out, the culture will

---

22. More accurately, one might say that the idea of the soul appeals in particular to those who are ready and eager to realize themselves, but have not yet done so—men who sense but have not experienced "transcendence." Paradoxically, those who have experienced it—have achieved a radical freedom in mind—are apt not to believe in the doctrine of the soul as it is usually taught and thereby lose an important clue to their own origins. They dislike, perhaps, to think that powers as splendid as their own may owe anything to what they regard as the superstitions of the humble.

have reached the final Toynbeean stage of fossilization. Like China of 1900 or Islam still, it will be a world fixed in the mold of ancient custom which none can find the inner resources or the outer consensus to break. Even know-how fails: all of life, including the practical, proceeding by rote. The same culture which once produced large clusters of great men within a few centuries and often from quite a small population may now go for millenniums and produce no more.[23] Such may be the sequence by which societies once great lose the "secret of progression," at first living on their intellectual capital as "late" civilizations do, showing an unparalleled ingenuity and outward splendor; at last losing even these, sinking to a state in which they are borne along only by the forces of habit or crude self-imitation. Vulnerable now to conquest, but possessed also of a massive all-swallowing inertia, they stand as immense obstacles to further human growth and therefore as monuments to the hopelessness of the human condition. For just as a tradition, while still young and in the process of elaboration, can confer undreamt-of powers on the individual and lead whole societies into new ways of life, the same tradition, disintegrated to become a mere collection of totems, practical rules of thumb, and superstitious prejudices—no longer the instrument of a people, but now its automatic conscience and prescribed world view— blocks the mind of rising generations more effectively than any mere want of in-formation could do.[24]

23. The population of England at the end of Elizabeth's reign has been estimated as 5,000,000; in 1750, as 6,500,000; and the census of 1831 showed it to be 13,800,000 (H. O. Meredith, *Economic History of England* [Pitman, 1936], p. 233). The adult male population of Attica reportedly declined from 35,000 to 21,000 in the fourth century B.C., which gives an idea of the per capita production of great men during the earlier Periclean age (J. B. Bury, *A History of Greece* [Modern Library, 1937], p. 571).

24. Western visitors to India or China (for instance Kazantzakis, whom I have quoted below, page 111, fn.) are often struck by what they regard as a paradox—namely the odd mixture of superstition and shrewd practicality, of resignation and violence, which they find in these peoples. However this combination of characteristics is what one might expect. The shrewdness and practicality represent simply the ancient adaptive self; the tendency toward superstition and violence correspond to a decontrolling of the Id and an invasion of conscious mental life by primitive fantasies; and the resignation or "fatalism" is a natural consequence of living in a world in which, while an appearance of civilization is maintained, all real progress, inner or outer, has ceased.

What seems to bring this situation about is the break in living continuity between a people and their tradition which occurs in sceptical-materialist epochs like our own. In effect, they opt for a simpler, more animalistic mode of existence,

The question is why that should occur—why traditions should lose their power to produce intelligent change and become instead the nemesis of those who inherit them, encasing late civilized man as inexorably as tribal tradition encased the Iroquois. A part of the answer is perhaps to be found in what are called Ages of Enlightenment, and a part in the fact that even at its best, no human society has ever been more than an amalgam of Neolithic and "higher" features—a graft of the human upon the animal. The paradox of man's nature is that he is these two selves at once: the one necessary, given, biological, and conservative, the other merely latent, requiring long nurture, both collective and individual, to come into being and maintaining its dominance, if at all, only by continuous inner struggle.

While it is true, as many religions seem to have held, that biological success is the platform on which men can stand and at last be men, it is also true that throughout history a majority have labored to provide that platform for a few; and many of those who have stood on it did not deserve to do so. The net result, over centuries, has been that mankind has evolved into separate races, not genetically along blood lines, but psychologically along class lines. Nor can one say that in any era more than a handful of those at the top have been delivered in the sense meant here, since that clearly has not been the case. And especially since the end of the eighteenth century, with the emergence of the industrial classes as the dominant arm of modern society, there has come to exist a huge grey intermediate mass, neither as penalized in spirit as the poor nor as concerned with ideals of self as the best of the older aristocracies had been.

and the resulting psychic deficit in their descendants makes the break with tradition irremediable. At the same time the tradition, although no longer understood and so incapable of further development, persists in many outward forms, perpetuating the illusion that culture is once and for all complete and human achievement incapable of going further.

So while the barbarian, in his nakedness, is comparatively openminded and optimistic, the man of fossil civilizations while often approaching the barbarian in ferocity, is trapped in a far more elaborate network of mental and social habit which he has neither the intellectual power nor the opportunity in fact to change. He may disrupt it from time to time; but when his rebellion is over, it is still there—"eternal", as massive as Fate or as the instincts which, in its fixity, it resembles. When evidence comes to him from the outside world that men in other civilizations are continuing to change and progress, he can only reject it with a fierce uncomprehending pride, as the Chinese for centuries rejected the West, or as De Gaulle today is rejecting twentieth-century politics and the new fact of French insignificance.

This is the mass of yesterday's poor, now half-delivered by education, who carry in themselves and bequeath by daily example only crude special remnants of the tradition, the most usable residues, so to speak, together with a few nobler pretenses easily seen as such by their heirs. Whereas education, when available, may come too late in life to be of help to the poor man, education in the hands of the middle classes becomes something else altogether: a means to social promotion out and out. With this, its original object—to produce the whole man, *l'uomo universale* capable of disinterested interest in all things—is lost, and no amount of talk among university humanists seems likely to revive it, given the public which education now serves and those responsible for its practical support and management. "The greatest innovation in the world," Burckhardt wrote a hundred years ago, "is the demand for education as a right of man; it is a disguised demand for comfort."[25]

It is, one might add, as the older ideal of education is replaced by largely practical motives for becoming educated that the educated community itself begins to split up into specialist enclaves. The educated man, including the educator, is increasingly after the models described by Ortega y Gasset[26] or Lewis Mumford: a literate half-man, highly skilled in some directions, indifferent and next to uncouth in most others; a man more committed to a career than to culture or learning as such. One hackneyed excuse for this state of affairs is that science (for instance) has become too vast for any one man to make it his province. In an article in *Science* several years ago, a geologist and geophysicist named Hubbert[27] was at some pains to show that that argument is nonsense. The object of science, he points out, is to reduce the "chaos of phenomena" to some sort of order—to clarify our mental picture of the world; and this it does, with some success. It makes considerable domains of reality intellectually and practically manageable by reducing what happens in them to a handful of rules. Provided a man has the brains to learn and understand some tens or, at most, hundreds of these rules, he

25. Jacob Burckhardt, *Force and Freedom* (Pantheon, 1943), p. 152.
26. The "disregard of science as such appears, with possibly more evidence than elsewhere, in the mass of technicians themselves—doctors, engineers, etc.—who are in the habit of exercising their profession in a state of mind identical in all essentials to that of the man who is content to use his motor car or buy his tube of aspirin—without the slightest intimate solidarity with the future of science, of civilization." José Ortega y Gasset, *The Revolt of the Masses* (Norton, 1932), p. 94.
27. M. K. Hubbert, in *Science*, Vol. 139 (1963), pp. 884 ff.

can turn to any branch of scientific investigation he likes; he may not have time to learn the experimental techniques involved, but he can at least understand what is going on there. All of which means to say that the modern scientist has no real need, apart from his "motivation," to be as narrowly specialized as in general he is. Unfortunately, the requirements of career often force him into it; but that sort of careerism is a matter of consensus too. Most are agreed on it. Therefore it exists.

The same argument applies to the modern man in the street. With the resources of information which are available to him, with the shorter work week he enjoys in modern Western nations, with the mobility afforded by his automobile, there is little but a lack of motivation to explain his specialization in self-interest, his massive incuriosity regarding most things that do not directly concern him, his narcotic or sensational tastes in entertainment, his indifference to the arts except when debased or presented *as* entertainment.[28] As surely as the scientific specialist, the scholar immersed for life in an analysis of Coptic texts, the officer immersed in war and service-politicking, he too is a man half-grown: a limb or organ of society rather than a member of it in the full human sense. This is the race which Lewis Mumford called the "new barbarians," Ortega y Gasset's *hombre-masa*. It was perhaps not the industrial world with its division of labor which produced them, but the other way round.[29] As inheritors of selected fragments of their tradition—men informed (*sic*) from boyhood only in certain directions; in whom mechanical aptitude, for example, may flourish at the expense of human warmth and esthetic sense—they might be defined as Jefferson's Citizen of the

28. Regarding the change in intellectual tastes of the Common Man, A. H. Dupree writes: "T. H. Huxley, one of the greatest moulders of scientific opinion in history, worked out many of his most effective essays not in learned journals but before audiences of workingmen. . . . The audiences of the middle 19th century responded with . . . enthusiasm. The crowd in Boston which broke a plate-glass window trying to get tickets for a Lowell Institute lecture is not easily duplicated in 20th century America. And the audiences flocked in to hear the straight science of the day. . . . Both scientist and audience shared a belief that the common man could understand science, that the professional had a duty to explain science to the public, and that a massive uplift in society would result from their joint activities." *Science*, Vol. 134 (1961), p. 716.

29. Just as, in classical times, it was perhaps not the accumulation of learning —by modern standards, trivial—which produced Alexandrianism, but rather a certain psychological change which disposed the scholarly to overdepartmentalize such learning as there was.

Future *manqué*. Rather than becoming the truly enlightened, responsible majority which he and other theorists of democracy (and Marx) expected, the Common Man, together with many of his social superiors, seems to have settled for far less—in essence, for a specialism of the spirit, a resigned partiality. The result is a world in which, despite its enormous debt to the past, real contact with the past is failing.[30] In the same period in which its expression in the form of applied science has reached an apogee scarcely imaginable to men, say, of Voltaire's day, the culture itself is perhaps even less a common property than it once was, surviving if at all, piecemeal, no more than a tiny fraction in any one.

It was apparently New Men of this sort who built and administered the Roman Empire. In our own era they are the superspecialists of business and learning and statecraft, the experts, whose logical, not to say indispensable counterpart is incurious Common Man. Although differing greatly in rank and "advantages", these two basic classes, the directors and the directed, share an outlook without which, one guesses, the whole process of industrialization might never have developed the phenomenal momentum it has, more particularly since the latter half of the nineteenth century. A most important part of that outlook is negative—a matter of what men tacitly agree *not* to trouble themselves about any longer, of the stringency with which they will limit their interests and sympathies, in some cases even their ambition. There is much comfort to be gained from such co-operative sacrifice; just as, at higher social levels, much mental pain and effort and uncertainty are saved by a sacrifice of real breadth and intellectual mastery to specialism and *expertise*.[31] While quite unequal in its rewards and by

---

30. "Real contact" meaning not ritual preservation of the past, as in Manchu China, but the sort of intelligent retention of it which causes tradition to be both respected and adapted to present circumstances, as in Britain.

31. With this, the scientist becomes a technician in the sense meant by Ortega y Gasset, neither he nor the general public understanding the ideal expressed in the past century by John Tyndall after his successful lecture tour in the United States: " 'What, I may ask, is the origin of that kindness which drew me from my work in London to address you here, and which, if I permitted it, would send me home a millionaire? Not because I had taught you to make a single cent by science am I here tonight, but because I tried to the best of my ability to present science to the world as an intellectual good. . . . It is especially on this ground of its administering to the higher needs of the intellect . . . that I urge the claims of science on your attention.' " See René Dubos, in *Science*, Vol. 133 (1961), p. 1211.

In this passage, one hears a last echo of the Renaissance ideal of universality. It

no means agreed upon by all, this is essentially the compact which has made the modern middle class world possible. At bottom, the success of that enterprise depended upon turning to account not merely the results of science and mechanical invention, but also the profound psychological change which was beginning to take place in the western world at about the same time. A part of that change—the most useful, from the standpoint of businessmen anxious to recruit a permanent civil service of white collar workers and minor executives—was the one I have just described, an increasing resignation of the semi-privileged to being in every sense simply that, men reasonably comfortable and secure, reliable and competent in their work, and without curiosity or serious involvement outside of it.

The difficulty, as we shall see—are already seeing in daily life—is that this stability and passive acceptance in the middle ranks of society is a passing phenomenon. It represents, in fact, the initial and temporarily covert phase of a general atheism[32]—our reasoned denial of the impulse to transcend ourselves, to realize the soul. The first few generations to practise this denial had the advantage of coming to adulthood as beneficiaries of the tradition they were repudiating. So for a time, Christian ideals continued, almost unnoticed and from sheer force of collective habit, to shape the minds and govern the conduct of large minorities who at heart no longer believed in them. Likewise the benefits of liberalism continued for awhile to accrue after the faith from which they derived had passed. This was the situation obtaining in the nineteenth and into the forepart of the present century. In our day however, matters have reached a new, and possibly critical stage,[33] in which the "grey intermediate mass", the middle or-

also expresses the psychological premise underlying that ideal—that mind has "needs" of its own, unrelated to practical necessity.

32. This being, of course, a reference to Victorian hypocrisy, of whose debunking and demise we once hoped so much.

33. This was the stage Germany had reached with Hitlerism which the rest of the world at first watched with incredulity. The Germans (we recalled) were so correct and docile, so vocal in their admiration for culture. How then could Hitler have arisen and, almost overnight, commanded such a vast following, even among the apparently decent and cultivated? The answer may be that even in these more of the past had already died than any outsider could have guessed; so that the culture (as in imperial China) had become mere appearance, while the resignation and the returning ferocity were real. It was in this profound sense that Hitler corresponded to his time and achieved therefore such prodigies of unification and conquest.

ders, have started to suffer from the same psychic contraction which has long since afflicted the lower. Since the 1920's the covert rejection of our traditional ideals has finally become overt; and with that their transmission by parental example has, almost by definition, been drastically curtailed. The results, which are now beginning to cause us some alarm, amount to a psychic levelling—a forcing down, through deliberate neglect, of the interior development of the young, to the point that those of the more favored classes have started to approach or even outdo the children of the poor in vulgarity and amorphousness of mind, in an inclination to anesthetic excess (drug-taking; mass sex) and in an anarchic violence whose moral content is largely fake, being for the most part a coarsely rationalized hatred of any obstacle to immediate self-gratification.[34]

The paradox of our age is that while it has, to some extent, raised the (white) poor to the material level of the middle classes, it has simultaneously acted to undermine the psychic stability on which the success, if not the very existence, of our production system depends, threatening us with profound upheavals and retrogression in the midst of real social advances and an unprecedented abundance. My object, in the remainder of this book, will be to show this paradox in a variety of other lights—ultimately to show it is not one, but a quite logical consequence of the principles according to which we are trying to live.

In Europe of the thirteenth century, with its great fairs and thriving chartered towns, the business classes were evidently well started on their slow climb to the top of the social order.[35] They perhaps owed their eventual arrival to the fact that business, by its nature, encourages habits of intense factual analysis—of foresight, calculation, and adroit maneuver, hardly matched except in the cleverest nobles or most ambitious churchmen. Significantly, some of the earliest overt unbelievers

34. Including not only sexual freedom and the "right" to considerable rudeness and self-assertion, but also the student's "right" to set up university curricula. The notion that those whose minds are not yet formed are capable of deciding how to form them is surely odd. We perhaps owe it to Rousseau, our first doctrinaire primitive.

35. How strenuous that climb was in the beginning may be seen from an account in Guizot of the miseries of the burghers of Laon which resulted from their attempt to buy a lasting charter (that is, a reasonable independence) from their local overlords and Louis the Fat, in the early 12th century. See F. Guizot, History of France, Robert Black transl., Aldine, 1886, Vol. 2, p. 166. The later history of the Flemish towns, during the Hundred Years War, was not dissimilar.

were from this mercantile burgher class, which drew the wrath of the church accordingly.

> As heresy followed in the wake of trade, the Inquisition followed in the wake of heresy, and the beginning of the thirteenth century witnessed simultaneously the prosperity of the mercantile class and the organization of the Holy Office. . . . Jacques de Vitry breathed the ecclesiastical spirit. . . . His sermons burn with hatred of the bourgeoisie "That detestable race of men . . . hurrying to meet its fate. . . . But of all other evils of these Babylonish cities, there is one which is the worst for there is hardly a community to be found in which there are not abettors, receivers, defenders of, or believers in, heretics.[36]

It is not, of course, until the French Revolution and the nineteenth century that that "detestable race of men" comes into ascendancy and, with them, the outlook of scientific materialism. The core of that view —which predated modern science by some centuries, having been quite prevalent in late classical times—is explicitly that there *is* no further purpose, no principle of transcendence, in human life. The history of the nineteenth and twentieth centuries is, at bottom, a record of the social consequences of that belief, which in a formal philosophic sense began almost secretly among the enlightened[37] and has spread since to include all ranks. While some of its effects on the several classes have been quiet different, its major consequence has been substantially the same for all: namely, a dissolution of what one could call the centrality of our tradition, a loss, through disbelief (and hence through perfunctory teaching and contrary example), of certain ideals and concepts which linked together all the rest. Such ideas are like copestones in the architecture of abstract memory. Without them what might have been a single edifice remains an assortment of smaller structures or, at worst,

---

36. Adams, *The Law of Civilization and Decay,* pp. 183 ff. In the same passage he recounts the story of the sacrilegious burghers of Saint-Riquier, who in 1264 conducted a mock-religious festival, in which they carried a dead cat in procession and made a horse-bone a sacred "relic."

37. Loren Eiseley, in *The Firmament of Time* (Atheneum, 1960), p. 61, quotes from a lecture given by Coleridge in 1819: "Whoever is acquainted with the history of philosophy during the last two or three centuries cannot but admit that there appears to have existed a sort of secret and tacit compact among the learned not to pass beyond a certain limit in speculative science.'" The issue here was that of man's evolutionary origins, but the principle at bottom is the same: one of doubt concerning man's uniqueness and his soul.

a mere heap. The chief of these master concepts was the idea of the soul,[38] or possible higher self, whose realization would in theory (and sometimes did in fact) give men new unity and light, altering all that they did or thought through the agency of "grace." This was the ideal lying at the root of the notion of Universal Man. As belief in it and related ideals—for instance, that of the gentle knight, or later the gentleman—failed, our tradition gradually dissolved in its inheritors into the miscellany of special truths and principles it now is, and in parallel with this dissolution, the type of the specialist came to prevail on upper levels of Western society and the type of the revolutionary nihilist or desperate amorph at the bottom.

At first the new business oligarchs of the nineteenth century imitated the older aristocracies they had displaced, a phenomenon illustrating the power of our mimetic and competitive instincts when these converge on the same end. Among other things, business aspired to be cultural in its leisure as the nobility had been, to live with style and to conserve the decencies, as represented by Christian ethics and decorum. For a time it seemed to achieve these aims, but as the Victorian age moves on, something increasingly freakish and dismaying, an unrest, an air of profound pretense, a confused theatricality in taste and feeling, begin to show themselves. Because the arts, including those of casual decoration, most deeply and directly mirror the inner condition of man,[39] it is perhaps first in these that the loss of "centrality" in a tradition becomes evident. The arts, one might say, reflect the state of coherence of the human spirit, including prevalent relations between the rational I and the Id and the stature and degrees of freedom of the I proper.

38. Speaking of Aquinas' doctrine, Henry Adams says, "The soul existed as a form for the body, and had no previous existence." The medieval notion of form he refers to suggests the process of in-forming often mentioned here. He adds that "the soul has always refused to live in peace with the body" and that idea also translates into physiological terms, as I have tried to show. From *Mont St. Michel and Chartres* (Houghton Mifflin, 1933), pp. 358–359.

39. Burckhardt arbitrarily divides society into three "constants" State, Culture and Religion. Of Culture he says: ". . . It is the critic of [the other two], the clock which tells the hour at which their form and substance no longer coincide."

He is here speaking of culture in the form of overt criticism à la Voltaire, but might equally have spoken of the dilapidation or grotesqueness of popular styles, or of the unconscious and as it were, prophetic preferences of the fine arts in periods such as our own. (See Jacob Burckhardt, Force and Freedom, Pantheon Books, 1943, p. 140.)

From this standpoint, it is particularly significant that poetry, which was a flourishing folk art as well as a literary one in the time of Elizabeth and Cromwell and Queen Anne, dies out in nineteenth-century England.[40] Nor had urbanization and conversion to factory employment gone far enough, by the time that occurred, to be its sole or even its major cause. One might guess rather that it was due to a slow spread of the "realism" of the business and scientific classes to the lower ranks. The result was to undermine and finally destroy that optimism and imaginativeness released in the mass of men with their conversion to Christianity centuries before. Psychologically as well as materially, the position of the poor had always been precarious. By ancient custom recipients of the least and most adulterated of spiritual goods, they necessarily relied to a far greater extent than did their betters on their faith as a bulwark against the terrors of existence. It was, in effect, the more childish promises of religion—for instance, that of an afterlife, offsetting the fear of death and mitigating somewhat the trials of this world—which enabled them to keep the Id in check. As the suspicion got abroad that these promises might be mere fictions, and disingenuous ones at that, an immense change began in the depths of society. The relative stability and poetic good humor of the Elizabethan age now give way to a glum and dangerous resignation—really a psychic contraction, threatening those who can least afford it with a loss not

---

40. Thenceforth poetry will be the accomplishment of a special caste, at first enjoying the patronage of the middle class; at last, in the twentieth century, barely surviving.

In view of the discussion of "creativity" in Chapter IV above, it is perhaps also logical that poets not to mention artists of other kinds, suffer especially keenly in ages of psychic contraction, reflecting in life as well as in their work, the increasingly decontrolled Id. Poe, Rimbaud and Verlaine announce this development in the nineteenth century. In the twentieth, two older poets—Yeats and T. S. Eliot—write of man's inner collapse without sharing it; while two younger men, Dylan Thomas and Theodore Roethke, do both. Roethke, in his lifelong struggle with insanity, might be called the poet of the dying self:

> Semblance, Semblance, I'm cursed by the half-perceived.
> Something has thickened my sight:
> A scared dog cowering in a dream.

Or:

> I must be more than what I see. Oh Jesus
> Save this roaring boy riding the devil's blast.

(Quoted by James Dickey, from Roethke's notebooks; in The Atlantic Monthly, November 1968.)

only of self but, in the extreme, of sanity. As result of psychic deprivation and the new materialism combined, the poor and the lower middle
classes become increasingly a prey to envy and bitterness and to the
violence latent in all of us. Paralleling the collapse of styles on higher
levels of Victorian society, the folk arts of the poor disappear, and the
mass begins to become revolutionary in the modern sense. Unstable,
all but ineducable, clinging to a primitive respectability as its last forti-
fication against the onslaughts of the Id, full of dreams of the Better
Life, yet incapable of respect except for power, as vulnerable to psychic
disease[41] as to physical, as suggestible, as prone to cartoon thinking
and superstitious terrors and impulsive frightfulness as a race of children, this mass is the modern "masses"—the psychological type of
shapeless industrial man. With his appearance, late civilizations become,
in a sense, permanently revolutionary,[42] and the same characteristics

41. T. A. C. Rennie *et al.* studied a random sample of 1,660 New Yorkers,
drawn from the same (one-mile square) area in the city. Anxiety was nearly twice
as prevalent among upper-class vis-à-vis lower-class subjects (but considered prevalent at all levels). Probable psychotics: 13 per cent lower class, 3.6 per cent upper.
Probable neurotics: 28 per cent lower, 18 per cent middle, 9 per cent upper class.
*American Journal of Psychiatry,* Vol. 113 (1957), pp. 831–837.

42. Compared to those of the nineteenth and twentieth centuries, the revolutions of the Middle Ages—for instance, Wat Tyler's—were mere episodes. Because
"modern" revolutions arise in part from psychic causes neither well understood
nor in any way much affected by their outcome, they tend to continue indefinitely
and to occur in their most devastating form in nations which, like modern Germany had seemed most "advanced."

The Negro uprisings in the mid-1960's in this country, though they have good
ostensible causes, may nonetheless be part of a more general rebelliousness which
in the case of our middle-class young people is much harder to rationalize. From
this standpoint it is significant that large numbers of whites, according to the
newspaper reports, took part in the Detroit riots of '67. The fact that crime and employment rates have risen together over the past several decades is likewise difficult
to explain on the old-fashioned ground that material deprivation is a (or the)
main source of "antisocial" behavior.

Since the Berkeley demonstrations, student rioting has gained considerable
momentum. Between September and December, 1967, there were demonstrations
"on at least 62 different campuses of 4-year schools," all of these being "prior to
the major student revolt at Columbia." *Science,* Vol. 161 (1968), p. 21.

It is apparently becoming obvious, even to the experts called in to help us in
our travail, that the supposed causes of student unrest, including Viet Nam, do not
entirely account for it. Something new, we feel, is manifesting itself.

"The present series of student protests might be compared to a succession of
earthquakes, some minor and some major. They have come unexpectedly and
with an impact which has produced visible tremors in the structure of higher

which make mass man a perennial natural resource for demagogues lead to outbreaks of primitive religiousness, which serve to release his instinctive energies in less destructive form, if not, in some small degree, to "save" him. In Sargant's opinion,[43] it was Wesleyanism which may have prevented the equivalent of the French Revolution from occurring in England; and had the rulers of Rome had better sense, they would have indulged the mystery cults, of which Christianity was one. Mommsen's description of the Republic at the end of the Scipionic age suggests the atmosphere of Hitler's Germany, with its torchlight processions, its return to Wotan, its mystique of blood, its almost envious destruction of the past, in favor of the newer, more primal way, the "ideology":

> The wild worship of . . . Bellona, to whom the priests in their festal processions shed their own blood as a sacrifice, and the gloomy Egyptian worships began to make their appearance. . . . Men had become perplexed not merely as to the old faith, but as to their very selves. The fearful crises of a fifty years' revolution, the instinctive feeling that the civil war was still far from being at an end, increased the anxious suspense, the gloomy perplexity of the multitude. Restlessly the wandering imagination climbed every height and fathomed every abyss where it fancied it might discover new prospects or new light amidst the fatalities impending. . . . A portentous mysticism found in the general distraction—political, economic, moral, religious—the soil which was adapted for it, and grew with alarming rapidity. It was as if gigantic trees had grown by night out of the earth, none knew whence or whither, and this very rapidity of growth worked new wonders, and seized like an epidemic on all minds not thoroughly fortified.[44]

A little more than a century afterward, the same populace was to worship the emperor as a god—the paradox of "realism" being that it leads back not merely to a simpler life[45] of reasoned adaptation but

---

education. . . . What is not known is how severely the foundations of the academic institutions have been damaged or where the fault really lies. . . . Although the characteristics of student activism have been examined by behavioral scientists and others since the events at Berkeley in 1964, recent instances of student protest raise new questions about the dimensions and nature of this phenomenon." *Ibid.,* pp. 21–22. *I.e.,* we do not understand it.

43. William Sargant, *Battle for the Mind* (Doubleday, 1958), p. 95.

44. Theodor Mommsen, *History of Rome* (Everyman's, 1930), III, 412.

45. Simpler in the sense of being unencumbered, as our life increasingly is,

in time much farther—to the superstition and psychological chaos of prehistory. Such is the power of modern know-how that Hitler was almost able to accomplish the same miracle of regression roughly in a decade and a half. (In reality of course, such successes as his are a matter not of technique but of a latent consensus.)

In short, as the idea of the soul dies—as men lose faith in the ideal of self-realization which it represents—the soul itself dies. The rational conscious I, no longer given centrality or that coherence of organization which results from inculcation of a unified more-than-practical view of life, subsides into the partially grown specialized self it is becoming in most of us today, at last dwindling away to an almost prehistoric feebleness. This is the self one finds in "fossil" peoples like the modern Arabs or Chinese: one obsessively concerned with private advantage, yet so unstable, so readily invaded by fantasy or overwhelmed by primitive emotion, as to seem slightly mad to Westerners.[46] The loss of larger interest, of the capacity for detached effort and identification with the not-me, which centuries ago cost these peoples the "secret of progression" in the arts and intellect, has of physiological necessity also cost them much self-control or that minimal morality needed to maintain an efficient, materially progressive state.

The Arab world of Nasser, the China of the war lords or the recent Red Guard purges, are ramshackle structures continually threatened with collapse because of the massive inadequacy of rulers and ruled alike to the real task in hand, which is to say the psychic reconsti-

by many of the ideals and aspirations of former times. Our relief and liberation, however, come at a price to be paid, if not by us, by our descendants.

46. "Generals are sold and bought; they move from camp to camp dragging the hungry, ragged masses behind them. . . . There is no country, no race, no language, no religion. A mixture of races. And every Chinese has in his yellow bosom a multitude of souls. Barbarism and refined decadence, senile infantilism and primitive crudity, atheism and mysterious complex religious preoccupations . . .

In his everyday life, the Chinese gathers his wrath and swallows his tongue. But suddenly his eyes blur and he is seized with a mania like rabies: that is the ch'i, the black mania. You can see children, women and men fall down and foam. A woman often faints or takes a knife or a stone or a pot of boiling water and kills her husband or her mother-in-law. . . . This black mania, the ch'i, sometimes captures the Chinese in groups. And then horrible slaughters take place. . . .

When the Chinese bows deeply and submits himself to your voice, you shudder because you feel that this silence of his is terrible, full of wild silent wings."

(Nikos Kazantzakis, describing China as it appeared to him in 1935. From *Japan and China*, Simon and Schuster, 1963, pp. 181 and 229–230.)

tution of a whole people. The notion that that can be accomplished simply by a grafting on of alien techniques or ideologies may be mistaken in the first place. It is not, I believe, in the mechanisms of society as such, but in the brain—in the architecture of abstract memory and therefore in the realm of unifying ideas—that high cultures are born and die. Nor is it likely that the process can be run in reverse; the outward forms of a culture, imposed on primitive or regressed peoples by their own rulers or by a foreign conqueror, have seldom resulted in much beyond a *reductio ad absurdum* of the forms themselves.[47] Democracy, as practiced in the United States, Britain, and Scandinavia, has not proved exportable, even to other parts of the West.

Finally, it is probably not true that *any* coherent far-reaching body of doctrine will do, only provided it is dinned hard enough into large enough numbers of people. The saving feature, for instance, of Christianity was that it contained sufficient truth to produce in time a minority, at least, of fully developed men. It was true in the sense that its morality required seemingly unrealistic forms of self-denial which, as they were based on correct intuitions about human nature, turned out to be a means to greater self-fulfillment in the longer course. Through it, the abstract memory system expanded and articulated itself over generations until mind achieved a power and imaginative range without equal in history. (It is a question whether any purely political ideology has ever had the necessary disinterestedness and validity to be capable of producing the same results. The best available evidence is the present state of Russia; and there, from what I read and from what scientific colleagues report, learning and the arts thrive despite, rather more than because of, Marxist orthodoxy.[48] I have also been given striking examples of the way in which, in that country, even after the fiasco of Lysenko, authoritarian habits of mind continue to cripple scientific

47. Celebrated, for instance, in Evelyn Waugh's *Scoop* and *Black Mischief* and Joyce Carey's *Mr. Johnson.*

48. Several years ago, in a bound volume of the Russian journal *Biophysica,* I was startled to come across a brief editorial, or rather testimonial, apparently occasioned by the anniversary of some great event in the Revolution. It attributed the glories of Russian science, if not of science generally, to Lenin, and not merely as their political protector and champion but as a *participant.* That such an extraordinary piece of sycophancy could appear in a learned periodical in this century says much about the power which adaptive man in the U.S.S.R. continues to hold over those whose business is ostensibly to speak the truth.

inquiry. However, this is not far from the situation of Western science vis-à-vis the church in the seventeenth century; in short, one cannot tell yet what sort of men generations of Marxist upbringing may produce. The puristic, and somewhat antiquated, practicality of that doctrine is not reassuring, the real question for Russia perhaps being how much of its former religious idealism is surviving in disguise.)

We are by now so accustomed to it that it is hard for us to see how revolutionary the idea of experiment—experimentation as a consistent approach to nature—was for mankind. Prior to it, we had made abstract inquiries in the shape of philosophy and mathematics, and a few had done experiments in the strict Western sense. But for the most part, man had studied or manipulated nature with some limited adaptive end in view and with correspondingly limited results. It was not until he ceased to concern himself with the possible returns of inquiry and concentrated instead on understanding or truth that the real conquest of nature began.[49]

Much as modern scientists may dislike the idea, and much as the

49. When chemistry, for example, ceased to concern itself with primitive objectives such as the conversion of base metals into gold, concentrating on what Bacon called "experiments of light" rather than those "of fruit," the results were spectacular. Whereas alchemy had been practiced for centuries and gotten almost nowhere, chemistry since the end of the eighteenth century has transformed medicine and technics and incidentally made for many the fortunes which alchemy never did.

Gibbon reports that Diocletian, after his punitive expedition against Egypt in A.D. 296, ordered the suppression of alchemical texts, not, Gibbon says, on the ground that he considered alchemy a real threat to Rome, but rather because "he was desirous of preserving the reason and fortunes of his subjects from the mischievous pursuit." The Decline and Fall of the Roman Empire, 3 Vols., Modern Library, Vol. I, Chapter XIII, p. 316. Some writers give alchemy more credit as a scientific enterprise.

"The idea of transmutation, in the country of its origin [Greek Alexandria] had a philosophical basis, and was linked up with Greek theories of matter then current; thus by supplying a central philosophical principle it to some extent unified and focussed chemical effort which previously, so far as it existed at all, had been expended on acquiring empirical acquaintance with a mass of disconnected technical processes." Encyclopaedia Brittanica (11th Ed.): "Alchemy." The point about this "central philosophical principle" is its very close relationship to money, which, as the means to any instinctive gratification, including those of status, might be called the central adaptive principle of human life. That closeness perhaps helped to keep alchemy from ever becoming a science in the same way that today it keeps a good deal of military or industrial research from getting results proportionate to the immense outlay of men, money and capital goods involved.

church has done in the past to make it seem implausible, the fact is that the impulse to scientific understanding may be a direct descendant of the Christian ideal of disinterested love. In its most general form that ideal stands for an active warmth or affection, a going out to all of reality, not for our own sakes as perpetually uneasy appetent organisms, but for its sake as something wonderful, to be understood and delighted in rather than merely used or fended off. This, I believe, is the notion which lies at the root of the ideal of Universal Man and once lay at the root of our education or culture of the young. To it we may owe much of our present technological virtuosity; and in proportion as it is no longer believed in or transmitted, our tradition is breaking up in us, disappearing into a hodgepodge of the Confucian and the merely self-serving. With that, there are signs that our virtuosity is already beginning to suffer (see above, Chapter V, note 34), to say nothing of our peace of mind.

For, in turning, as other cultures have done in their enlightened maturity, from an ideal and moral to a realistic and purely ethical world view, we have unwittingly begun to defy what may be a basic principle of human nature: namely, that man, given the brain he has, can never reach full psychic development if he regards himself as simply an animal with the gift of speech and tries to live accordingly. If my estimate of man's place in evolution, which is to say, of the functional requirements peculiar to his brain, is essentially correct, our present view of ourselves amounts to psychic suicide: the death, by reasoned neglect, of the soul. The evidence from historiography is that this phenomenon has occurred before, apparently from quite similar causes.

By the same logic modern specialism, as a *Weltanschauung* or rationalized insufficiency of mind, becomes simply an *étape* on the way to a general nullity and political chaos. After the Alexandrians[50] come the Roman mob of Marius' day and the Terrible Simplifiers of Caesar's; after Descartes' *cogito*, Dostoevski's "If God doesn't exist, everything is permitted" and Freud's grim caricatures of the human condition in *Totem and Taboo* and *Beyond the Pleasure Principle*. After the "inner-directed" man of the nineteenth century comes the relativistic amorph

---

50. That is, the Ptolemaic twilight of learning. In a literal, even in a scholastic, sense, Alexandria, of course, survived the Roman Revolution by centuries.

of the twentieth; after Bismarck, Hitler. In outlook and emotional tone, ours is quite like the era described by Mommsen in the Rome of two millenniums ago, an age in which the shrunken self threatens to surrender, *en masse,* releasing once more the terrors and mindless ferocity[51] which generations of our forebears labored with some success to subdue. It is an epoch announced by an odd mixture of frivolity and despair, the worlds of Lady Metroland and Miss Lonely Hearts, the sad, soiled, "romantic" Paris of Baudelaire, or of Colette and Céline:

The hall was lit by great white lights, low down, which emphasized the shadows on the faces; all the lights seemed to harden under it and the colors were most crude. . . . Philip leaned over the rail, staring down, and he ceased to hear the music. They danced furiously. They danced round the room, slowly, talking very little, with all their attention given to the dance. It seemed to Philip that they had thrown off the guard which people wear on their expression . . . and he saw them now as they really were. In that moment of abandon they were strangely animal; some were foxy and some were wolflike; and others had the long foolish faces of sheep. Their skins were sallow from the unhealthy life they led. . . . Their features were blunted by mean interests, and their little eyes were shifty and cunning. . . . They were seeking escape from a world of horror. The desire for pleasure which Cronshaw said was the only motive for human action urged them blindly on, and the very vehemence of the desire seemed to rob it of all pleasure. They were hurried on by a great wind, helplessly, they knew not why. . . . Fate seemed to tower above them and they danced as though everlasting darkness were about their feet. . . . It was as if life terrified them and the shriek which was in their hearts died at their throats. . . . And notwithstanding the beastly lust which disfigured them, and the meanness of their faces, and the cruelty, notwithstanding the stupidity which was worst of all, the anguish of those fixed eyes made all that crowd terrible and pathetic.[52]

51. One thinks of Charles Whitman in his tower, in Austin, Texas, gunning down passers-by (New York *Times,* August 3, 1966); of Lee Harvey Oswald or the strangely blank young killers in Truman Capote's *In Cold Blood*. See also the Campbell case (page 134 below); the Loeb-Leopold murders, the burning alive of derelicts on the New York Bowery by teen-agers during the past year, etc., etc.

52. Somerset Maugham, *Of Human Bondage* (Modern Library), p. 293. The description is of a Parisian dance hall, *circa* 1900.

*Chapter VII*

## MODERNITY

On upper levels of the Victorian world, one can trace psychic changes rather different in form but perhaps identical in principle to those which were occurring in the social depths. By the end of the first quarter of the nineteenth century, it is as if one had reached the summit of a mountain ridge and begun to look out upon streams flowing in a new direction, whose confluences were yet too distant to see. From that *Aussichtspunkt* Keats, Shelley, and Wordsworth appear quite distinct from the later romantics, seeming, like Goethe, to be the last of another era. Of the three, Wordsworth was perhaps the most profound, although, as with many poets, 90 per cent of his genius was concentrated in 10 per cent of what he wrote.

In the poetry of that time, the in-formed sensitivity of mind and with it an intensity of the warmer emotions—what Walter Bagehot (speaking of Shakespeare) called "this union of life with measure, of spirit with reasonableness"—reach a pinnacle perhaps only equaled in Shakespeare's day:

> . . . feelings, too,
> Of unremembered pleasure; such, perhaps,
> As may have had no trivial influence
> On that best portion of a good man's life,
> His little, nameless, unremembered acts
> Of kindness and of love. Nor less, I trust,
> To them I may have owed another gift,
> Of aspect more sublime; that blessèd mood,
> In which the burthen of the mystery,
> In which the heavy and the weary weight
> Of all this unintelligible world
> Is lightened;—that serene and blessèd mood,
> In which the affections gently lead us on,—
> Until, the breath of this corporeal frame,

And even the motion of our human blood,
Almost suspended, we are laid asleep
In body, and become a living soul:
While with an eye made quiet by the power
Of harmony, and the deep power of joy,
We see into the life of things. . . .[1]

In the same period the powers of intellect, matured over centuries, were about to produce that further explosion of scientific understanding from which most of our present technologies derive. Mind was in truth seeing "into the life of things" more deeply than it had ever done. The emotional timbre of Wordsworth's poems is perhaps equally significant if, as I believe, the neocortex of man, in freeing itself and giving rise to mind, in the fuller sense, enlists a part of the Id as its servant and natural ally—namely, that part responsible in us for attraction and warmth, whose primordial function was probably to prolong and deepen sexual ties and so to favor the protection and nurture of children. Just as olfactory functions of parts of the mammalian brain have generalized in their evolution to become emotional in man,[2] so

---

1. William Wordsworth, from "Lines Composed a Few Miles above Tintern Abbey." A. N. Whitehead, in *Science and the Modern World* (Pelican, 1948), pp. 77 ff., describes Wordsworth as reacting against the scientific mentality of the eighteenth century, whereas in fact his reaction may have been against a type of mentality which sprang from that one but did not yet exist—namely, our own. In the same chapter, Whitehead mentions that Shelley, unlike most literary men ever since, had some understanding of the ideas of science and delighted in them as reflecting the phenomenon Whitehead himself called "prehension." He quotes from Shelley's poem "Mont Blanc":

The everlasting universe of things
Flows through the mind, and rolls its rapid waves,
Now dark, now glittering, now reflecting gloom,
Now lending splendor, where from secret springs
The source of human thought its tribute brings
Of waters,—with a sound but half its own. . . .

[A scientist who read this book in manuscript wrote in the margin: "How could he react against a mentality that did not [yet] exist?" What I meant, of course, was that Wordsworth may have foreseen the sort of leaden literalism to which science might lead.]

2. Olfaction is perhaps the sense modality most logically suited to such a transformation, odors being characterized by quality and intensity, but otherwise dimensionless. They are not *things* having clear spatial or temporal outline, but climates, as our feelings are. Their nearest equivalent in diffuseness is visceral sensation, which has also remained closely tied to emotion.

one group of emotions may, with full development of the neocortex, depart from its primal role as an adjunct of familial behavior and become capable of attachment simply to others or to nature. This phenomenon or process is what underlies Christ's concept of love: an emotion basically as remote from the sexual as our emotions themselves are from our sense of smell. As a warmth, enlarged by reason to become forgiveness or tolerance of others, a compassion founded on understanding; as a love of métier apart from what our work repays us in advantage, a disinterested affection for the very fabric of things, for the qualities of existence, however they happen to show themselves, this emotion has never perhaps been very general. However, as the natural (physiological) auxiliary of reason and therefore as a possible consequence of the unified system of aspirations expressed in the notion of Universal Man, it and its parent ideals tend in late civilized ages to decline together. The "finer feelings" of the Victorian age seem more and more faked, until in our own day, along with Universal Man, they are on the verge of disappearing altogether. When they crop up, we tend to conceal them under a façade of "toughness," as if no longer daring to flout our own instinctive selves or to tempt too strongly those of others.

The 1830's are roughly the watershed of the present, the point at which the tide of probability, mentioned earlier, begins to set the other way. It is signalized politically by what are, in effect, continuations of the French Revolution: the upheavals of '48, the Empire and the Paris Commune, Bolívar, Andrew Jackson, Mazzini and Garibaldi, and, not least, the metaphysicians of the new materialism, Comte and Du Bois-Reymond[3] as much as Marx and Engels.

In everyday life, the same phenomenon, indicative of a general loss of centeredness or psychic "unity," appears as a sudden breakdown in taste.[4] The older architectural styles (in America, for instance, the

3. "In 1847, a year before the Communist Manifesto of Marx and Engels, (Emil) Du Bois-Reymond, speaking for the German school, enunciated the manifesto of mechanistic materialism: that all properties of living matter are subject to physical and chemical laws. H. W. Magoun *et al., The Central Nervous System and Behavior*, Trans., 1st Conf. (Josiah Macy, Jr. Foundation, 1959), p. 26.

4. Accompanied by a decline in intimate piety, as opposed to Sunday membership, or conspicuous attendance. "A feature of the times," Emerson wrote in his journal (in 1849, at age forty-five), "is that when I was born, private and family prayer was in the use of all well-bred people, and now it is not known." *The*

Federalist) fade out, while the Victorian aesthetic, not only in building but in *couture,* in minor arts such as ceramics, and in interior decoration, sets in with the gathering momentum of an epidemic. Who, seeing the relatively innocent Greek and Gothic revivals, could have guessed the nightmares to come: the riotous eclecticism, the proliferation of scrollwork and interior ornament, the Pullman lampshades and tasseled plush, the incredibly choked perspectives of the late nineteenth-century parlor?

Simultaneously, the winds of emotion in the arts start to blow from a new quarter. Beneath the medieval fakery of works like the Morte d'Arthur or the verse and painting of the pre-Raphaelites;[5] under the thick crust of pretension with which the aesthetes and critics of the age finally covered everything; even under the reformist zeal of Dickens and the jocose play acting of Mark Twain,[6] there begins a drift into

*Heart of Emerson's Journals,* Bliss Perry, ed., (Houghton Mifflin, 1909), p. 245. Conspicuous attendance continued much longer, of course, surviving even today in smaller towns and rural communities, as well as in the Presidency. Mrs. Trollope found it particularly oppressive in the late 1820's and marveled at the number of our sects, "each of which assumes a church government of its own; of this," she adds, "the most intriguing and factious individual is invariably the head"—a feature faithful to institutional Christian tradition.

"In order," she continues, "as it should seem, to show a reason for this separation, each congregation invests itself with some queer variety of external observance which has the melancholy effect of exposing *all* religious ceremonies to contempt." Frances Trollope, *Domestic Manners of the Americans* (Vintage, 1960), p. 108.

5. Perhaps the best example being the painting of Burne-Jones, whose logical successor, if not literally, at least in point of sheer nullity, was Alma-Tadema. Both, incidentally, were knighted.

6. It is interesting that Dickens and Twain both ended their careers with books rather ominous in tone (*The Mystery of Edwin Drood* and *The Mysterious Stranger*), as did H. G. Wells much later, with *Mind at the End of Its Tether.* Dwight MacDonald, *Against the American Grain* (Random House, 1962), pp. 79 ff., considered Twain a victim of the social machinery for turning talent into cash. "Mark Twain's difficulty was a peculiarly modern one—he was damaged by success, as later on Fitzgerald and Hemingway were to be. He was simply too popular for his own good. . . . He was overfed with praise and starved for understanding" (*ibid.,* p. 107). The fact seems to have been that Twain, like Hemingway and Fitzgerald, was a gifted juvenile, a man who started adult life with too little in this head to sustain or develop his talents. Like the more extreme exemplars of disintegration who came later, he was the self in bits (see page 125 below), but one that held itself together after a fashion, the nihilism and childish smuttiness never breaking through except in his secret writings, never damaging the façade. What he seemed to lack was the ability to learn more, to continue growing ("The

wildness and despair and surrender of the rational will. The surrender seems at first deliberate, and the romantics look to many, still, like men not indulging or abandoning themselves, but seeking in somewhat odd ways for a new vision of the world and a new mode of being.[7]

The vision and mode of being they arrived at were in fact those most likely to result, given the psychic changes then occurring. What they saw, and what some like Poe and Rimbaud vividly experienced, was man's nature succumbing once more to the irrationality and turbulence of mind induced by the Id, the ancestral instinctive self now slowly being released and coming back, like a rising storm, at the end of history.

Without, in most cases, the least awareness of being political, the romantics nonetheless were so, in that they represented an inner condition out of which the revolutions, as well as the art, of the time were arising. Delacroix with his literal storms at sea; Washington Allston's "Belshazzar's Feast"; Poe's grisly tales and musical, half-mindless verse; *Une Saison en Enfer;* Edwin Drood and The Mysterious Stranger; the peculiar worlds of Hardy and, later, Faulkner; Wagner's *Niebelung;* Stravinsky's *Sacre du Printemps;* Céline's *Mort à Crédit—* all prophesy a return: in essence the return to a mysterious, chaotic inner life in which rational control becomes more and more problematic and the visions of reason ever more limited and subject to violent invasions of fantasy, to primitive longing and destructiveness. The mild, harmonious emotions of Wordsworth give place by degrees to more powerful ones, to an unstable alternance of love and hate, to forms of love themselves more exclusively sexual and self-serving, above all to

---

period from which all his significant work came was his boyhood; he returned to it again and again."). MacDonald attributes this peculiarity to the break in our history which came with the Civil War. In itself, I believe that had little to do with it. In psychic type, Twain was in fact postbellum.

7. "It is not too much to say that the chief cultural effort of the 19th and 20th .centuries has been to raise art and confound . . . Intellect and Philistinism. . . . The battle of the artist . . . has been for over a century, a battle for the possession of the common educated mind. And it has been won not by showing the delights of art, but the dangers of Intellect. 'Save your soul alive' has been the watchcry. Intellect will harden your heart without damping its passions. . . . Most grievous, Intellect will destroy the wholeness of yourself by throwing doubt on instinct and making habitual the arresting of impulse, *until there is born within you a second man"* (italics mine). Jacques Barzun, *The House of Intellect* (Harper, 1959), p. 166.

fear—to dominance, once again, of the primal emergency system which all other feeling and behavior now come only to subserve and to placate.[8] It is in this profound sense that moderns are "compulsive"— have lost spontaneity and more and more respond only to the pressures of circumstance felt as commands or threats. In Auden's title phrase, ours is finally an Age of Anxiety, in which, as in late Scipionic Rome, men have "become perplexed as to their very selves." After the apparent moral "liberation" of the 1920's, sexual disorders in this country, contrary to what might have been predicted, have not died out, but appear to be still prevalent; and anxiety, if one can believe the clinical literature, is a frequent cause of them, a result of the subcortical emergency system competing too successfully, perhaps, with the one which embodies sex and which, in more fortunate eras, combined with the neocortical I to keep our fears in check. At the same time, the family, once held together by those same ties of affection whose more reasoned equivalents bound Wordsworthian man to his fellows and to nature, begins to disintegrate; and so deep-rooted is this change in the psychological constitution of our time that law and custom are powerless to stop it and, as usually happens, are adapting to the fact instead.[9]

8. "There are various kinds of fear . . . but we may narrow them down to two main categories; individual fear, which is a natural part of the human character, and collective or mass fear which comes from the lack of any character at all. . . . [The second] arises, not from man's definite consciousness of his own personality and a natural desire to defend it against encroachment, but rather from the absence of such personality, from the feeling that man has no existence apart from his participation in the vague and amorphous life of the collectivity.

"This collective fear is the root of mass movements and of totalitarianism. It comes from an incomplete and faltering consciousness of the self . . . an ignorance of concrete problems, and a tendency to spill over into a world of symbols and abstractions. This is the deep-seated ineradicable fear of the man . . . who cannot attain freedom and therefore feels unsafe and defenceless in a world where freedom is the only reality, the only true life. . . . The very existence of a totalitarian government is predicated upon such a fear, and once at the helm this government aggravates, through the application of relentless power, the very conditions which bring such fear about. Next come the . . . terrors of the police state, persecution, the sadistic cruelty of concentration camps, and finally war. There is created a vicious circle . . . from which, as we have seen, it is extremely difficult to escape." Carlo Levi, in New York *Times Magazine,* October 3, 1948. In terms of the physiology of the central nervous system, this diagnosis is, I believe, brilliantly correct.

9. It is well known that divorce became a problem in Rome roughly from 150 B.C. on and, as in America, paralleled the rise in influence of women in the national life. See Edward Gibbon, *The Decline and Fall of the Roman Empire,*

The coming of this unhappy epoch, in which men are a danger to themselves roughly in proportion to their own triviality, is announced in the middle of the Victorian age—in 1867, almost seventy years after Wordsworth's "Lines" quoted above, and a year after the close of our own Civil War (which was the watershed of American modernity, the period when the enormous expansion of business was about to begin in this country, and with it, the attitudes dominant among us today). I am speaking of "Dover Beach," perhaps the only first-rate poem Arnold ever wrote:

> The sea is calm to-night.
> The tide is full, the moon lies fair
> Upon the straits;—on the French coast the light
> Gleams and is gone; the cliffs of England stand,
> Glimmering and vast, out in the tranquil bay.
> Come to the window, sweet is the night-air!
> Only, from the long line of spray
> Where the sea meets the moon-blanch'd land,
> Listen! you hear the grating roar
> Of pebbles which the waves draw back, and fling,
> At their return, up the high strand,
> Begin, and cease, and then again begin,
> With tremulous cadence slow, and bring
> The eternal note of sadness in.
>
> Sophocles long ago
> Heard it on the Aegean, and it brought
> Into his mind the turbid ebb and flow
> Of human misery; we
> Find also in the sound a thought,
> Hearing it by this distant northern sea.
>
> The Sea of Faith
> Was once, too, at the full, and round earth's shore
> Lay like the folds of a bright girdle furl'd.
> But now I only hear
> Its melancholy, long, withdrawing roar,
> Retreating, to the breath
> Of the night-wind, down the vast edges drear
> And naked shingles of the world.
>
> Ah, love, let us be true

To one another! for the world, which seems
To lie before us like a land of dreams,
So various, so beautiful, so new,
Hath really neither joy, nor love, nor light,
Nor certitude, nor peace, nor help for pain;
And we are here as on a darkling plain
Swept with confused alarms of struggle and flight,
Where ignorant armies clash by night.

Not only have we come to accept the clash of "ignorant armies" and a climate of neurotic unease as almost permanent features of life; we have also tried to make a saving fetish of love. But love, as we understand it, or even as Freud understood it,[10] may not be up to the task. For to endure and to be the comfort we try to make it, sexual love needs to be enlarged by reason and its ally *warmth,* which is in reality not sexual at all but a despecialized Id function appearing in tandem with the developing rational-conscious I. Contrary to what Arnold and American popular songwriters (and apparently Freud) have supposed, the process cannot be run in reverse. We cannot, merely by stressing certain Id functions—by madly pursuing the perfect love, or even more so by capturing it—hope to deliver ourselves. On the contrary; *as* an Id function, sexual love is no respecter of persons, of the real identity of the loved. Once satisfied, it sooner or later shifts the lover's attention elsewhere. In its way, it is as ruthless as the Id functions related to fear and survival behavior; and as a "defense," or an alternative to these, it is in several senses bound to be temporary and unreliable. Nor is there much chance that, indirectly, sexual love will favor any major or lasting expansion of the rational I and there-

3 Vols. Modern Library, Vol. II, Ch. XLIV, p. 702. In view of the special role of America in the modern West, discussed later here, it is interesting that our divorce rate, as of 1954, was by far the highest among Western nations. See the New York *Herald-Tribune,* Tuesday, June 15, 1954.

10. In the last paragraph of *Civilization and Its Discontents* (Doubleday, 1958), Freud says that the "fateful question" for man is whether "the cultural process ... will succeed in mastering the derangements of communal life caused by the human instinct of aggression and self-destruction." We know our present capacity for exterminating ourselves; hence our "dejection." "And now it may be expected that the other of the two 'heavenly forces' Eros, will put forth his strength so as to maintain himself alongside of his equally immortal adversary." My own view is that he has already done so and failed. The modern world has soaked itself in love, only to worsen its divorce rates.

with, among other things, its own constancy. That process, as I have tried to show, begins with mind and works downward *into* the Id. In physiological terms, it proceeds from the neocortex down and cannot in the nature of the case be run from the bottom up. Arnold's hopes for romantic love and "togetherness," like ours, are rooted in ignorance of the way our natures are put together; and on the basis of the available evidence, they seem to be failing accordingly.

In the style and content of the arts, since Arnold's day, there appear, as it were prophesied, a gradual shallowing and finally a breakup of the inner world of mind itself.[11]

In painting, romantic "themes" give place to impressionism, or the art which sees simply what the eye sees;[12] after which in the twentieth

---

11. Stenham, in Paul Bowles's *The Spider's House* (Random House, 1955), p. 195 to p. 240, is an ex-Marxist and Party member who, after World War II, "had lived in solitude and carefully planned ignorance of what was happening in the world. Nothing had importance but the exquisitely isolated cosmos of his own consciousness. Then, little by little, he had the impression that the light of meaning, the meaning of everything, was dying. . . . One day . . . he had been forced to admit to himself with amazement and horror that there was no better expression for what he feared than a very old one: eternal damnation."

12. In the same period, Western music moves from its classical form—the "horizontal," based on counterpoint—into its romantic, impressionist, and finally its modern, phases. An important feature of that change is a shift toward the "vertical"; that is, the substitution of successions of tone masses or chords for simultaneous melodic lines. With this, music loses some or much of its temporal structure and becomes a matter of instantaneous "effects": an art which plays more and more directly upon the senses and emotion and requires less and less in the way of sustained attention and musical intellect.

The parallel of this change in literature, is the lapsing of the novel into a chaotic subjectivity à la Joyce or such *petites maîtresses* as Virginia Woolf and Anaïs Nin.

The meaning of this seemingly voluntary abandonment of larger temporal organization perhaps becomes plainer when one considers that most children grasp spatial relations (geometric pattern; pictures) long before they can handle notions of rate and acceleration. Likewise, in the history of mathematics, the first formal geometry comes some two thousand years before the calculus of Newton and Leibniz. Conversely, in the regression of intellect, the first faculty to suffer may be that involving the time dimension, one manifestation of this change being the loss of a sense of the past—that is, one's tradition and origins. Be they never so emphasized in our schools, the events of our history and the line of great ideas from which our world descends apparently move us less and less. In "modern" eras it is finally as though the past had never been. The failure of "time sense" in *avant-garde* literature and music is perhaps a complementary phenomenon, as is McLuhan's notion that the "mosaic" is now about to replace print,

century come the splintered worlds of the abstractionists. The paradox of the arts seems to be that at their best they are greater than whatever they happen to reflect or symptomatize. They have a validity, one might say, which transcends their origins. Renaissance painting is, in this sense, far more than religious and modern painting far more than "sick." In the latter, two predispositions in particular show through: one toward a radical simplification of the seen as in Chirico or Matisse, and the other toward presentation of it as jagged, exploding, dripping with blood, ominously visceral or mechanical, above all disordered— *ruined* (Kandinski, Bacon, Pollock; the "action" painters, and so on). Like much of modern writing, it is an art of the self in bits, of increasingly nightmarish emotion, and of a world whose pieces severally may have form or meaning but whose totality does not. To the modern mind the large, complex, organic view of things is no longer a source of ecstasy as it was to Wordsworth. It is no longer even possible. To live mentally at ease, we must simplify and fragment, avoiding great systems of thought, breaking reality up small—"reductionists" *faute de mieux*. Less and less do we feel *wonder,* or a kind of mystical oneness with forms of order newly seen; more and more the new is merely confusing and frightening to us; the less readily can we grasp or accept, let alone identify with, the not-us, the radically unfamiliar.[13] This is, quite literally, the state of alienation. As the larger organization of the

or step-by-step comprehension. (On the question of the representation of spatial and temporal relations in the brain, which relates to the peculiar difficulty we have with the concept of time, see C. M. Fair, in *Annals of the New York Academy of Sciences,* Vol. 138, Article 2 (February 6, 1967), pp. 912–913.)

13. In physiological terms, the more subject we have become to the "orienting reflex," or fearlike responses to the unfamiliar. Sokolov, in Russia, attributed this phenomenon to a failure of neocortical control over more basal systems. The corollary of his view is that the more informed the neocortex becomes—the more widely developed are its memory or recognition systems—the less prone the organism is to fear inspired merely by changes in its surround. In the case of modern Western man, the situation is complicated by the fact that even as his powers of apprehending the world, outside of his own special sphere, may be declining, the world itself, thanks to the techniques born of science, is becoming rapidly more complex and full of surprises. On the "orienting reflex" principle, the result is a huge build-up of anxiety, which then rebounds into other emotions (as, when one is frightened, fright may rebound into violent rage). "History," Eric Hoffer said, "is made by men who have the restlessness, impressionability, credulity, capacity for make-believe, ruthlessness and self-righteousness of children." In this passionate era, we have seen quite a crop of them. See Eric Hoffer, "A Time of Juveniles," *Harpers Magazine* (June, 1965).

mind crumbles, and with it the capacity for empathy or true identification, even the familiar can come to seem alien. Even the old instinctive ties of affection tend to dissolve, and the whole world appears to
us as a ravening wilderness. This is the *Weltanschauung* of writers like
Céline and Kafka. It runs like an underground river through much
of Faulkner and is the dark side of Henry Miller's bouncy ignorance,
of Huxley's elaborate comedies of despair, of Mann's *Death in Venice,*
of Cozzens' and John O'Hara's dreadful bourgeois, of Emma Bovary
and Carol Kennicott. With a few exceptions, writers up through the
1940's seem to have balked at readmittance of pure sensualism and
philosophic resignation à la Petronius Arbiter. It is as if they had felt
somehow that the Id might still be resisted, and life reorganized on
better lines. Like the purists of reason in physics and mathematical
logic, they destroyed in the hope of future, improved creation; but
already, perhaps, the effort came too late and did not, at bottom, understand itself. As writers, our impulse has been to mock and repudiate
the works of our immediate forebears in art or life with a thoroughness
out of all proportion to their actual errors and defects of character.
And this same judgment, springing from a mixture of petty observation and a rejection of things present amounting to embittered blindness, has now appeared as the attitude of a whole generation toward
its predecessors. Since World War II, particularly perhaps in America,
the young have suddenly come to form what some have called a "subculture"[14]—one in the extreme capable of (or one might better say, sus-

---

14. Sceptics maintain that this idea is nonsense—an illusion fostered perhaps
by better "communications." Youth, they say, is inherently rebellious. True, but
the quality and intensity of the rebellion seem recently to have changed. See,
for instance, Kenneth Keniston, *The Uncommitted: Alienated Youth in American
Society* (Harcourt, Brace, and World, 1965). A review in *Science,* Vol. 134 (1961),
pp. 1061–1062, of another such book—J. S. Coleman's *The Adolescent Society* (Free
Press, 1961)—gives some of the usual pros and cons. The reviewer takes the
position that the book fails to show there is *an* adolescent society (and complains
of the word, which he says should be *subculture*) "Do all adolescents form a unit?"
he asks, concluding of course that they do not and that therefore the author's
inference "that social disintegration is in process is—like Mark Twain's death
notice—premature."

It goes without saying that adolescents do not form *a* (sub)culture. Neither
do adults. That fact does not prevent many current ideas from being held, if
differently acted upon, by people comprising many different subcultures within
the same culture. Hardly an adult in any walk of life has not been touched by
modern agnosticism and our attempt to view ourselves, accordingly, as simply

ceptible to) a defiance and criminality of extraordinary senselessness. More commonly, its alienation takes the form of a gray obstinacy and withdrawal, only to turn into an equally gray conformism ten years later. Like the Menckens and Philip Wylies of the several preceding generations, like the iconoclasts, even, of pure reason,[15] the "subculture"

articulate animals.

In the same way, I think it is probably true that a large percentage of adolescents today—probably significantly larger than one would have found a century ago—distrust many ideas and stated convictions of their parents and other adults, even though a relatively small percentage of these same adolescents are outright delinquents or fomenters of riots. Therefore to be grown up, to inherit the "oldies" confusions, is not attractive to them; they share our scepticism—have improved upon it, even—and do not want our rat-race or our surviving "values." A teen-ager in the book under review says, " 'The adolescent borrows for his society the glamorous and sophisticated part of adult society. The goals and worthwhile activities of the adult are scorned because they involve responsibilities which the adolescent is not ready to accept.' " And he is not ready to accept them, one guesses, because he finds them not only beyond his resources of character and intellect but suspect as well, if not, in a sense, trivial. If we are all just animals, who cares? Besides the few who literally act out this proposition as hippies, delinquents, and the like, there are probably many who play along, finish high school, get their college degrees, enter some part of the system, some adult subculture, and still believe the whole undertaking to be pretty absurd. It is this want of conviction or attachment which no doubt contributes to our rising divorce rates, to an increasing fluidity in our morals generally.

The statement that our young people today form a more distinctly alienated minority than they once did, hence a kind of subculture, means that in them the processes of shedding the past have gone so much farther than they have in us that minorities among them have become overtly, almost mindlessly revolutionary, while many, including the nondelinquent, have developed a teen-age style only partially and superficially imitative of ours and in other ways peculiarly their own. We are still talking about a statistical phenomenon, not a monolithic movement. The fact, however, that it is not monolithic does not mean it is not a movement. How revolutionary it is, in the extreme, can be seen from this remarkable passage quoted from a student editorial (in the *Berkeley Barb;* Benjamin DeMott, New York *Times Magazine,* May 19, 1968, p. 104). The editorial exhorts students to sweep through "college campuses burning books, burning degrees and exams, busting up classrooms and freeing our brothers from the prison of the university. . . . The universities cannot be reformed. They must be abandoned or closed down. They should be used as bases for action against society but never taken seriously."

15. That is, the logical positivists and the purists of "operationalism" in physics, among whom an American, P. W. Bridgman, was pre-eminent. See his *Logic of Modern Physics* (Macmillan, 1949). Of operationalism, J. L. Synge, in *Science: Sense and Nonsense* (Jonathan Cape, 1951), p. 77, said: "There is about this new creed, an appealing modesty and matter of factness. It looks as if a lot of nonsense is being blown away. . . . Eagerly we shovel out of our minds a struggling mass of

of our youth has produced no new prophets to replace our false ones. It is merely the next stage in the general slide into a life of the Id, providing the public for novels like *Naked Lunch* and the following and *raison d'être* of saints like Timothy Leary.

All of this amounts to saying that a great many apparently unrelated aspects of life in this century may, in fact, have common origins and a common meaning. Our *terribles simplificateurs* are not confined to politics, but appear in the realms of art and intellect and common usage as well—even perhaps in our seemingly healthy urge to be "sincere" in word and deed, our determination to dispense with "frills." Like the undercurrent of envy in egalitarianism, which acts to destroy real and necessary distinctions, as well as arbitrary and unjust ones, there is in our modern purism an uneasiness about the past, almost a hatred of it, which may have its roots in a well-founded suspicion that we are not up to continuing what our predecessors began. This sort of primitive envy, in the form of a relentless competitiveness with all other writers, living or dead, is quite evident in Gertrude Stein, an iconoclast and simplifier of literature to the point of being herself almost unreadable. Few writers of her reputation have ever, with such consistency, combined the opaque and the trivial or achieved an egotistical dullness so unrelieved. Apart from a kind of stunted sentimentalism, one senses little warmth in her work, no great gift for ideas, nothing in the end but this incessant leaden affectation, this incredible will to persist and prevail. One feels that she has impoverished the language to no purpose—not really to purify or reconstruct it, but to *humble* it, thereby bringing down all the arrogant unassimilable past. In her odd way she is Sartre's type of the anti-Semite,[16] the Impene-

giants . . . and sit with ears and eyes open to gain the new wisdom. It is disappointing. The promise of hard rationality is not fulfilled."

It is clear that Synge (see above, Chapter V, footnote 22) connects this phenomenon with the decline in imagination which for hitherto obscure reasons has gone with a decline in faith—all the more paradoxically since organized *official* faith has long been the enemy of scientific insight.

16. See Jean-Paul Sartre, *Anti-Semite and Jew* (Schocken, 1948), pp. 18–22. In contrast to the "rational man" who "groans as he gropes for the truth," who "never sees clearly where he may be going," the type of the anti-Semite is "attracted by the durability of a stone." He wants to "exist all at once and right away" and at times plays with his audience. "They know that their remarks are frivolous, open to challenge. . . . They are amusing themselves, for it is their adversary who is obliged to use words responsibly. . . . The anti-semites have the *right* to play. . . . They seek not to persuade by sound argument but to . . . disconcert."

trable One, mysteriously, implacably in possession of a treasure, her Idea, her ticket to absolute superiority.

In the same way Fascism was not content merely to come to power —to take over the state and the tradition as was. Eric Hoffer's "True Believer,"[17] the foot soldier of Fascism, needs a cause which meets several needs at once—among them the need to be massive (and therefore simple) in his opinions, to strike awe into others as the superpatriot and scourge of Jews and radicals. Perhaps equally he needs to revenge his own awe and envy by destroying everything that once inspired those emotions in him, which means not only the existing political order but the whole apparatus of learning and tradition which lies behind it. The very fact that he has become, in psychic type, too coarse and rudimentary to assimilate his own heritage is (as with Gertrude Stein) all the more reason for destroying it, since it is both an odious reminder of all that he is not and also in fact now useless to him.[18] For the same reason, he becomes less and less grateful or responsive to leaders of the older liberal type who may have done him much actual good, because these represent a world grown too complex for his understanding and too slow in its workings to satisfy his increasingly restless, decontrolled nature. In the end he will forsake them to follow leaders in mentality more like himself and so bring the revolutions of nihilism, begun in 1789, to their conclusion. The state, at last consolidating as a primitive autocracy, will then begin to turn its psychic energies outward and from the same almost irresistible impetus become an imperium.[19] In the meantime, within the state, every vestige of the past will be uprooted, either by deliberate book burning, as in the age of Shih Huang Ti in China or in Hitler's Germany; or simply as part of the incidental destruction occurring during prolonged civil war, as in the Rome of Marius and Sulla; or more gradually and subtly,

17. Eric Hoffer, *The True Believer* (Harper, 1951).

18. "The new élite [of Hitler's Germany] is far too primitive and of far too crude a mentality to be able even to understand the Marxist language, much less to elaborate its principles and doctrines. . . . In present-day Germany the new and unschooled leaders of the workers have thrown all social theories overboard; on the other hand there is a clear will to radical revolution. . . . The anti-intellectual attitude of 'dynamism' is not mere chance, but the necessary outcome of an entire absence of standards." Hermann Rauschning, *The Revolution of Nihilism* (Alliance, 1939), pp 28, 72–73.

19. As France did briefly and prematurely under Napoleon, or Germany under *der Führer.*

by the debasement of learning into a miscellany of special skills, the misuse of egalitarianism to discourage real distinction or dissent, the subornation of intellectuals,[20] and the slow spread of a *de facto* morality of success, as in the United States today.

With these changes, the historical cycle which started with the diffusion of a parent religion through the barbaric countryside of fifteen hundred years before[21] begins to come to an end. Arising, one might say, as a reaction in the majority of men against the perpetual fear and uncertainty of life, as well as from a sense that, as men, we may be capable of more than mere survival or brute success, the religions of early cultural time engender in spite of themselves a spreading optimism and to that degree a real and increasing probability of change for the better. But as religions are invariably abused by their princes, and as the grip of instinct on man guarantees that for every advance in any direction, a price will have to be paid in enlarged opportunities for the unredeemed, the progress of Progress suffers from great internal friction and presents to the observer an appearance of inextricable muddle and contradiction. One thing seems clear: almost nothing that men of the higher type have accomplished, in any civilization, has ultimately escaped debasement (*vide* $e = mc^2$). The profoundest insights, the most well-intentioned institutions, causes most nobly conceived and bravely fought for—all, one way or another, have come under control of men of the practical animal type, whose gift is to use in the service of themselves whatever the world may offer and who as often as not give it ashes in return. The ascendancy of such men, in late civilizations, is what finally brings them down.

It is not just, however, to say, as Brooks Adams did,[22] that Rome fell because it had been destroyed "by men of the economic type of mind." One cannot, like Marx, blame a particular class or particular techniques of rising in the peck-order for the fact that peck-orders have remained universal in human society. The real enemy is the animal within us, which contrives still to subordinate the individual to the tribal, worth to force, and truth to facts. It happened that by Marx's

20. J. Epstein, "The C.I.A. and the Intellectuals," *New York Review of Books,* April 20, 1967, surveys considerably more than the stated subject.

21. For example, the France of Clovis I, from which I have more or less arbitrarily dated the rise of West Christian Culture.

22. In *The Law of Civilization and Decay* (Knopf, 1943), p. 96.

day business had become the prime instrument by which men could come to power over their fellows. It had, and still has, much to be said for it, when compared to the sword or to power outright.[23] It has meant much incidental service, much easing of the physical miseries of life, even for the poorest; much accumulation of wealth and energy, and therefore much potential leisure and fulfillment. The sword alone never accomplished these things, except by plunder or the essentially inefficient means of slavery.[24] Marxism has tended to see modern science as in some way the handmaiden of business and in Russia has kept it in that role, in that scientists there remain politically accountable, as the opponents of Lysenko found to their cost. No one familiar with the history of West Christian civilization or really interested in an objective appraisal of events could conclude that our science has, or had, such a relation to big business. The original enemy of both business

23. The history of medieval Genoa rather strikingly illustrates this point. Besides the naval wars of that city with Pisa (after their joint expulsion of the Moslems from Sardinia in the eleventh century) and later with Venice, the Genoese "were an unceasing prey to intestine discord—the . . . commons and nobles fighting against each other, rival factions amongst the nobles . . . striving to grasp the supreme power in the state, nobles and commons alike invoking the arbitration and rule of some foreign captain as the sole means of obtaining a temporary truce." Matters apparently improved somewhat with the appointment of the first doge in 1339, but the continuing struggle with the Venetians "ended by establishing the great relative inferiority of the Genoese rulers who fell under the power now of France, now of the Visconti of Milan."

"The Banca di San Giorgio with its large possessions mainly in Corsica formed during this period, the most stable element in the state until in 1528. . . . Andrea Doria succeeded in throwing off the French domination." *Encyclopaedia Britannica* (11th ed.), II, 599–600.

The article on banks and banking in the fourteenth edition of the *Britannica* describes this enterprise as follows: "The Casa di San Giorgio . . . had gradually extended its commitments and powers until it was not only a deposit bank but also acquired many of the functions and powers of the Government itself. In 1453 Corsica, Péra (a suburb of Byzantium) and the Genoese Black Sea colonies were ceded to it, and according to Machiavelli, its administration was more efficient and less tyrannical than that of the state. It had an honorable history until 1797 and it is arguable that it is a direct ancestor of the present Banca d'Italia."

24. Alexis de Tocqueville compares the free state of Ohio with its slave-owning neighbor Kentucky. "At the present day," he concludes, "it is only the Northern States which are in possession of shipping, manufactures, railroads and canals. . . . Were I inclined to continue this parallel, I could easily prove that almost all the differences . . . between the characters of the Americans in the Southern and in the Northern states have originated in slavery." *Democracy in America* (Cambridge Ed., 1862), I, 464 ff.

and science was the church. It was primarily fear of the church which enforced that "secret and tacit compact" of which Coleridge spoke (page 106, fn. 37). And almost from the beginning science has gone its own way, seldom capitalizing on its own discoveries or directing its work along lines laid down for it by others. Nor can one blame either business or science for the spread of an enlightenment which has done much to destroy the last of our religious faith and with it, for reasons I hope to have made clearer, the psychological ground both of our interior freedom, our full stature as rational beings, and of the warmth and serenity of spirit which are a natural part of that condition. It is not enlightenment alone which in late ages causes the disastrous changes precluding man's proper inner development, wearing out his optimism and handing him back at last to the ancient dominion of tribalism and fear.

One reason that periods of enlightenment, intervening between the Spenglerian springtime and the final ages of scepticism, revolution, and empire, have invariably hastened, rather than retarded, the fall of cultures is that enlightenment itself has never been the real possession of more than a few. Nor have we ever known, except in the intuitive way of the saints and poets, enough about the principles on which our own natures are constructed to form ourselves or our descendants properly. Of the few things we have managed to learn, those most important to our own future have remained the least clearly understood or communicable and therefore almost blessings by chance. Worse, those who in general most desperately need them are apt both psychically and economically to be the furthest beyond help.

To the poor boy whose first five or six years have been spent in a world where Darwinian survival tactics count for more than words and whose mind, for lack of early seeding, may resist later cultivation except along the same essentially primitive lines, it is useless to talk religion except if it appeal directly to the Id. The same applies to academic learning and "values." These cannot promise immortality, though they can do the next best thing: offer him a hand up to a better life on earth. In this psychic scheme, appeals to cultivate gentleless in oneself or disinterested interest in others or in the world around have no place. For this reason teachers of the more old-fashioned idealistic type are simply ridiculous to students in a modern urban public school. Their very ideals mark them as weaklings and people hopelessly out of touch; and in fact there are probably few such teachers left. The concept of the gentleman has fallen into similar disrepute— not merely the manner but even more the substance ("He's a regular little gentleman"); and even the word *liberal* has acquired the same taint, connoting absurd pretensions, "do-goodism," virtues contemptible because they do not work and only make nuisances and victims of the virtuous.[25]

However, to people of this mentality the more negative findings of science *do* have meaning: one which, on the whole, fits quite well with the brutality of life on the lower tiers of society and contributes to it. The view of man as simply a creature of "glands" and functions, of life as no more than biological or adaptive, a senseless perpetual combat with circumstance, ending finally in death and vanishment of the self —this notion, which general education has helped to make universal, deals the older forms of faith a heavy blow. For the poor boy is of necessity practical. The fact that his fifty-dollar car runs, that there are TV and radio and cures for sickness, tells him that science works. That is what he and most grownups think science *is*. And science, by strong implication, tells him that religion does *not* work—is just words.

Convinced, he ceases as a grownup to go to church, puts most of the moral talk he may have heard in his childhood behind him, and raises his own children by a system of slam-bang example whose basic precepts are largely practical and whose tone is authoritarian; that is, a reflection of belief not in superior principles, but simply in his factual superiority as an adult and a parent. This is no more than the world of nihilistic autocracy in miniature, the germinal form of the revolutionary state. This type of family life, cut adrift from the influence of ideals or principles once felt to be real and realizable and therefore worth emulating, becomes subject to the same caprices and the same violence which later appear in political form as the sheer arbitrariness, the Terror principle of modern dictatorships.

We have no statistics to tell us whether the frightful crimes which erupt in modern families—the wife-beating, the brutal, sometimes fatal

25. Worse still, *liberal,* as in the phrase New Liberalism, connotes something like the opposite of its original meaning: an authoritarian zeal for ramming "progressive" ideas down the throats of the multitude or promoting a Rusk-Rostow type of foreign policy which works on the principle of protecting democracy here by force and bribery there.

beatings of infants, the murders and suicides springing from jealousy or simply from perpetual argument and squabbling; the "model students" who for no apparent reason shoot Mom and Dad, or dismantle their sweethearts, or go on killing sprees—were as prevalent, say, in seventeenth-century England or America. The records which survive from those times suggest that brutality then took somewhat different forms—was more a monopoly of brigands or religious mobs or the armed upper classes and rather less a feature of the domestic life of the people. An early indicator of change in the supposedly happier existence of those days may have been the appearance and sudden popularity of cheap gin in England at the beginning of the eighteenth century.[26] And certainly by mid-Victorian times, the connection between parental *Schrecklichkeit* and the Demon Rum had become well advertised. It was typical, in fact, of the Victorian mind to give alcohol as such so large a share of the blame.[27] It is a cliché, but unfortunately

26. G. M. Trevelyan, *English Social History* (Longmans, Green, 1944), p. 341. At first encouraged, for economic reasons, gin-drinking had such alarming results, especially in Hogarth's London, that it was virtually taxed out of existence after 1750.

27. More recently, "thrill killings" such as the murder of nurse Pauline Campbell by three teen-agers in Ann Arbor, Michigan, have evoked similar attempts at explanation. A police officer, speaking of that case, said, "I think people *wanted* to blame narcotics." It is obviously easier to accept a single physical cause for such actions than to consider the alternative which intuitive common sense suggests, namely, that they result from sheer emptiness, a nullity which delivers the criminal to his primal self almost without a fight and with little emotion before or after the fact. What we call emotion arises, I believe, in one of two ways: when a basic drive is denied expression or when the rational I sees a gross discrepancy between conscious intentions and results. A cardinal feature of the I, properly formed, is that it enables man to "identify"; that is, it gives him the objectivity to grant equal existence to others. If one's adaptive (self-serving, self-indulgent) acts lead one to violate others in some way, the I causes one in imagination to assume the role of the violated, the result presumably being horror and remorse.

As traditions decay and the I dwindles, such processes of "identification" tend to fail, the result in the extreme being "psychopathic" killers like Bill Moyer (and his accomplices Max Pell and Dave Royal, in the case mentioned above). One of the defendants, Pell, was a gifted mechanic who was precipitated into making a full confession when the police threatened to cut up the upholstery of his car to test for blood stains ("You don't need to tear my car apart. I'll tell you. It's blood.") At the trial: "A newspaperman remembers: 'They never tried to avoid the cameras. In the anteroom they were always smiling and laughing together.'"

The psychiatrist who diagnosed Moyer as a psychopathic personality admitted that no one knows what that phrase means. "Our prisons," the writer (John Bartlow Martin) adds, "are full of men labelled 'psychopathic personality'—indeed,

true, that alcohol or drugs tend only to unmask what is already in us
—in this case, a defectively controlled Id. As men in our society have
drifted in that direction—toward a precivilized amorphousness, a weak-
ening of the I, and a proportionate release of the primal self—the emotional climate of family life may likewise have changed. Even at social
levels where brutality is rare, there is perhaps more of coldness and
anxiety now, more of a tendency to *use* children, to put our emotional
relations with them on a kind of economic basis, than there was, say,
a century ago. With the waning of affection and of intellect, in the
older sense, together, father even when "educated" may have less to
pass on, and also less of an impulse to pass on what he has, than he
once did. With this, women, to whom at least the primal forms of
affection probably come more naturally and whose situation often protects them from the anxiety and tense competitiveness of daily life,
begin to take over, as it were by default. So long as the family stays in
existence—that is, escapes divorce—they tend to be its rulers.[28]

Since the "modern" state of mind described here implies a statistical
shift away from imaginative reason and warmth, it also implies a shift
toward dominance, once again, of the primal emergency system and

running through prison classification files in some states one gets the impression
that prisons contain few people other than psychopaths." He may be quite correct.
According to the view of human nature outlined here, the psychopath is simply
modern man taken to a logical extreme. He is capable of quite violent emotion
when balked, but then indulges himself readily. His emotions seem to us "shallow"
because, being seldom concerned with long-range intentions or inflamed by self-
restraint, they pass off quickly; while the sort of emotion resulting from identification with others and from objective self-awareness is almost unknown to him.
(Citations above are from J. B. Martin, *Why Did They Kill?* [Ballantine, 1953],
pp. 98, 104, 110.)

One should add that there is also apparently a minority of delinquents and
criminally insane who show sex-chromosome abnormality (the so-called 47 XYY
type), a condition often accompanied by exceptional tallness, dullness, and sometimes atrophy of the testes. They are described as occurring in "small but consistent numbers" among recidivists or "antisocial aggressive males who are
mentally ill" (M. A. Telfer *et al.,* in *Science,* Vol. 159 [1968], 1249–1250). Whether
the psychopathic population includes other such genetically determined minorities
we do not know.

28. Many statistics have been published showing that women control a considerable per cent of this country's wealth. It has been repeatedly suggested, though
never incontrovertibly shown, that there is a close connection between "Momism"
and male homosexuality. Mommsen describes a similar rise in the power of women
in the Rome of the first century b.c. *History of Rome* (Philosophical Library,
1959), p. 505.

fear. As already mentioned, instinctive functions related to self-protection tend in any case to be the most massive and the most difficult to subject to rational control, if only because survival is the first condition of existence. In animal experiments, one can show that cooling of the neocortex is accompanied by apparent "release" of the primitive activating system in the midbrain reticular formation. This experiment perhaps crudely demonstrates what happens in man when the functions of the rational I fail to come to proper development. A similar release of survival systems, manifested by intense competitiveness and intense chronic anxiety, may occur, the man of this type acting as though continually threatened and treating all about him as potential enemies or rivals. For such a man, relations of easy warmth and equality with others become difficult if not impossible. He inclines to view the whole world in terms of power and status relations, to be a snob and compulsive succeeder, literally driven into a lifelong scramble for goods and honors he may neither want nor really enjoy, because the getting of them in no way lastingly relieves the pain which produced these prodigies of effort in the first place. With the decline of religious idealism and the accompanying diminution of the I, this may be the psychic type which comes to predominate, giving modern eras such as our own their peculiar dynamism—as if men only yesterday on the way to greater rationality and self-control, were seized suddenly by a mindless energy and propelled, as it were, into crises of outward achievement (witness the incredibly swift rise and the Wagnerian *finale* of the recent Nazi state).

A prime feature of emergency responses is that they favor survival if need be at a considerable cost to the organism in states of pleasure or mental clarity,[29] sometimes, paradoxically, at the deferred cost of its life. Similarly, the more man acts, not "spontaneously" from affection or positive attraction, but on the rebound from external circumstance or from inner promptings equivalent to fear, the more "compulsive" by definition he is. This is the man perpetually "anxious" to be doing something, always "on the go," and not primarily, but, as it were, only derivatively happy in that fact. The best that he can hope for—the

29. See, for instance, Maier's rats, driven to near madness by the "no-solution" problem. N. R. F. Maier, *Frustration* (McGraw-Hill, 1949). Of course we cannot say what an animal is feeling, but strong inference is possible, particularly in experiments like these.

basic purpose served by his dynamism—is to deliver himself from the constant unease of anxiety, the continual pressure of his own emergency system, by an endless round of work. Only then, by the mechanism of physiological rebound which I called the "answering effect,"[30] may he temporarily shift the balance back in favor of the instinctive system related to pleasure, creativity, and sex. It is for this reason that many moderns feel real only when frenetically engaged or committed. They are incapable of leisure in the older sense[31] because they must constantly be challenging and outmaneuvering their own fears. In literature and in life as well, Hemingway was a superb example of the type. He made a career of outwitting his fears, of courting them even, the more primal the better.[32] He worked at sex and bravery with a

30. The "answering effect" can produce "opposite" feelings of proportionate and, as it were, paradoxical intensity: wild sexuality out of grief, wild courage or enthusiasm out of fear or discouragement. In the following passage, quoted in H. S. Commager's *The Blue and The Grey* (Bobbs Merrill, 1950), p. 1057, from "Sheridan's Personal Memoirs," Sheridan is describing his return to the front, after Early had surprised the Union Army at Cedar Creek and all but routed it.

"At Mill Creek my escort fell in behind and we were going ahead at a regular pace when . . . there burst upon our view the appalling spectacle of a panic-stricken army—hundreds of slightly wounded men, throngs of others unhurt but utterly demoralized . . . all pressing to the rear in hopeless confusion. . . . Some of the fugitives . . . assured me that the army was broken up, in full retreat, and that all was lost; all this with a manner true to that peculiar indifference that takes possession of panic-stricken men. . . . When most of the wounded and wagons were past, I returned to the road which was lined with unhurt men who . . . had halted without any organization and begun cooking coffee. . . . When they saw me they abandoned their coffee, threw up their hats, shouldered their muskets, and as I passed along turned to follow with enthusiasm and cheers. . . . In this way the news was spread to the stragglers off the road when they, too, turned their faces to the front . . . changing in a moment from the depth of depression to the extreme of enthusiasm. I already knew that even in the ordinary condition of mind enthusiasm is a potent element with soldiers, *but what I saw that day convinced me that if it can be excited from a state of despondence its power is almost irresistible*" (italics mine).

31. "The point and justification of leisure are [that he who works] . . . should continue to be a man—and that means he should not be wholly absorbed in the . . . milieu of his strictly limited function; the point is . . . that he should continue to be capable of seeing life as a whole . . . that he should fulfill himself, and come to full possession of his faculties, face to face with being as a whole. . . . It is only through leisure that the 'gate to freedom' is opened and man can escape from . . . that 'latent dread and anxiety' . . . [which are] the mark of the world of work." Josef Pieper, *Leisure: the Basis of Culture* (Pantheon, 1952), p. 57.

32. In her biography of T. H. White (Doubleday, 1968 p. 75), Sylvia

monotonous intensity which men of some later time, less crippled and "compulsive" than we, may well find absurd. And with the sickness and subsidence of his physical self, he lost his prime instrument and was driven to suicide, as if cheating fear of final victory after all. His poverty of ideas, his purism in language and choice of theme, are the intellectual parallels of his emotional life style—and necessarily so, if my analysis of the structure of human nature is approximately correct. He was ourselves taken to a logical extreme: grotesque, brave, intolerant, miserable in his successes, but to the end dynamic. Like us, he was less the driver than the driven: a man of the "response" type, pure; a modern.

Chronic dominance of the emergency system, while it may produce an extreme keenness (which is one of its functions), also produces a chronic overworking of physiological stress mechanisms and therewith a tendency to certain types of degenerative disease, among them arteriosclerosis, inflammatory diseases of the joints, hypertension due to overactivity of the sympathetic nervous system, ulceration of the gut, and renal or cardiac failure. It is interesting that there is paleontological evidence of arthritis in prehistoric man, who must on the whole have had a very stressful existence. The prevalence of certain of these diseases in modern man—in particular, for instance, of heart trouble, hypertension, and ulcers among business executives—may not be without meaning. However we do not know whether these disorders have shown a statistically significant increase; and even if we did, could not say precisely what it meant:[33] All one can say is that if my appraisal of the principles governing man's psychic life is at all accurate, one would expect these diseases to prevail and stubbornly resist eradication, especially in this age, and in any era to be most frequent among those with the strongest drive to rise in the peck-order, those most "anxious" to succeed.

Townsend Warner says: "When he took up flying, he was after more than a technique. He wanted to learn a new variety of fear. He was drawn to fear."

33. A very interesting study by S. A. Rudin in *Science,* Vol. 160 (1968), 901–903, suggests a clear connection between children's stories which encourage competitive achievement and a relatively high incidence, twenty-five years later, of ulcers and hypertension among adults raised on such stories. The same study suggests a negative correlation between a highly aggressive, competitive population and bookreading and a positive correlation between (encouraged) aggression and alcoholism.

While the dynamism of modern business and political life provides deliverance or fulfillment via relief of tension for a few, it cannot, in view of the actual allocations of power, do the same for a large majority. Neither in these fields, nor in organized sport, nor in the mass-entertainment industry is there a way up or out for most—which means they are stuck, not only in a socio-economic sense but also in the psychological. Burdened with a mass of "bad" feelings daily renewed, like a well which will not be pumped dry, bored by jobs which neither fulfill nor release them, they turn, if they can afford it, to psychiatry; or else to alcohol or drugs; to strenuous sports or hobbies as a way of "blowing off steam"; and to increasingly violent and sensational forms of entertainment which vicariously convert fear and tension into their "opposites": the release and sense of self-expansion which go with a rebound into ferocity and tumultuous sex. Our sexual behavior in real life has much the same character—is obsessive and driven, not to say grossly mechanical and often grossly competitive—anything but simply sensual and joyous. Quite naturally, the older-fashioned sentimentality, notions of romantic love and of fine "high" character and achievement, get no more than a nod in the new entertainment. The modern American movie combines a bravura appeal to the senses with an almost total lack of content or of the gentler emotions; it is driven and dynamic to the point of defeating its own purpose. Who can identify with action so incessant, a ferocity and contempt of human life so gratuitous and without issue, sex so bald and transitory that there is scarcely time even to make love properly, let alone noticing the girl you are making love to? Its sheer literalism, its effort to push us too fast in the direction we were already going, nearly cost Hollywood its economic life in the early 1950's. The Alan Ladd pictures were ahead of their time, but there is, of course, always TV to bring them back.

Still other forms of emotional redemption, in this country, are provided by our lunatic sectarianism (especially in California), by political religions of violence (also concentrated in California), and by alcoholism and drugs. Two points about drug addiction are worth noting. One is that it is particularly prevalent in cultures long fossilized, like that of China or Islam, or among tribal peoples such as the betel-chewing Pacific Islanders or the American Indians who use peyote—societies which have either been static for centuries or which have never had a history in the full sense at all. Drugs are simply the, or an, *ultima ratio* for men who see no way out for themselves, in whom tension, as Aldous Huxley put it,[34] has become a disease—whose reason, whether used reflectively or as an instrument of adaptive self-management, is unequal to the task of keeping the primal emergency system and its corresponding emotions from dominating their lives. Drug addiction, being essentially passive, is a quite logical refuge for those men of late civilizations who have no great gift for worldly success, who in their mental lives are not driven to extremes of calculation and self-seeking, but are merely further impoverished and made miserable by the unrelenting pressure of anxiety in its variously rationalized forms: doubt, aversion (or Sartrean nausea), the "fear of life," the "guilt of modern man," and so on. One might say that the use of drugs is a later and more extreme solution to the problem of the vanishing self, reaching epidemic proportions long after "dynamism" has become the general way of life, and in fossil civilizations, surviving it.

These, then, are some of the roads which I believe we—meaning West Christian civilization—have begun to travel since the forepart of the nineteenth century. The art and politics and intellectual history of the period, its emotional climate and fashions in crime, mental disorder, and popular entertainment, have, I think, an internal consistency and a meaning we may prefer not to see, but which we would do well to try to understand, nevertheless. One may doubt that history unfolds in a prescribed way, in obedience to laws of its own. This view, which appeals to the always Hegelian German mind, is suspect to the Anglo-Saxon, and I think rightly so. It is perhaps more economical and more plausible to suppose that there are no laws of history as such, but only certain principles, equivalent to "laws" of human nature, whose collective effect is to make certain sequences of historical change highly probable, but no more than that. The *Geist* of an era is then a certain pattern of odds, and history a sequence of such patterns.

It is always a temptation to give human doings, one's own included, an air of the *destined,* a coherence in retrospect, which they may not have had at the time. It does not however follow, as many modern his-

34. In *Annals of the New York Academy of Sciences,* Vol. 67, Article 10 (May 9, 1957), p. 676. Huxley points out that tension or anxiety increases man's isolation and also his boredom with himself, culminating in an egotistical self-hatred. "Correlated with this distaste for the beloved self, there exists in all human beings an urge to self-transcendence"—a drive, really, toward completion and freeing of the I, whose more corrupt manifestations include drug addiction.

torians appear to think, that the converse is therefore true: that there are *no* detectable regularities in man's history, *no* principles except accidental, short-term ones which determine the course of human events on a scale of centuries. The truth may be that higher cultures do originate as I have described, in the process developing a momentum of inner growth and consequent outer change, which is ultimately self-reversing. If true, this means merely that such cultures will *tend* to follow the same curve of rise and decline, will have roughly homologous ages, in art, philosophy, religious reform, and the like, and succumb in time to roughly the same evils. In this approximate statistical sense, it is perhaps correct to see Napoleon and Alexander the Great as historically more akin to each other than Napoleon was to Frederick II or Alexander to the Spartan commanders of the Peloponnesian War. Similarly, the Alexandrian scholars of the Hellenic age and playwrights like Plautus are perhaps more in the spirit of twentieth-century specialism and modern Broadway than they were in that of the Athens of Plato or of Aeschylus. The two Gracchi may have had more in common with the two Roosevelts than either pair did with leaders like Hitler and Marius, who represent a later stage in revolution.

There may even seem to be a timetable to great events, such that cultures pass from one major *étape* to the next at about the same rate. It was the Punic Wars which evidently converted Rome from an agrarian republic into an urbanized oligarchy and finally into an imperium. Its opponent in those wars, Carthage, was apparently descended from the old, essentially Semitic culture of Phoenicia. But by the time the wars began, Carthage had taken on many of the forms and institutions of Roman life, which is to say of the classical culture of that period. In that it was a "pseudomorph," or graft of alien new ways upon much older ones, Carthage rather strikingly suggests modern Japan. And if one is not too strict in drawing analogies, dating the beginning of our own "Punic War" period—Toynbee's Time of Troubles—from Bismarck and the rise of modern Germany, then the time relations of these events (the rate of onset of "modernity" in the West Christian and classical worlds) appears to have been about the same. From Alexander's death in 323 B.C. to the start of the First Punic War is fifty-nine years; from Waterloo to the start of the Franco-Prussian War, fifty-five years.[35]

35. It is interesting that the first Roman gladiatorial show was apparently put on in the Forum in 264 B.C., the year of the beginning of the First Punic War.

It is perfectly obvious that such parallels as these cannot be pushed very far. The Seleucids in the Near East and the Ptolemies in Egypt survived Alexander's passing by centuries, whereas the rule of Napoleon's marshal-princes was swept away almost at once. While America, as I shall try to show, in the next chapter, is perhaps uniquely fitted for the Roman role in the twentieth century, it faces far different and more formidable adversaries in the "pseudomorphs" of modern Russia and China than ever the Romans did in Egypt and the Near East.

All that the very crude and incomplete parallels between cultures tell us, perhaps, is that there are certain trends in collective human affairs which are apt to repeat themselves, arising again and again in the form of a chain of probabilities such that given the first, the whole sequence then tends to follow. This phenomenon is possibly related to the fact that our natures are organized according to essentially conservative principles which, like the "answering effect" or rebound principle in physiology, guarantee a certain *round* of probable results from a given cause, in time always bringing the organism or the collectivity back to where it started: not to identical *circumstances,* but to approximately the same set point or formal time zero. It is as though there were a homeostatic principle in history according to which, with the rise of each new culture, mind or the "soul" comes to threaten the ancient dominion of instinct.[36] In later ages of the same culture, the by-products of mind—scepticism and technics—strengthen the hand of instinct, which is to say of practical men of action, to the point that culture is at last destroyed in favor of civilization, which is really the life of instinct in fancy dress. With that the cycle is complete.

The whole process is, however, far more intricate and far less uniform than this drastically simplified description of it would suggest. One rea-

---

In the Western world, modern prize fighting (as opposed to the earlier, more or less amateur pugilism) dates from 1866 in Britain and the United States. *La boxe française,* which included elements of *savate,* reached a kind of peak at about the same time. See H. G. Wells, *Outline of History* (Macmillan, 1920), I, 490–491; and *Encyclopaedia Britannica* (11th ed.), "Boxing."

36. A process not incidental to cultures, but one of their defining features. Religions are "great" to the degree that they challenge the older tribal gods (as Christianity or Zoroastrianism did) and by means of a new repertoire of ideals encourage ways of life and being which far transcend the tribal. It is just because cultures represent, at bottom, man's determination to exceed his creature limits that they have more capacity for growth than do tribal societies, which are more strictly Id-bound.

son is of course that the orders and activities and institutions which comprise a society do not take shape or fall into decay at the same rate. The rise or decline of cultures is not smooth, but an irregular alternance of crises and of eras of relative stability. Nor is any age fully in step with itself; more often several coexist in one. Roman literature, while it never reached the level of excellence of the Greek, thrived during the dissolution of the Republic. American literature thrives in the twentieth century; and simultaneously with our emergence as a heavily armed aggressive world power, our internal policies (the belated manifestation, perhaps, of the idealism of another day) have become more humane and enlightened than they were even thirty years ago. As our homicide and general crime rates rise, we move toward nationwide abolition of capital punishment. While doing much to relieve the distress of our own poor and spending millions more supposedly in aid of the needy abroad, we also support vicious dictatorships in the name of anti-communism and corrupt and ravage nations like Viet Nam or Guatemala, which have proved to be reluctant clients. The history of imperial Rome (and doubtless of Egypt after the Hyksos, of Aztec Mexico, or of any other late civilization) is full of similar contradictions. They are that only if one insists on a monolithic view of the historical process. In truth, of course, strict contemporaneity is more a matter of clock time than of historical fact. The *Geist* is not *the* outlook, but simply that combination of feelings and ideas which is deepest in the grain of the age and therefore most prophetic of what is to come.[37] The beautiful periods and noble sentiments of Cicero were less prophetic of the Roman future than were the ruthlessness and gifted practicality of Caesar. The former had echoes in Seneca and Marcus Aurelius; but the latter became the foundation of imperial polity.

Perhaps the chief difference between the rising and descending phases of a culture is that in the rising phase, religion or a profound belief in the improvability of oneself and one's world exists in the majority. The consequence of that psychological fact, granted it may be one, is that the higher human self which it forecasts tends slowly to come into being. As that occurs, the struggle between men of faith and the unregenerate men of instinct intensifies, tending for a time to go in favor of the former. As in any war, however, the odds are continually changing, and

---

37. That is, we are still talking about odds, not certainties.

the real outcome can only be judged long afterward. By a variety of criteria, the trend of European civilization from the time of Clovis I in the fifth century, to the Reformation was on the whole upward. Taken decade by decade or even century by century, however, that progress was wildly erratic. Between the death of Charlemagne (814) and the accession of Hildebrand as Gregory VII in 1073, the papacy became a political spoil of the Roman nobility, and as Bertrand Russell remarked, "the disorder and weakness of Western Europe was so great . . . that Christendom might have seemed in danger of complete destruction."[38]

While mixed in their motives, the Gregorian reforms, as represented in men like Anselm or Hugh of Lincoln, may have owed much to genuine piety, both in the leaders and in the led. The principal result nonetheless was to consolidate the church as a great secular power and in proportion to attract to it the sort of man who would inevitably pervert its ideals and drive the faithful elsewhere—in the thirteenth and fourteenth centuries into a suicidal heterodoxy.[39] In this sense, Bernard of Clairvaux was a transitional figure, a man of profound faith on the one hand and of stringent, one might almost say reflex, orthodoxy on the other. The latter might be taken as representing the concealed animal element in his Christianity, the primal coercive self whose only object is to prevail—in this case to enforce the sanctity of certain ideas as surrogates of one's personal supremacy. He seems to have felt this contradiction in himself, saying at the end of his life, "All of my works frighten me, and what I do is incomprehensible to me."[40]

---

38. A *History of Western Philosophy* (Simon and Schuster, 1945), p. 397.

39. Writing in the 1850's, Buckle said, "We have now no great poets; and our poverty in this respect is not compensated by the fact that we once had them. . . . The movement has gone by; the charm is broken. . . . Hence our age, great as it is, . . . has . . . a certain material, unimaginative, and unheroic character which has made several observers tremble for the future."

He adds that it has become "doubly incumbent on physical philosophers to cultivate the imagination" not only because it might improve their work but because they might, through their example and prestige "correct the most serious deficiency of the present age" and "make us some amends for our inability to produce such a splendid imaginative literature as that which our forefathers created and in which the choicest spirits of the seventeenth century did, if I may so say, dwell and have their being" (Henry Thomas Buckle, History of Civilization in England, 3 vols., Longmans Green, 1885, iii, pp. 381-382). See footnote 37, Chapter V.

40. And Peter the Venerable said of him: "You perform all the difficult religious duties; you fast; you watch; you suffer; but you will not endure the easy

No such duality appears to have troubled Innocent III, who, less than a century later, was to say of himself, "I have no leisure to meditate on supermundane things."[41] With him—which is to say with the destruction of Provençal culture in the name of orthodoxy and the subsequent establishment of the Inquisition (in 1233, by Gregory IX)—the church formally commits itself to a policy of ferocious enforcement. By the time of Philip the Fair, its combination of riches and pretensions to worldly power bring it into disastrous collision with the rising power of the crown; while its attempted exactions on the Rhenish towns strip many of pastoral care and literally expel the faithful into a heretical mysticism for which not a few will pay with their lives. It is probably fair to say that the destruction of the "medieval synthesis" was begun at its apogee, in the early thirteenth century, and by the institution to which, more than any other, it owed its existence—namely, the church—then passing into the hands of men with the gift of Realpolitik unalloyed.

The striking fact is that Christianity was to survive centuries more of such dreadful abuse, repeatedly expressing itself in new heterodoxies (George Fox, Wesley, Joseph Smith) as the Establishment became too corrupt or too staid to contain it. Moderns would perhaps interpret this phenomenon as meaning that superstition, in particular the craving to be free of the fear of death, is unquenchable in the ignorant and that the survival of ignorance guarantees the survival, in some form, of the ancestral faith.[42] The analysis may be correct so far as it goes, but it may

ones—you do not love." Nevertheless it must be said that in comparison to Innocent's treatment of the Albigensians, Bernard's of Abelard was mildness itself.

41. In fairness one should add that Innocent was evidently a man of some piety, who preached often and well and meditated on "supermundane things" sufficiently to write an exposition of the Psalms. What he may have lacked was the humility which, in Bernard, led to self-examination and doubt—a defect of character most fortunate in one who, like Lyndon Johnson, was destined to attain such power and to be responsible for the death of so many.

A most significant difference between Bernard of Clairvaux and Innocent III can be seen in their attitude toward Jews. Whereas Bernard "heroically protested" against the persecution of Jews which occurred during the second crusade (1145-1147), Innocent "gave strong impetus to their repression, especially by ordaining the wearing of a badge." (Encyclopedia Britannica, Eleventh Edition Vol. 15 p. 405).

42. If that were all there is to it, it seems unlikely that even the most corrupted of religions would have been forced into reform, but in truly religious ages that has repeatedly happened, implying not merely a few enlightened idealists but a

also omit two crucial points. The first is that man's religious impulse may contain something more than these primitive elements—namely, a sense of his own incompleteness or lack of "soul"—it being this sense, as well as his yearning for deliverance after death, which causes him to adhere to certain ideals and see in life more promise than any realist would agree that it holds. It is this element in faith which I believe to be real; and the evidence that it is so—that it tells us of potentialities in ourselves which are actually there—is that in the wake of man's higher religions have come social improvements and triumphs of art and intellect which few realists would have been likely to predict before the fact[43] and which, one might add, have never been equaled in tribal societies or in "late" ages of imperial aggrandizement.

The second point is that urbanization, as much as a general enlightenment, may be responsible for the scepticism which, in later times, finally undermines religiousness and returns men en masse to a life of instinct. In ancient Rome educational standards, even among the upper classes, were quite low,[44] but this general ignorance in no way prevented the Romans from becoming sceptical and materialistic as Rome itself became megalopolitan. In fact, the average citizen of modern New York or Chicago or Hamburg is not educated either, except in the most superficial sense. He can probably read after a fashion and knows a smattering of his national history, a few scientific rules of thumb, a few names from literature. He is still far from equipped to think out his own agnosticism. What he has is not enlightenment, but "savvy": a reflex sort of sophistication which tells him what the going ideas and attitudes are. But what turns him away from religion, killing the poet in him and inclining him to increasingly crude ideals of self and of accomplishment, may be not the enlightenment which dribbles down to him so much as

considerable consensus in support of them. If ignorant self-concern were the root of religion, would such a consensus ever come to be?

43. In the same way that in the mid 1960's Lyndon Johnson could ask for a more direct "pay-off" from government-supported medical research, despite a centuries-old precedent that pure research is in the long run apt to be far more productive. The realist, in short, knows all the Darwinian truths—the "facts of life"—but finds learning anything beyond them exceedingly difficult.

44. See Mommsen, *History of Rome,* III, 413 ff. The Mystery Cults of the masses in the same period (*circa* 100 B.C.) represent a regression to violent superstition with a minimum of ideality or moral content, nothing of stoic dignity.

the interaction of this cartoon "philosophy" with the life he lives daily in the big city.

As studies of animal colonies suggest, crowding in human societies may lead to an automatic rise in psychic and physical stress and thereby to a massive shift in the mental and emotional tenor of life when large populations come to be concentrated in cities. In a sense this is the reverse of the psychological shift which occurred centuries before, when a nomadic, warlike population gradually settled down in Europe to become agricultural and mercantile and in so doing transferred emphasis from the emergency functions of instinct to those concerned with sustenance and procreation. Whereas that shift, as I have tried to show, may be conducive to enlargement of enthusiasm and the imagination (and so to the hopeful mascent self-awareness which is a major part of the religious impulse), the shift back again which occurs with urbanization inclines men to a new nomadism: a life of continual anxiety and of fierce daily competition with their fellows. Urban entertainments reflect that habit of life, playing upon the tensions and the mental grossness of the mass audience, appealing more and more nakedly to the Id—witness the Roman theater versus the Greek, or our own versus the Elizabethan. The essence of big city life is not merely that it exposes large numbers to the scepticism of the enlightened; it is that it prepares them, physiologically, to abandon an incoherent idealism for an equally incoherent belief in animality as the sole real principle of life.

Finally, a characteristic of "modern" ages is that their natural leaders —those adaptive geniuses of which any age has more than enough—find themselves obliged to make fewer and fewer concessions to traditional standards in order to rise to power. In fact, when the age is sufficiently "modern," they can triumph through their *anti*-idealism, their repudiation of notions of goodness and excellence which the majority no longer believes in and would like to be rid of as a nuisance and an accusation. In substance, that was the Nazi "platform." The late Senator Joseph McCarthy and his aides represented a similar drift in this country, with their violent revisions of judicial procedure in the interests of a paranoid anti-Communism. The character of the riots in our universities in the 1960's suggests that the generation now in its late teens or early twenties may shortly become quite receptive to this sort of revolutionary leadership. By contrast, the earlier periods in Western history mentioned above represent a time in which men were moving away from tribalism into a more diversified, mentally freer type of life; and in proportion as they did so, they seem increasingly to have eluded or mitigated the control exerted over them by their primordial masters. The latter, for their part, were often forced to extremes of hypocrisy, maintaining an appearance of "honor," or probity, or piety and humility, which the modern dictator can dispense with. The division of the powers of state, begun earliest and most faithfully adhered to in England, represents a workable common-sense approach to the problem of Darwinian man in politics; but it is one presupposing a general public such as has perhaps never existed in Germany or elsewhere.[45] The success of the English system rests essentially on a realized ideal which combines tribal notions of obedience and loyalty with Christian notions of personal responsibility and fair play, the result being a nation which has remained both cohesive and flexible and on the whole more decent than most.[46]

The basic difference between tribal life and that of high cultures is

45. Reading the history of the Thirty Years War, one cannot but wonder if the fearful destruction not only of life but of decency and morale in the survivors, may not have made that period a critical one for the Germans. Although for a long time concealed under the forms of a civilization rebuilt, its effect may have been to undermine the Christian Idea to the point of making Germany the first of modern nations, not merely in technology but in the politics of retrogression. It is possibly significant in this connection that the recrudescence of anti-semitism seems to have set in earliest and continued with the greatest intensity in Germany, starting (somewhat ironically) with the Lasker inquiry of 1873. It should be added, however, that the percentage of Jews relative to the whole population was at that time considerably higher in Germany than France or Italy (1.2% vs 0.14% and 0.12%), and higher still in the big cities (4.36% in Berlin). A feature of racism, as we have since discovered, is that peoples seemingly free from it may suddenly develop violent prejudices when the density of the minority population becomes sufficiently high. The roots of racism itself may be exceedingly primitive, related to ancient mechanisms governing sexual selection (including active rejection of those too deviant from innate norms). As such, it is perhaps akin to our "instinctive" horror of the mutilated. The fact that antisemitism (which throve in the Christian Middle Ages) is recurring among us today suggests a reversion to a precivilized Id-directed type of life such as I have been describing.

46. Which is not to deny the ruthlessness of the English in colonial nations even as nearby as Ireland. The fact remains, however, that their colonial administration was somewhat less brutal than that say of the Belgians in the Congo or the French in North Africa; and the English are almost the only nation in history to have given up its empire without a bloody rearguard action. While not necessarily humane in intent, such realism—as compared to the French—is far more humane in the result.

that in the former neither the clear aspiration to break free in mind or in fact nor the real moral and intellectual means to do so have developed. The rate of change in such societies is accordingly very low and is so largely determined by outer circumstance and so little by what one could call inner momentum or choice that we regard them as outside of history. In the deepest sense they are. They have only annals, which, as these chiefly reflect the zigzags of fortune, are scarcely worth preserving and scarcely ever preserved, except as vague oral traditions, or legend.

By contrast, when we come to believe that life may hold some possibility beyond mere adaptation, and when events in our world begin to take on the identity or radical newness which is often a direct outgrowth of that belief, we are likewise moved to make detailed records of them from an intuition that they may embody important meanings which, if not immediately apparent to us, may in time become so. Modern historiography arose when enough information of that kind had been accumulated to enable scholars to detect what seemed to them the outlines of a larger pattern of recurrence in human affairs. What they lacked was a means to account for the pattern they saw, and much of their description suffered from a proportionately naïve intrusion of the predispositions of the scholars themselves: in Spengler from a German propensity for Absolutes, Iron Law, Destiny, and the like; in Toynbee from an incantatory piety; in Sorokin from a kind of industrial, filing-system mentality. Nonetheless something roughly resembling the larger form they discerned in history may actually be there—a form dependent on the fact that man has, after all, a limited repertoire of feelings and modes of response and with that a foreseeable tendency to progress, either individually on a small time scale, or collectively on a larger one, from one "set" or complex of feelings and ideas to another, according to definite rules—that is, in a certain preferred or most probable order. Once one understands something of the fundamental logic of brain processes and their mental and emotional equivalents, a way is perhaps opened by which one may come to see the significance and probable consequences of human behavior on a historical scale. This book is a preliminary attempt at that sort of understanding. And from the argument to this point, one can conclude that it is at least plausible that there *is* such a thing as the *Geist* or dominant outlook of an age; that the *Geist* consists essentially of a predominant emotional tone and a predominating trend toward the expansion or contraction of mind; and that these phenomena are of necessity complementary to one another in clearly definable ways. From this and related principles discussed earlier here, it follows that we may, in a very rough way, be able to forecast the next stage in the history of a society (provided it is "historical"), if we have on hand enough information about it. An odd but important corollary is that the most desirable events, like the actions of mind itself when properly formed , are in general the least predictable; while those we would most wish to avert, like many of the actions which arise out of the Id, are highly predictable if not near certainties. It is for this reason that the prospect immediately before us appears so terrible. It is clear enough how the odds on "bad" events are running; for instance, the odds on mass extermination via the Bomb or mass wretchedness through over-population. As direct outgrowths of the Id these events loom over us with nearly the same quality of the inevitable that we feel vis-à-vis our own primal functions. (Other things being equal, we are certain to eat tomorrow, nearly certain to sleep and perhaps to make love.) What we *cannot* see, and therefore can feel little confidence in, is those remark-able ameliorations or reversals in the historical odds which reason and its natural ally good will might still bring about. For if, in fact, man should succeed in getting sufficient control over his own nature and do so in sufficient numbers, there might lie ahead of us not the nightmares we foresee but a life more splendid and in every sense more free than any our ancestors dared dream of, since the practical means to such a life are now, ironically, quite within reach. For this reason, *the* problem is not even to understand our historical situation; it is primarily to under-stand what we are and therefore the principles by which our children might become more affectionate and larger in mind than we. Only in this way—in final terms, only by an understanding of the physiology of self-fulfillment—are we apt to break the grip which ancient mechanisms have, not only on us as individuals but on the course of our collective affairs, or history.

It is not fate in the older sense, but fate in the form described by Herrick[47] which makes history "cyclical." Each "cycle" represents an upsurge or new critical phase in the struggle between the conservative Id and the newer self, the soul or I, for control of the whole self, and each has so far ended with a "homeostatic" return to power of the Id.

47. C. J. Herrick, The Brain of the Tiger Salamander (University of Chicago Press, 1948), p. 122. I have quoted the passage in question in Chapter IX, below.

It cannot be denied that the soul has made some progress with each re-
newal of that struggle nor that each time it has finally lost. Its defeat
results in the roughly predictable course of events I have outlined, always with the proviso that the course of late periods of regression, once
under way, is by its very nature the easiest to forecast. Given Caesar,
one might have predicted Trajan or Nero or even Marcus Aurelius, who
represent, after all, nothing new in human life or radically unlikely under the circumstances. Given Greece of the seventh century B.C., one
could less easily have predicted Plato or Democritus or Zeno; or still
less, in Galileo's and Malpighi's day, have guessed the incredible things
soon to come in mathematics and physics, not to mention philosophy,
literature, art, and the physiology of the nervous system. These events
were clearly of *some* order of probability, since they occurred. It is also
true that great saints and geniuses are often far less easy to recognize as
such in their lifetimes, let alone to foresee, than is the imminence of
great catastrophes such as we now face. One knows the type of era likely
or downright certain to produce those calamitous "great statesmen" of
which we have recently had so many; but there is no telling if, or just
in what form, man's higher powers will show themselves in even the
most fortunate of epochs. If the religious "springtime" of a new culture
were to begin in another part of the world in our day, we might well
not see it for what it was, any more than the most intelligent of Byzantines probably understood what was germinating among the Frankish
barbarians of ninth- and tenth-century Europe.

Finally, one should be cautious in supposing that the chain of probabilities which has led all other great cultures into internecine war ex-
haustion and decline cannot at this late date in our own history be
broken, so as to prevent our suffering the same fate. One can only state
the facts and judge accordingly. The cardinal fact is that we are already
committed, as a matter of scientific faith, to a sceptical-pragmatic way
of life which all but guarantees that the "fatalities impending" cannot be
materially changed or warded off. From Darwin and Nietzsche down
to the absurd Robert Ardrey, we have by degrees convinced ourselves
that the life of instinct into which, in the same period, we have been
slipping, is the only and inevitable way. In a sense our "scientific" view
of ourselves is a rationalization, a way of making present circumstance
appear justified by Higher Law. We may thus, by general intellectual
consent, be returning ourselves, as the Romans and Chinese and ancient

Egyptians and Byzantines did before us, to the "historyless" existence of animals. In the final analysis it is only as man *has* history, has risen out of tribalism, that he really differs from the beasts. However, he has intermittently managed to do so; and to misconstrue that fact—to use a crude scientism, as many now do, to blur and trivialize the distinctions between ourselves and the rest of the animal world—is almost willfully to compound our mistakes and worsen the odds on our survival. It is perhaps because we dimly *do* know what we are doing that we look toward the future with such horror, living in the shadow of calamities we feel both responsible for and in some way fated to see through to the end. Nothing could be more absurd, more contrary to the spirit and even to the present facts, of science, as I have been at some pains to show. In fact, science has little to do with it; the Romans managed to arrive at the same infantile "realism" with almost none. Our situation is perhaps best described by Santayana, who said, "Those who cannot remember the past are doomed to repeat it." That is, of course, a statement not about history as such but about psychology—ultimately, perhaps, about the relations between the neocortex, with its complex memory systems, and the subcortical apparatus, embodying the ancient, infinitely exigent, infinitely monotonous functions of the Id. It is, I believe, through a grasp of these relations that man's future may be read, if not one day shaped to become as we might in our better moments wish it to be: an age freer than any has ever been of the determinism imposed on most of human life by human bestiality.

*Chapter VIII*

## AMERICA AND THE TWENTIETH CENTURY

In the seventeenth century and through much of the eighteenth, America was, in its outlook and style of life, not materially
different from the mother country, and both seem to have stood in
about the same relation to the rest of the West Christian world—that
of members of a larger common culture with their own distinctive differences from it. Early seventeenth-century American Puritanism, as
represented by men like Thomas Hooker, was a faith of some depth
and subtlety; and in New England, as in England, the persecution of
witches,[1] despite all the attention we have given it, seems to have been
minor and sporadic and in the case of the Salem trials was followed by
a public recantation. The leaders of our Revolution were not, in any
modern sense, revolutionary. Essentially, they were eighteenth-century
men, the majority of whom, like Washington, were simply dissenting
members of the upper class, driven by a combination of principle and
practical considerations to break with their peers overseas.[2] Their object
was to revise society, not to subvert it, and some, like Hamilton and the
Federalists, felt that a tight rein should be kept on all such reasoned
improvements. Even Jefferson was not a liberal of the type we have
become familiar with since. He was rather the model of the enlightened aristocrat—a Universal Man[3] and one of the few we have had—

1. Comparative statistics relating to the execution of witches in America, England, and Europe in the seventeenth cetury are given by C. P. Smith in *Yankees
and God* (Hermitage, 1954), p. 213. The estimated absolute and per capita figures
are lowest for America, highest for the Continent. See also G. M. Trevelyan, *English Social History* (Longmans, Green), 1942, pp. 256 ff.

2. Some years ago I happened upon a small volume containing George Washington's maxims of conduct. These were startling in that they could well have
been written by Frederick the Great, but not possibly by Jackson or Lincoln.

3. Jefferson was, by modern standards, a scholar of almost unbelievable versa-
tility. He read Homer and Virgil as a boy (on outings, according to Van Wyck
Brooks); and at the college of William and Mary he learned French, Newtonian

whose faith in reason extended to the theorem that ordinary people may have enough sense to decide, by due process, what is likely to be best for their society and themselves.

Not until the 1830's and Jackson do we begin to be "modern," showing some of the characteristics which a century and a quarter later will set us apart, as de Tocqueville clearly foresaw, from England and much of Europe. In his banking policy, as well as in his enthusiasm for the Union and in the strength he brought to the Executive, Jackson foreshadowed the Presidency as it would become under Franklin Roosevelt. His outlook was less suited to the primitive republic he actually ruled than to the urbanized democracy it would come to be roughly from the time of Grant onward. There is only a superficial paradox in the fact that both Jackson and Franklin Roosevelt aimed at breaking up the concentration of power represented by money, while (apparently contrary to their own liberal principles) increasing the power concentrated in themselves. It is perhaps this feature in particular which distinguishes modern liberalism from Jeffersonian. The latter viewed the world as, at bottom, capable of rational self-management, provided only reason were given sufficient opportunity to set things running in the right direction to start with. Liberalism of the Jacksonian or Rooseveltian type goes on a different assumption, partly because its most successful practitioners necessarily know their era and their constituents quite well, partly because they and their constituents are fundamentally men of the same kind. They see the world not from the same intellectual distance that Jefferson, the cultivated libertarian, did and in proportion are less inclined to laissez faire, less scrupulous in the use or retention of power.

To many eighteenth-century minds, human affairs came down, at least potentially, to logical arrangements, to *equilibria*—a notion probably descended from Christian ideals of order, on the one hand, and scientific discoveries of order, on the other. Like the laws of planetary motion, the laws of the market, à la Smith, could be trusted to give

physics (including the calculus), Italian, Spanish, and Anglo-Saxon. For some years he studied and played the violin. He was an energetic agronomist and developed the first accurate formula for the moldboard plow; he knew a number of American Indian dialects, practiced law, was as inventive of gadgets as Franklin; revised the laws of Virginia; designed Monticello and its gardens; and so on and so on. He was also said to have been an emotional, affectionate man. See *Encyclopaedia Britannica* (11th ed.), "Thomas Jefferson."

a kind of rhythmic reliability to business and moral laws a viable and generally acceptable form to the state. So, as a Jeffersonian liberal, one makes a few necessary adjustments, sets up the right institutions, and steps back to let things at last follow their proper course. Something of these concepts, this assurance of Ultimate Order, seems to be reflected in the lively yet serene and profoundly integrated tonal worlds of Bach, of whom Hindemith said, "We always sense in him a sober pre-eminence over any of his actions that prevents him getting lost in nebulousness or ebbing away into platitudes."[4] As in the warmth and perceptiveness of Wordsworth at his best, there is here expressed the deepest ideal of learning—the ideal of intellect and character matured together; as a result of which the universality of *l'uomo universale* consists in more than his knowing most of what is available or having superb mastery of some of it. Francis Bacon, supposedly the father of modern pragmatism,[5] remarked that "the unlearned man knows not what it is to descend into himself or call himself to account . . . whereas with the learned man it fares otherwise, that he doth ever intermix the correction and amendment of his mind with . . . the employment thereof."[6] Jefferson was perhaps after this latter model, while many moderns, including our great Leaders of the People, à la Roosevelt and Johnson, are more in the style of the "unlearned man," descending into themselves and calling themselves to account only as professional necessity forces them to do so. They are, in short, *adaptive*, without ideals which in any significant way alter their drive to personal success or interfere with their purely expedient use of moral issues of the time. (Hence the "paradox" of Johnson's liberalism at home and his clumsy authoritarianism abroad; the latter, one may guess, is the reality, the former like his folksiness, the pose.)

Such men have the enormous advantage of seeing life, not as it might be, but as it is: that is, as a phenomenon whose equilibria are often momentary and always at bottom unstable, because it is not a *process* that is involved, but a battle. One reason that economics has failed to become a science, in the sense of being able to make predictions as reliable as those of physics or physiology, may be that some of its

4. Paul Hindemith, *J. S. Bach: Heritage and Obligation* (Yale, 1952), p. 21.
5. But who really only urged objective testing of hypotheses and said that "experiments of light are more to be sought after than experiments of fruit."
6. See Loren Eiseley, in *Science,* Vol. 133 (1961), pp. 1197–1201.

most fundamental assumptions have been wrong.[7] For although forced to give more service than, say, the army or the church, business is simply the battle carried on by other means, as anyone even casually familiar with it knows. All efforts to stabilize business relations by law, to shift the odds permanently in favor of small enterprise or the consumer or labor, have resulted merely in a subtilization of tactics of aggrandizement and a multiplication of power blocs, but no real equilibrium. Businessmen themselves, including many small ones, regard such interventions of law as "artificial," which, properly understood, they are.

Jackson's strength lay in his clear understanding of the relations, both actual and possible, between the political executive and the financial community of his day. Hardened by personal combat and professional soldiering himself, he knew at once who his real friends and his most vulnerable and useful political enemies were, and acted accordingly.[8] In doing so he set the pattern for the revolutionary Presidencies of the twentieth century. One cannot but wonder if, with his experience of men, he ever really had much regard for the majority whose cause he did so much to promote.[9] If at heart he was a Jeffersonian idealist, the secret died with him.[10] The same might be said of Franklin Roosevelt, who, for all the real good he did, remained surprisingly elusive and ambiguous in his views, if not in many of his policies. It is a cliché, but also I think not accidental or without meaning (see page 71), that men of action often make poor memoirists and seem, at the end of brilliant careers, to have nothing to tell us. Too often the medium of

---

7. I believe Keynes was led to the conclusion that without government intervention the depression of the 1930's might become chronic. This might be taken to mean that certain segments of business tend to win decisive victories over the rest, resulting in the same sort of stagnation as often follows military conquest. The business-as-battle concept is well expressed in the "Jekyll and Hyde" theory of management in Walter Gutman's book *You Only Have To Get Rich Once* (Dutton, 1961), pp. 56 ff.

8. See Arthur Schlesinger, Jr., *The Age of Jackson* (Book Find Club, 1945), pp. 36 ff.

9. " 'Such has been the scenes of corruption in our last congress,' he wrote in 1833, 'that I loath the corruption of human nature and long for retirement.' " V. L. Parrington, *Main Currents in American Thought* (Harcourt, Brace, and World, 1954), II, 142.

10. However, Parrington (*ibid.,* p. 144) considers his position to have been Jeffersonian in principle and cites one of his speeches to that effect. Its tone strikes one as more Rooseveltian, though his position on the national debt was not.

their lives has been the message, and plain enough if we cared to read it. De Tocqueville understood Jackson's place in our history far better than his contemporaries did or even than many do today.

> We have been told that General Jackson has won battles; that he is an energetic man prone by nature and habit to the use of force, covetous of power, and a despot by inclination. All this may be true, but the inferences which have been drawn from these truths are very erroneous. It has been imagined that General Jackson is bent on establishing a dictatorship in America, introducing a military spirit and giving a degree of influence to the central authority which cannot but be dangerous to provincial liberties. *But in America the time for similar undertakings, and the age for men of this kind, is not yet come* [italics mine].[11]

The changes which since Jackson's time, and even more so since Grant's, have split us off from England and Europe can be described, I believe, as resulting from the action of our peculiar circumstances on those same psychological processes which, in retrospect, give the Victorian era, in all Western nations, its somewhat odd and ominous character. The fundamental feature of that era was a gradual loss in the "centrality" of transmitted ideals and so in the psychic "centrality" of succeeding generations. The outward manifestations of this change were an increasing tastelessness and fakery in the arts and moral discourse and conduct, a trend in life generally toward specialism (development of parts of mind only), and toward a relativistic (amoral) practicality.

Without our realizing it, the difficulties of pioneer life, the very virtues it bred in us, may have favored the psychological changes I have been describing and so hastened us faster along the road which, by the midnineteenth century, the whole West Christian world had begun to take. The wilderness, the Indians, the savage climate of the plains states, the need to catch up, even in the settled east, with the industries[12] and standard of life of Europe, all presented enormous practical problems. To solve them, something had to be sacrificed; and

11. Alexis de Tocqueville, *Democracy in America* (Cambridge Ed., 1862), I, 532.

12. Alexis de Tocqueville (loc. cit., p. 551): "Nothing can be more virulent than the hatred which exists between the Americans . . . and the English. But in spite of these hostile feelings, the Americans derive most of their manufactured commodities from England, because England supplies them at a cheaper rate than any other nation."

much of what Tocqueville or the less disinterested Mrs. Trollope describes is simply an early stage in that process.

What we sacrificed were essentially intangibles in the interest of the tangible, depth for miscellaneity of knowledge, concern with reflection and truth for concern with calculation and facts. As men moved west, the farther the more so, there simply was not time to preserve the "frills." Once a frontier community had been set up—its land wrested from the Indians and brought under cultivation, its log-cabin church and elementary school built—its inhabitants might spend decades far beyond the reach of fancy manners or higher learning, far outside the periphery, say, of Emerson's New England, whose climate of ideas seems hardly to have extended as far as Buffalo. We tend to think of this phenomenon, still, as one of temporary deprivation, a lack pro tem of certain "facilities"; but it may turn out to have been much more than that.

What was lost—more on the frontier perhaps than on the eastern seaboard, but to some extent there also— was exactly that body of more-than-practical or antipractical principles which the human brain needs, as abstract memories, if the human mind or I is to reach full development and thereby to come more fully into control of the Id or the self as a whole. These principles or abstract memories were the frills which we sacrificed in favor of practical competence or know-how; and their disappearance over several generations was directly reflected in an increasing ferocity of life on the frontier.[13] Seen from that standpoint, the bloody histories of Billy the Kid and Wild Bill Hickock, the drunken and generally frowzy tone of life in the old west, are no longer quite as picturesque, or as irrelevant to the present, as we seem to think them. What is striking, rather, is how rapidly the Id can come back—how easy it is for once staunch self-respecting people to become frozen into a state of demoralized acceptance by the frightfulness released in a few— how quickly, in short, civilizations can slip into barbarism when frills are dispensed with. The gangsterism prevalent in America in the

13. "The indications are . . . that the present trend toward juvenile behavior has been gathering force for over a century and has affected people who cannot be classed as revolutionaries. Such behavior was rampant on the frontier and in the gold-rush camps; and the American go-getter . . . is as much a perpetual juvenile as any revolutionary." Eric Hoffer, "A Time of Juveniles," *Harper's Magazine* (June, 1965).

twentieth century is perhaps a later variant of the same phenomenon—the more striking because, by our own testimony, we have the world's most efficient police force, the F.B.I., and often excellent local constabularies as well. Our only serious rivals in this sort of organized crime appear to be modern China and Sicily. And for all the improvements in crime control of which Mr. J. Edgar Hoover perennially tells us, the Mafia and the Syndicate are evidently still with us, as is a kind of half-organized hoodlumism in our larger cities, whose brutality is scarcely equaled in the lower depths of London or Marseilles. It is customary to blame Prohibition for gangsterism in the United States. However, its real line of descent, like that of Dillinger and Pretty Boy Floyd or of the "mad dog" killers of this decade, may reach back much further, to the heyday of the gun-toting heroes of our "westerns" in the second half of the nineteenth century.

What all of this comes down to is that the same processes which were destroying Christian tradition elsewhere, and thus eroding away Western man's "consciousness" and his self-control together, may have been greatly accelerated in America because of the practical demands which this continent was making on its new inhabitants during the same period. It is highly significant, I think, that nothing resembling the frontier life of Gold Rush times or of the 1870's seems to have developed on the New England frontier of two hundred years earlier. It is unlikely that life in outlying settlements of Massachusetts, say, in 1650 was much easier. And if one compares communications in the two eras, it is doubtful whether the New England colonists were tied much more tightly to England by the sailing ships of that day than the men of the old west were to the east by stagecoach or the Pony Express. The fact that modern police forces only begin to appear in the early nineteenth century (for example, in 1829, in England, under Sir Robert Peel)[14] is itself perhaps significant, indicating a general social change of which our frontier life was only an extreme.

That seventeenth- and eighteenth-century England and New England could live without police and that in the latter no hoodlumism or "mad dog" killings seem to have broken out suggests that in those times something besides external force acted very strongly to keep the Id of men in check. By the same reasoning, the character of life in the American

14. Trevelyan, English Social History, p. 482.

west after about 1850, and some of the character of life in all parts of the world today, suggest that that internal control has since progressively failed,[15] and in proportion as it has done so, has required a more and more elaborate (and still not very efficient) machinery of justice to maintain civil order.[16] In this, we in America differ only quantitatively from the rest of Western civilization; our crime[17] and drug-addiction rates may be somewhat higher than those of France or England. Though small, that quantitative difference may be an important one in that it reflects certain fundamental characteristics which, in addition to sheer power, may peculiarly fit America for ascendancy in the twentieth century.

It was not perhaps until the last of the eighteenth-century men had passed out of our politics, and our frontier had begun to reach beyond the Mississippi, that the revolutionary era announced by Jackson—in psychological terms, the era of massive attrition of the rational conscious I—began in earnest. About 1833 de Tocqueville visited the cabin of a settler in Tennessee and described in his journal what he saw there:

> Above the hearth, a good rifle, a deerskin, and plumes of eagle's feathers; on the right hand of the chimney, a map of the United States, raised and shaken by the wind through the crannies in the wall; near the map,

15. This is the conclusion of Dr. Philip Zimbardo, a psychologist currently making a study of vandalism and other forms of violence in this country. "What we are observing all around us" he says "is a sudden change in the restraints which normally control the expression of our drives, impulses and emotions." We are succumbing to a process he describes as "deindividuation" whose effect is to "make each of us a potential assassin". (*The New York Times,* Sunday, April 20, 1969, p. 49: The report covers a presentation made by Dr. Zimbardo at the Nebraska Symposium on Motivation at the University of Nebraska in March of 1969.)

16. Sir Richard Jackson, a barrister who from 1953 to 1963 was Assistant Commissioner in charge of criminal investigation with Scotland Yard, remarks in his memoirs: "The chief cause of crime is not, as the liberals of previous generations believed, poverty. Poverty can cause crime; few people would really prefer to starve rather than steal. But the relief of poverty and a drastic reduction of economic inequality have brought no comparable lessening of crime. On the contrary, booming crime rates seem to be characteristic of an affluent society." *Occupied with Crime* (Doubleday, 1968). J. Edgar Hoover tells us much the same thing at least once annually.

17. According to M. E. Wolfgang, Professor of Sociology at the University of Pennsylvania, our current annual homicide rate is 5.6 per 100,000—eight times that of England and Wales, four times that of Japan, Canada, and Australia. See the *Wall Street Journal,* June 25, 1968, p. 1, col. 6.

upon a shelf formed of a roughly hewn plank, a few volumes of books—
a Bible, the first six books of Milton, and two of Shakespeare's plays . . .
in the centre of the room, a rude table with legs of green wood with the
bark still upon them . . . but on this table a teapot of British ware, silver
spoons, cracked teacups, and some newspapers.[18]

A generation or so later, in a cabin in the far west, how many of the
volumes he mentions would one have been likely to find? If any, most
probably the Bible, along with the deerskin, the rifle, and possibly a
bowie knife, a revolver or two, and a barrel of whisky. The point is
overstated, but may also have meaning.[19] In the process of expanding
into the wilderness, we may more and more have dropped off the intangible goods which were our real heritage, in favor of the simpler tools,
mental as well as material, by which our immediate success was assured.
In the very process of making this exchange we began to pay a price for
it—in the bestialization of life, in the chilling and narrowing down of
our feelings and interests, ultimately in a kind of ineducability[20] which

18. De Tocqueville, *Democracy in America,* II, 436. In the same entry from his
travel journal, de Tocqueville describes the owner of this cabin as the poker-faced,
Gary Cooper type discussed below, here.

19. Some will say that it has none. If our tradition ran out, or at least
desperately thin, in the western reaches of the continent, how does it happen
(they may ask) that San Francisco today is so "cultural" or that the universities
of California are among the nation's best? One might equally ask why Boston
and New York have remained the intellectual and artistic capitals of the nation,
while Southern California has become a center for odd religions and cults of
political extremism (not to mention the movies).

20. Oliver La Farge, who spent some years teaching in the west (at the Universities of Utah and New Mexico), reports that "in a class of 30, at least 15
will dread what they call 'essay exams.' . . . They are semi-literate in a sense. . . .
They can read but they cannot write. They cannot spell, punctuation is quite
beyond them, the mere formation of a written word troubles them. . . . In these
classes one finds, also, a resistance to any discussion that roams beyond the
literal confines of the subject. In teaching general anthropology, the teacher can
feel that he is losing some of the class if he refers to *Babbitt* or to Shakespeare,
or speaks of the urban modernism of Rome as shown in Horace's *Satires*. A
good part of the class will never have heard of Horace. . . . There is a definite
resistance to erudition as such."

La Farge is speaking, of course, of state universities, and suggests that the
situation may be somewhat better in eastern private schools, in particular since
there, teachers are still selected on the basis of character and merit.

"By and large, the private schools have not bought the dreadful theory that
if a teacher has studied education he does not have to have real mastery of the
subject he is teaching." (Quoted in Time Magazine, Feb. 8, 1954)

persists in us to this day, a resistance to learning as such, a rejection of intangible qualities of all kinds if not self-evidently useful. This is the era we regard in retrospect as "romantic," a great saga, particularly as seen through the eyes of writers like Jack London (who, interestingly enough, ended as Hemingway did, a suicide). If, in fact, one reads the records and looks at the photographs from those days, it is apparent that this "romantic" era must have been incredibly dreary. For the few men who shot and roistered their way to an early and pointless end and possibly enjoyed themselves doing it, there were thousands who lived lives merely squalid and empty, diabolically bored when they were not actively uncomfortable. The majority, being from natural timidity denied even the pleasures of an outright indulgence of the Id, contented themselves with grubbing along and controlling their wilder impulses as best they might.

The basic psychological type of the period was perhaps not the hard-drinking bully boy, but the stoical nihilist: the wooden-faced man, strong and silent like Gary Cooper, incapable of the nuances of warmer emotion and equally without interest or real belief in "higher things." This man, in his sheer numbers, was perhaps to become the basic type, the ancestor, of ourselves. In effect so much of his tradition had died in him that he (and we) became "mechanical-minded" by default, because this was the one limb of the psychic self which circumstances had combined powerfully to force into growth, while they combined just as powerfully to suppress or stunt the remainder.

To understand what we are today, it is necessary to see our "mechanical-mindedness" as a talent of greater generality than the mere aptitude for fixing gadgets. More accurately, it is a faculty of *practical* thinking in whatever mode, abstract or concrete, consisting essentially of causal analysis and causal (that is, mechanical) reassembly of a given set of elements into a working system. This is, in many respects—even in its results—very like the faculty of imaginative insight and synthesis which have been the basis of West Christian intellectual life since the Middle Ages. What differs in us now is the motivation for these actions of mind; for the contraction of our psychic inheritance *means* that mind

However, other sources I have cited below (page 205, footnotes 20, 23) indicate that even in the Ivy League, things are not what they might be, and one is left with the strong suspicion that the educability of all, including the most favored classes, has for some reason declined.

has lost much of the momentum proper to itself—has largely ceased to be disinterested or spontaneous—and to the same degree has become more and more strictly tied to objectives sanctioned by our older drives—objectives of use or status. That is, we have reverted to a more adaptive Id-directed style of life, even in spheres of endeavor where it is out of place and apt to produce only second-rate results. Unless circumstances impel us via our primitive motivational apparatus—unless there is some concrete need, some "sense" to a project, such as the possibility of a career and money or influence—we do not move. Conversely, when we do move, we tend to go only so far as circumstances, or the Id, push us. In the intellectual life of universities this type of mind or psychic being leads to the dreadful dry careerism mentioned earlier[21]—to a pride in petty excellence or petty advantage and a cold dislike and incomprehension of the unusual or original, which frighten young academics and undermine their respect for their nominal superiors, if not for their calling itself. What is surprising is not the resistance of our young people to learning; on the contrary; with the odds there are against them, internally as well as externally, it is remarkable they learn as much as they do.

In the nineteenth century, even New England, which had psychologically lost the least ground, produced few writers or thinkers on a par with those of Europe; and among them at least one, Melville (see footnote 53 page 186 below) suffered from a devastating pessimism as if aware of what was wrong with the age and what it prophesied. In science, we have to this day produced only one man certainly of the first rank, Willard Gibbs,[22] though, especially in recent years, we have

21. A development which may have been a long time in the making. Mrs. Trollope, after visiting Philadelphia *circa* 1830, wrote: "It is said that this city has many gentlemen distinguished by their scientific pursuits; I conversed with several well-informed and intelligent men, but there is a cold dryness of manner, and an apparent want of interest in the subjects they discuss that, to my mind, robs conversation of all its charm. . . . *The want of warmth, of interest, of feeling, upon all subjects which do not immediately touch their own concerns, is universal,* and has a most paralysing effect upon conversation" (italics mine). Frances Trollope, *Domestic Manners of the Americans* (Vintage, 1949), pp. 278-279.

22. In fact, it is hard to know the first-rate in one's own time, so this is a question better begged. Linus Pauling, however, may well be one; and it is worth mentioning that he and Russell and Einstein have been among the most liberal of contemporary intellectuals: that is, the emotions which favor, and are favored

excelled in the production of first-rate second-raters. The same can be said of our industrial production, which in general has set utility and quantity above quality. Our greatest geniuses have been in the fields of mechanical invention. And as the circumstances of our national life have changed, we have put the same basic ability to work in other fields, elaborating the machinery first of law and corporate business, and latterly of government and the military, with a formidable energy and thoroughness. In addition to these, we produce numbers of smaller-scale social machines: associations, lodges, fraternities, civic groups whose ostensible functions are often trivial, but whose real one seems to be to reassure us and fill us out as individuals, much the way physical machines, our cars and hi-fi and TV sets, do. Much of this tremendous constructive drive may result from the peculiar kind of psychic specialization we were unwittingly forced into, back in our formative days in the last century, by the practical demands of life on a new continent. We entered that century as simply one wing of West Christian civilization, slightly more provincial than the rest, but otherwise unremarkable. We emerged from it as, in a sense, leaders of the world, so far ahead of most of Europe in modernity that we have since, to the chagrin of some Europeans, become its model, and not in the practical conduct of life alone.

The psychic type I have been describing—the man whose conscious self is like a tree with all its branches but a few pruned away, and those few enormously hypertrophied—is still far better off and far less of a menace to himself or his society than is the type of the spiritual amorph described in the last chapter. The latter, the type of mass man or the modern urban poor, is especially prevalent in countries such as those of South America (in *rus* and *urbs* both) as result of a combination of gross maltreatment and gross neglect. Such countries have apparently trapped themselves in a condition of nearly perfect stasis. Because the Id, in the majority, is by definition ill-controlled,[23] those who rule do so almost necessarily by fear and are always threatened by their own inefficiency and their own excesses. Exploiting the easily available violence

by, intellect fully developed are apt to be the warmer ones resulting in "Christian" behavior, with or without formal Christianity.

23. In contrast to our own homicide rate of 5.6 per 100,000, which is high by comparison with England, Canada, Australia, and Japan, Colombia's present rate is reportedly 34 per 100,000, Mexico's, 30, and Guatemala's, 12. Wolfgang, *loc. cit.* (footnote 17 above).

of the mass, new and still more brutal leaders continually spring up to overthrow the old, and the revolution, which never gets anywhere, never really stops either. Like the Rome of Septimius Severus, these miserable lands combine, to a remarkable degree, permanent arrest with a permanent instability.[24] It is more truly said of them than it was of us that they have made a direct jump from barbarism to decadence with no interval of civilization. Like the history of imperial Rome, or of China for many centuries, that of Latin America is trivial and depressing— scarcely history at all, in fact, but a collection of tribal annals illustrating the monotonous brutality of life in societies in which realization of ideals of the self, or soul, has from the outset been precluded by the abuse of power—in which those at the top have usually been such psychic primitives that they were incapable even of successful despotism.

This is perhaps the kind of deadlock into which all late civilizations tend finally to sink: the end result of the "homeostatic" return to power of the Id. However, in North America, while we may have lost psychic stature more rapidly or become as individuals more narrowly grown than many Europeans or Englishmen, we also appear to have less of a base in brute poverty and therefore less of a reservoir of the psychological amorph type than some other Western nations do. One thinks not only of South America but of Germany of the early Nazi days, as described, for instance, in Christopher Isherwood's *Berlin Stories*. It was precisely the stratification of the German world, its *order,* with arrogant long-established castes at the top and a deceptively quite subservient *Lumpen-proletariat* at the bottom, which made it vulnerable, after World War I, to subversion by Hitler. In his resentment of learning and tradition, his savage impatience, his intellectual shapelessness, his lack of real aims beyond revenge, and the expansion of his own power and Germany's, Hitler represented mass man with the wraps off. He was, as Shirer said, a "genius" of a special sort—one of the Darwinian élite of the *Lumpen-proletariat* who defied the police as the rest dared not do and, at the

24. Even those like Colombia (noted for the purity of its Spanish and its "city of poets," Bogotá), which seemed most advanced and stable, have not been proof against violent backsliding: witness the revolution of the Right which recently devastated that country. Our Guatemalan policy, inaugurated by Eisenhower in 1954, has precipitated a similar catastrophe there, perhaps forestalling indefinitely that nation's brief experiment in less authoritarian government begun by Arévalo two decades ago. See Henry Giniger, "Guatemala Is a Battleground," New York *Times Magazine,* June 16, 1968, pp. 14–26.

risk of his neck, ended up in control of everything. In quite a real sense, he was, as our press frequently called him, a gangster.

What distinguished Hitler from the Sicilian *mafiosi* or their American equivalents was the scope of his intentions. Like most of South America, Sicily represents a society perennially trapped at a low level of development, in which men are so resolutely "realistic," so primally adaptive, that the rule of terror never ceases and the "fit" never fall from power, except to give place to the more "fit." Centuries of this life, which some have attributed to former Spanish rule, have so stunted the Sicilian that he not only can scarcely be brought to help in his own deliverance[25] but is, as a *mafioso,* incapable of more than a kind of strong-arm parasitism. The Hitlerian vision of revolution and imperial expansion is totally beyond him, appearing to his "realistic" intelligence as not only unthinkable but in a way silly. Why take such risks? What the *mafioso* wants, essentially, is village prestige—to become "a man of respect" with lots of money and sex and eats and influence, in return for a minimum of work. Like man the primitive hunter, he lives by sporadic violence, but, unlike the hunter, preys upon other men, an arrangement resulting in the permanent bestialization of all concerned.

This simple program coincides in many respects with that of mass man anywhere and in America has led to the remarkable success of the Italians in racketeering. The latter, especially Neapolitans and Sicilians,

25. See the series of articles on the Mafia in the *New Yorker* by Norman Lewis, February 8, 15, and 22, 1964; also Luigi Barzini's *The Italians* (Bantam, 1964), pp. 207 ff. While distinguishing the northern from the southern Italian outlook, Barzini makes the point that a certain "realism" has been a mark of Italian life since medieval times and clearly sets the *novelle* of that period apart from the more idealistic literature of northern Europe. "The lesson the reader drew was not meant to edify him. . . . The cruel and ruthless ways of the world are accepted as unchangeable. . . . The rich in spirit, the clever and strong men . . . without scruples or charity, always come out on top." *Ibid.*

The same tradition appears in movies like *Divorce Italian Style,* or in the *novella, A Man's Blessing,* by the gifted Sicilian writer Leonardo Sciascia. The former, perhaps intended for more than a local audience, ends on a note of farcical retribution. The protagonist, having brought off the murder of his wife and married the girl of his dreams, seems about to be cuckolded by her, apparently with the helmsman of the yacht on which they are spending their honeymoon.

No such concessions to alien notions of a happy (that is, morally satisfactory) ending are made in Sciascia's brilliantly spare tale. His hero-victims, Dr. Roscio and Professor Laurana, struggle against the Darwinian fates but are in no way equal to them: and there is not a hint that the villain (in this story, also, a designing lover) derived anything but profound satisfaction from his triumph.

comprised some of the last waves of immigration to this country; and along with the Negroes and Puerto Ricans, these form the bulk of our present *Lumpenproletariat.* What makes American gangsterism a less ominous force than many abroad think it, is the fact that its practitioners are still too mentally stunted to entertain really big, dangerous ambitions; while on the other side, the social order in which they operate is as yet too cohesive and well organized to find them much more than a local nuisance. It is possibly more significant—though not for the future of gangsterism as such—that the older native American population put up with racketeers to the point of giving them a secure foothold in the first place. In earlier times, when men's moral convictions, like their religious beliefs, tended to be more intense, such a phenomenon was perhaps less likely to arise; in fact, the *Mafia* seems to be the corrupt descendant of a secret organization whose original object was to help fellow Sicilians against the alien oppressor. In becoming what it now is, it simply moved with the times—modernized.

The point is that racketeering is merely one among many forms of crime which now require external constraint because the internal constraints which might either have precluded it or led to its speedy extirpation have broken down. This situation is, in turn, a logical consequence of other psychic changes discussed here—changes which may have gone furthest in America because of our special circumstances. The modern specialized man, with one particular segment of the world and one particular competence as his sphere, has much difficulty in thinking clearly about events outside of it. It is not just science, but reality, which has gotten too big for him. He lacks the imagination to take in, let alone developing sensible convictions about, things happening Out There;[26]

26. "We are deluged with facts, but we have lost, or are losing, our human ability to feel them. . . . Why we are thus impotent, I do not know. I only know that this impotence exists and that it is dangerous, increasingly dangerous. . . . Slavery begins when men give up their need to know with the whole heart . . . to bear the burden for themselves." Archibald MacLeish, in the *Atlantic Monthly,* March, 1959, p. 46.
A part of the danger MacLeish is talking about consists in the fact that when men cease to "bear the burden for themselves" and cultivate a strict business-is-business, stick-to-the-facts attitude, the result can be a grotesque, almost moronic complicity in the most horrible of crimes. There is in existence a correspondence between the I. G. Farben chemical trust and authorities at Auschwitz. It was cited, in part, by Emanuel Litvinoff in the Manchester *Guardian Weekly,* May 4, 1961, p. 10:
" 'In contemplation of experiments with a new soporific drug, we would appreciate your procuring for us a number of women.' "

and the very fact that he is potentially better informed than he has ever been may only worsen his confusion, as casual conversations about politics or world affairs often seem to demonstrate. As a scientist, the

" 'We received your answer but consider the price of 200 marks a woman as excessive. We propose to pay not more than 170 marks a head. If agreeable we will take possession of the women. We need approximately 150.' "

" 'Received the order of 150 women. Despite their emaciated condition, they were found satisfactory.' "

And the final note in the series:

" 'The tests were made. All subjects died. We shall contact you shortly on the subject of a new load.' "

The conditions under which slave labor at the Krupp Works were forced to live (see the testimony given at Nuremberg by Dr. Wilhelm Jaeger, Krupp's senior physician in the camps, as reported in William Shirer's *Rise and Fall of the Third Reich* [Simon and Schuster, 1960], pp. 948 ff.) were almost inconceivably bad. Here men were herded into dog kennels; women suffering from "open festering wounds and other diseases" were maintained in huge barracks in which " 'there were no medical supplies. . . . They had no shoes and went about in their bare feet. The . . . clothing of each consisted of a sack with holes for their arms and legs. . . . Food in the camp was extremely meager."

In other barracks there were almost no toilet facilities ("ten children's toilets . . . for 1200 inhabitants); the floors were covered with excrement. . . ." "The Tartars and Kirghiz suffered most; they collapsed like flies [from] bad housing . . . insufficient . . . food, overwork and insufficient rest.' "

The worst abuses of the coolie traffic in Peru in the 1850's scarcely equal these: the horrors of Manchester or of American child labor in the same century do not even approach them. It was hardly common sense to maintain a labor force in such a state of feebleness and degradation, unless the object, besides exploitation, was to kill people (and not merely Jewish people) en masse. And what really was the object of that, one may ask: practical (to create Lebensraum) or aesthetic? As a practical program it presented great difficulties, as some of the gruesome correspondence in Shirer's book, concerning ways of improving the killing rates in the camps, shows. Much evidence suggests that the element of sheer fun was important. It is hard to imagine that the degradation of our species can go much further, although other attempts may be made. But what of the thousands, or even millions, who had a hand in these sadistic games, not really as sadists themselves, but simply as bystanders, or as poker-faced professionals doing a job? Their deadness is almost more frightening than the savagery of their superiors, representing a contraction of human character and imagination to the point that men will condone or even endure anything because they have really ceased to be men. On this point Hermann Rauschning says, of the Germany of 1939: "Once more we may observe the degeneration which struck observers in the age of the decay of Hellenism—faces and figures grown ugly; nowhere any nobility . . . of intellect or soul; no sign left of any inner struggle or any genuine repose; only eyes that flash for a moment and are blind again; brutal expressions . . . the gestures of the inane." Hermann Rauschning, *The Revolution of Nihilism* (Alliance, 1939), p. 36.

typical modern is apt to protest that it is not "operational" for him to dwell on matters so far beyond his practical reach. Whatever his *métier*, he is inclined to feel that in social emergencies some other sort of specialist should be called in: in the case of gangsterism, J. Edgar Hoover; of Communism in small foreign nations, the army; and so on. Our tendency as a nation today is to "let George do it." But the fact also seems to be that we still do not lack entirely for men intelligent and courageous enough to rise after a time against a Senator Joseph McCarthy or to denounce our present dismemberment of Viet Nam.

However, the fact that we have not yet reached the point of complete "relativism" in moral matters and complete specialization in outlook does not imply that we are not headed in that direction or may not suffer serious losses of political freedom and of ordinary human decency on the way. If there is anything to the model of mind-brain relations, and to the corresponding principles of human psychic development which I have proposed, it follows, I think, that we *are* headed that way, nor is there a lack of historical evidence to that effect. Just as the art and conduct and politics of the Victorian era make a kind of internal sense or complement each other in a quite logical way, so does much that is happening in our own country now, particularly when seen in the light of our frontier past.

The term *provincial* connotes a kind of stuntedness or specialism in outlook forced upon men by their too-narrow beginnings. It might be said that provincialism is our national problem—not that since World War II we have not been increasingly aware of the fact. It may also be true, however, that a people which has become provincial, in the deeper sense I have tried to convey here, needs more than city life, public education, and a few good newspapers to become really grown up. The very fact that our society is a "leveled" one militates against that sort of improvement. In England, for example, it is mass man who reads the "yellow press," whereas it is most probably the middle class which supports the better papers, literature, and higher-quality entertainment such as the B.B.C. third program. Here, it is the middle classes as well as the lower which support cheap journalism and fourth-rate entertainment, along with the dreary productions of our middle-brow culture.

If one compares publishers' sales figures, for books of comparable quality, in Britain and the United States, it appears that the British, per capita, read far more than Americans (as do the Russians, incidentally) and that in this country the number of consistent adult, non-technical readers is on the order of a few hundred thousand out of a population approaching two hundred millions.[27] If one argues that the public which might have existed for books has been diverted to other media such as TV, the question arises as to why the quality of entertainment offered by these supposedly educational media has remained so low—why it has remained "entertainment" and almost never been either real art or really educational.

The old argument as to who is to blame for this state of affairs, the public or the impresarios, seems to me quite futile. For anything to "go over" requires a consensus; and within limits consensuses can be made, rather than simply being born and exploited. But common sense suggests, and facts to some degree support, the conclusion that people of our time and country cannot yet be made to believe or accept *anything* which those in control of the machinery of information happen to decide upon.[28] It is more reasonable to suppose that Lords of the Media get

27. A sale of 25,000 to 40,000 copies may make a best seller in the United States. *Science* published this brief survey of the situation (Vol. 127 [1958], p. 562): "A 1955 Gallup poll disclosed that 61 percent of American adults had not read a book, other than the Bible, during the previous year. . . . Only 17 percent were reading a book at the time of the survey. From other surveys we learn that America is only one third as literate as Great Britain and only one fifth as literate as Sweden, in terms of adult book reading. We are told that one half of American adults live within a mile of a public library, but only one fifth of them ever enter it. . . . The average reading [of American college students] is one book a month, and it is reported that many find it possible to complete a college curriculum without any reading other than assigned textbooks. Is the fact that only 12 percent of the homes constructed during the past decade have built-in bookshelves a clue? We think it is."

The situation may have been much the same in the 1820's and 30's: "The only reading men I met with were those who made letters their profession," said Frances Trollope in *Domestic Manners of the Americans* (Vintage 1949), p. 93.

In *Walden* (which was written in 1845-1847), Thoreau remarked: "There is in this town (Concord), with very few exceptions, no taste for the best or for very good books, even in English literature, whose words all can read and spell. Even the college-bred and so-called liberally educated men here and elsewhere have really little or no acquaintance with the English classics; and as for the . . . ancient classics and Bibles which are accessible to all who will know of them, there are the feeblest efforts anywhere made to become acquainted with them." *Walden* (Houghton Mifflin, 1893), p. 167.

28. For an amusing analysis of the powers of propaganda, see Bertrand Russell, *Unpopular Essays* (Simon and Schuster, 1950), pp. 95-95. He suggests that if a powerful and intolerant government were to lay it down that water boils when put in the refrigerator and freezes on the stove, people would accept that

their best results by playing upon existing prejudices or tendencies in their audience—that they frequently owe their success to the fact that they have much the same outlook as their public, are men of much the same psychological type. It takes a vulgarian like Hearst or a rough customer like Beaverbrook to know his own.

One can object—as Edmund Wilson, among others, has done[29]—that what then results is a vicious circle, a kind of degradative process or antieducation which gradually reduces all to the lowest common level. The answer is that something of the kind undoubtedly occurs, the aesthetic sins of the fathers being visited upon the sons either as a love of TV and bowling or in the shape of writers like Jack Kerouac and William Burroughs. This line of (literal) descent begins with the grandfathers and mothers who read Ouida and Richard Harding Davis and Elinor Glyn, who went in for "conspicuous consumption" when they could afford it and began to believe in their hearts that culture, like religion, was bunk. But with that we are brought back to the principal point made in this book; namely, that culture represents, at bottom, an ideal of mind or psychic growth which springs from our religion and is dying with it. Realized, that ideal results in a type of intelligence not merely obligated, but joyously able, to contemplate a wide range of things not to any special or predetermined end but simply for the hell of it—out of the mind's reckless affection for its own proper objects. Between them, the scientific enlightenment and the frontier lured us back into fragmented, "interested" ways of being and looking at the world which are, in principle, like those of tribal man. And in proportion as we ceased to achieve "centrality"—the breadth and momentum of mind which the earlier ideal of universality produced in a few and

dictum as a "Sunday truth" while discreetly continuing to heat or cool water as they had always done. The same applies to dicta concerning political freedom when the consensus supporting such freedom in daily fact has passed (as in imperial Rome with its show-window Senate) or has never really existed (as in Russia).

29. In *Memoirs of Hecate County,* p. 263: "The most immoral and disgraceful and dangerous thing that anybody can do in the arts is knowingly to feed back to the public its own ignorance and cheap tastes." The same might be said of the scientism which feeds out to the public, as certainties, those inferences from modern biology which present man as in no way basically different from the beasts. The result is to push our hope and idealism still farther to the wall, and that not by the power of superior insight, perhaps, but from what amounts to cocksure prejudice.

held up as a possibility for all—the ideal itself, the notion of the soul, lost its reality for us, to the point that now those rare men who manage to become psychically whole are often little understood or appreciated by their contemporaries. Their example[30] is wasted, since no one any longer knows what it means.

Once this process of fragmentation, essentially the production of part individuals, was well started, it was only a question of time before culture began to suffer. The poets, who were kept on as sometimes prosperous and respected ornaments of society in the Victorian age (Browning, Tennyson), are today all but out of work, rarely honored, as Robert Frost was by the late President Kennedy, almost never able to live on their royalties, and enjoying only the impersonal patronage of universities or foundations.[31] The situation of most painters and serious composers, even of not a few fine jazz musicians, is hardly better. Our theater has been moribund for decades, and even in its better days it never amounted to much. It has become harder and harder, particularly in America, to get commercial publishers to bring out a "quality" novel by a new author. The Metropolitan Opera and most of our symphony orchestras are in chronic financial trouble. In short, rich as we are, we cannot find the money to support the same culture which our forebears did, not because the cost of culture is now so high, but because interest in it is so low.

In the mass "culture" of the movies and TV, the trend, as mentioned earlier, has been toward an increasingly bald Id art—toward public enactment of primitive fantasies of violence and gratification without even a pretense of content or a nod to older "inhibitions" (that is, taste). What strikes one about American movies is their combination of action, gaudiness, and psychic poverty. Emotionally they tend to be one-track. The parts our actors do most convincingly are those requiring a show of *strain*: the unrelieved brutality of the gang chief or Gauleiter, the girl made compulsively bitter and venomous by an unhappy childhood, the wooden-faced cowboy or dry irascible businessman-father, who

30. For instance, the liberalism of Pauling and Russell and Einstein, mentioned earlier.

31. "Poetry still survives with us, survives with vigor and inventiveness. . . . But the poem itself has lost its power in men's minds. . . . We seem unable to know as Shakespeare knew, who makes King Lear cry out to the blinded Gloucester on the heath, 'You see how this world goes,' and Gloucester answers, 'I see it feelingly.' " Archibald MacLeish, in the *Atlantic Monthly* (March, 1959), p. 46.)

stick to their guns, are the same admirable or hateful automata through thick and thin. When, as sometimes happens in the last reel, things take a turn for the better and these people are suddenly called upon to show their warmer, more "human" selves, the results are usually embarrassing. The emotional timbre of our times is not warm, nor are we much interested in, or really able to understand, the complex dramas which may be going on inside of others, their subtleties of thought and feeling—in short, their identity. Hollywood, as usual overworking a good thing, exaggerates this nullity and presents us as even more rudimentary than we are. Many European films seem to have a warmth and subtlety which ours lack—are much more "human" and believable in detail; and to that extent their recent popularity here is reassuring. The difference between American and European films is still, I think, significant and fits in with something which Camus said about the American "realistic" novel:

> The American novel claims to find its unity in reducing man either to elementals or to his external reactions and to his behavior. It does not choose feelings or passions to give detailed descriptions of. . . . It rejects analysis and the search for a fundamental psychological motive. . . . This is why the unity of this novel form is only the unity of the flash of recognition. Its technique consists in describing men by their outside appearances, in their most casual actions, of reproducing without comment, everything they say, down to their repetitions, and finally, by acting as if [they] were entirely defined by their daily automatisms.[32]

While unfair to some of our novelists, his description fits most of the productions of Hollywood quite well. The real reason that we tend toward the method Camus describes may be that there are many emotions we no longer very much feel, and a good deal in ourselves which, in step with that change, we cannot very clearly understand either. So minute portrayal of externals becomes for us a *faute de mieux* technique, but with the important qualification that *certain* emotions we still do feel, and portray, with great vividness—namely, those arising out of the

---

32. Albert Camus, *The Rebel* (Vintage, 1956), p. 265. Also: "One may say that the fear of prose as much as any other single element, has hampered the American novelist. This is a . . . logical consequence in a tradition that has been dominated by an aimless and uncritical naturalism, and that has never been quite able to distinguish between fiction and journalism." Mark Schorer, in a review, New York *Times,* October 9, 1949.

primitive emergency system: anxiety, strain, a rebound anger against circumstances, resentment, and so forth. Significantly, these predominate in the new *avant-garde* fiction and poetry as well.[33] There is little gentleness, little of nuance or real eloquence—of coherence even—in many of the liberated young, their tragedy, like that of the modern revolutionary mass, being that they may be too like what they are rebelling against, too crippled by the fate they would change, to change it.

The method of portraying man in fiction by way of a painstaking assembly of facts, never interpreted, has its parallel in the straitened, almost fanatical empiricism of our science. In the field in which I have worked, to name but one, there has been an explosion of discovery in recent years, a deluge of new information which threatens to swamp our libraries and has made "retrieval" of data a major problem. Not only have very few tried to knit up these new facts into a major theory of mind-brain relations but, as I and others can testify, those who do try are not encouraged, the currently accepted approach being to devise small special hypotheses and wait for the larger synthesis, as it were, to make itself—to emerge, suddenly self-evident, from the pile of facts, when the pile has at last got big enough. Possibly that will happen, although it looks as if we may be buried alive first. My object here is not so much to dispute that concept of scientific method as to examine the type of mind that inclines to it. Basically it is the same type which has produced the American movie, the "realistic" novel, and, at lower levels, the mechanic and factory pieceworker. Its predominance in our science has given the latter its peculiar, one might say lackluster, excellence.[34] The same type also prevails in our business and statecraft, and in the latter, over the past two decades, has had predictably poor results (witness the contributions of the Dulles brothers or latterly Rusk and Johnson).

We make a good deal in America of our sense of humor, to the point

33. Louis Bogan, in the *New Yorker*, April 1, 1961, p. 129, remarks that "mid-century American verse . . . has failed to explore, except in rare instances . . . variety, depth and delicacy of emotion. Delight, tenderness and a continuing refreshment of the ancient attitudes of wonder and awe have become unfashionable and very nearly unapproachable. The limiting of feeling to hostility (open or disguised), violence, guilt, anxiety, and fear has brought about a situation in which the gentler emotions have become suspect."

34. That is, much drive and production, but little depth or originality; hence a huge body of second-rate work, some of it nevertheless quite useful.

that hardly a man among us will admit to not having one. Aside from the fact that it is "in" to do so, having and respecting humor are signs of essential sanity, just as the German lack of humor, we feel, may say much about the sort of mind which gave its consent and support to Nazism.[35] One of the fundamentals of humor is the continually perceived contrast between what is and what might be, between fact and ideality. As such, it is often the result of mind or the waking I catching itself at the tricks which the Id forces it into. One of the things which made W. C. Fields funny was his odd blend of the seedy and the grandiloquent. In general, the grossly self-deceived man is a comic figure, as is the hypocrite who thinks he is deceiving others, or the innocent who takes the world's self-justifying nonsense at face value (for instance, Evelyn Waugh's John Boot, the bird watcher and nature columnist who becomes, by accident, a war correspondent in Ethiopia).

American folk humor makes much use of exaggeration, the tall story told with a poker face. This is a primitive comic genre which often tries to have it both ways, the Id of the teller being gratified by a kind of boasting in fantasy, even as the teller is by implication debunking the boasting. This sort of quasi-lying is more anarchic than satirical. A fundamental theorem in our humor seems not to be "there is an underlying truth to events, or an ideal way of life, in contrast to which . . . " but rather "all supposed truths or ideal ways are bunk, therefore . . . ." In this sense, it is a long jump from Fielding and Sterne to S. J. Perelman or the "sick" comics of our night clubs and TV. And in contrast to Waugh (who was nevertheless more of a modern than he knew and whose attempts at "values" produced his worst, really "sickest" writing), there is little suggestion in American humorists, from Twain[36] and Petroleum V. Nasby to the present, of a further standard against which our absurdities can be seen as such. On the contrary, the basic absurdity is that there *are* no standards, so that much of our humor has become simply an attack on supposed futility, on what remains of our pretensions

35. "How dare a man have a sense of humor when he considers his immense burden of responsibilities toward himself and others. However, I have no wish to pass censure on the humorists. After all, does one have to have a conscience? Who says so?" Quoted from "Goethe's Conversations and Encounters," by W. H. Auden, in the *New York Review of Books,* February 9, 1967, p. 10.

36. There is, of course, the famous passage in which Huck Finn reproaches himself for helping Jim; but more of Twain is, like his essay on the German language, simple burlesque.

to Higher Things. Perelman, though a genius in the construction and misuse of rhetoric, is not far from Hollywood's grosser caricatures, or even from the comic books, in the peculiar violence of his little scenarios. One senses in him not the moralist outraged but the demolition expert— a man obviously happy in his work and uniquely good at it. Like the folk art of exaggeration, our modern professional humor inclines to the hectic and overblown. That quality was already well developed in American movies and in the radio comics of thirty years ago. The "Comic Books" in the meantime have mostly stopped trying to be funny, but simply present bloated fantasies of power and blood and sex; and it is startling that large numbers of grown men, for instance in our armed services, seem to read them in preference to anything else.[37] We do not

---

37. Perhaps the strongest case against the comics has been made by Dr. Frederic Wertham in *Seduction of the Innocent* (Rinehart, 1954). At the time of the Senate hearings on the comic book industry, Max Lerner ran a series of articles in the New York *Post,* April 20–22, 1954, covering both the hearings and some of Wertham's findings. "The highpoint of the day was William M. Gaines, publisher of Entertaining Comics. . . . He saw himself as bringing thrills into the lives of millions; and he saw anyone opposing or doubting the comics as most probably either a Communist or a 'Red dupe.' "

The question of whether the horror comics do inspire some or many of the crimes of frightfulness committed by children (as Wertham maintains, with evidence), or are simply a precipitating agent in a few clinical cases, but otherwise a healthy outlet for "aggressive impulses" (as a Dr. David Abrahamsen held, at the hearings), is in a sense beside the point. The point is that while the human appetite for violent adventure or for tales of the uncanny is perennial, the *quality* of those in the comic books puts them in an entirely different universe from Grimm or *Treasure Island* or the *Pit and the Pendulum.*

" 'I look at the pictures a long time,' " one of Wertham's child subjects reported. " 'I just imagine as if they are real. They go around stabbing people. They have 8 knives and they rob a liquor store. . . . One man started killing people; 5 cops, 6 women and 18 others. If anybody ever crossed him he didn't give them no chance.' "

" 'The girls are always on the gangsters' side,' " another said. " 'The gangsters pick them up, like. They just roam around with the gangsters. . . . The dresses have a V-shape in the front. The girls are in the room. They do something bad or something, and then a man slaps them and beats them up.' "

"Then there is the erotic 'hanging' fantasy" (Lerner speaking). "In one comic book a man who 'kills for sport' is shown with a sequence of half nude girls. 'Ho ho! What a hangman I make! . . . My noose will fit around that pretty's neck!' Then a girl, scantily clad, is shown hanging from a tree . . . in a death struggle."

The old-fashioned tale was a *story.* The heroes and villains had objectives. Violence or cruelty, overdrawn perhaps, were still incidental to the action, as in

have a body of "serious" comic writers to compare with those of England, though we do have a humor magazine, the *New Yorker*, which, I think, is of higher quality than its overseas equivalent, *Punch*. The striking thing about *New Yorker* humor is that it is confined to a small public (amounting to perhaps 1 per cent of the population, or four to five times its circulation) and is almost totally opaque to a vast majority. Another rather noticeable feature of the magazine is the queer, almost sinister tone of some of its more memorable prose pieces. This genre, which seems to have descended from Henry James's *Turn of the Screw*, suggests a world lapsing into a kind of cold frightfulness as seen through the eyes of men themselves afflicted in varying degrees with the same disorder. (E. B. White's "The Door"; Thurber's "The Cane in the Corridor"; Shirley Jackson's "The Lottery"; most of Roald Dahl's stories; J. D. Salinger's "Great Day for Bananafish".)[38]

daily life. Here the story has all but vanished; there is no pretense of a vehicle any more; just a wild indulgence of primal fantasy, a running together of sex and ferocity, a reversion to almost mindless undifferentiated being in which even the several branches of the Id have not clearly separated out. What is startling is not only that children "read" these "comics" but that they are "written" by adults—that a whole industry, in this supposedly civilized country, is based on them. "The . . . estimate . . . given by the staff director of the Hendrickson Committee, Richard Clendener, [was that] crime and horror books comprise one fourth of the total—about 20,000,000 copies a month" (Lerner).

What this says about the degree of psychic regression which is occurring in quite large numbers of our people is so serious as to put the whole matter outside the realm of censorship entirely. The comics are, in fact, only a sort of caricature of changes taking place in our arts—for instance, in the novel à la William Burroughs, or the *avant-garde* film. Amos Vogel (New York Sunday *Times,* January 21, 1968), under the title "Goodby Alienation, Hello Nudity," has this to say about the recent film festival at Knokke-le-Zoute, Belgium: "Perhaps most significant . . . were the paucity of social comment, the emergence of nudity as a mass-phenomenon and the growth of the unblinking-observation-of-reality school of Andy Warhol. . . . There has never been a more voluminous progression of nudes, assorted genitals, and full-frontal shots of both sexes than at this festival. . . . The metaphysical 'Self-Obliteration' (USA) ends in a free-for-all body-painting sex-orgy. . . . The affirmative eroticism of 'The Bed' (USA) with its charmingly polymorphous-perverse tumblings of one or more stark naked boys and/or girls into and out of bed remained a rare exception at the festival." One Japanese avant-gardist showed a ninety-minute film "which consisted of 365 buttocks of London's artists and intellectuals, each on screen for 20 seconds."

As usual prophetic, the arts are telling us what our real concerns are narrowing down to. Nor does it, in the present case, take much of an art to do so.

38. Especially since World War II there has been a vogue for authors like Kafka, who present the world as a kind of vast concentration camp, in which

Salinger's hero Holden Caulfield (in *Catcher in the Rye*) is a kind of sensitive upper-middle-class amorph, part of whose immense appeal seems to lie in his shapelessness, which we find not repulsive or grotesque, but touchingly familiar if not, in this era, an inevitability—Man's fate. A lower-class version of the same character—the gabbling, incoherent high-schooler—has lately appeared on TV (played by one of the Smothers Brothers). In psychological terms, these are natural complements of comic book reading and the garish violence of the comic books themselves—man the amorph's life of the "imagination." All are logical, if remote, descendants of the civilized melancholy of Matthew Arnold's "Dover Beach" and began, perhaps, with the reappearance, by invitation, of primal emotion among the Victorian romantics.[39]

men are forced to endure senseless frustration or persecution by the powerful, without any hope of escape.

"But the actuality of the literature of extreme situations is due ultimately to the fact that in the concentration camp is realized nothing more than the logical extension of certain aspects of modern society. This is obvious in the totalitarian states where . . . it is terror which holds the society together. But even more in democratic states, social disintegration and irresponsibility, the forerunners of terror, are playing an increasing role. The subjugation of individual initiative to the enervating and unpredictable pressures of almost every aspect of a mass-production society is not unconnected with the naked brutality of a forced labor camp. The popularity of the concentration camp literature is one indication of the unconscious fear that in these books [lies] a prediction of man's fate." Albert Votaw, "The Literature of Extreme Situations," *Horizon* (September, 1949), pp. 157–158.

39. Writers of this school, which includes moderns such as D. H. Lawrence, Wyndham Lewis, and Julien Benda's "clerks," appear to enjoy indulging ferocity. But note that it is still in civilized security that they do so, like the superpatriot who is past military draft age. In an earlier chapter I mentioned that, like rats which have become secure in their social life (see Konrad Lorenz, *On Aggression* [Harcourt, Brace, and World, 1966], p. 158), men of late civilizations tend toward ferocity. In men, however, this is a more complex phenomenon, involving mass release of the Id as the restraints of mind and the opposition of the warmer emotions begin to fail. (In rats it simply reflects a shift from dominance of emergency functions and fear, in the disorganized rat world, to dominance of sexuality and ferocity in the organized.) But the first general outbreaks of ferocity, as in the major wars of this century, produce such a worsening of (real external) conditions, and so darken human prospects, that ferocity indulged soon leads back to the dominion of fear outright, or to a type of psyche run largely on the rebound from "emergency" states. Hence our present Age of Anxiety.

A news dispatch of May, 1968, on the radio quotes Senator Stennis as saying that even if the Viet Nam War is settled in Paris, we will probably spend as much as it cost us, or more, per annum on new, still more fearsome missile

The modern nation-state, like modern revolution, represents, in short, a reversion to Id-determined behavior on a large scale: a kind of supertribalism. This is not to say that war in any era is not basically the same phenomenon. Only its declared objectives or "causes" change. The so-called religious wars of the seventeenth century resulted in part from those enormous perturbations, or outbreaks of primitivism, which are apt to occur when men's faith, never in the majority very rational, seems to them to have been threatened or violated in some way. The persecution of witches comes under the same head, as does the earlier slaughter of the Albigenses. Such atrocities, which have done much to discredit religion in modern eyes, are a kind of retribution brought upon man by his inability to purge himself of Neolithic leaders—to bring himself up, by his bootstraps, far enough and in sufficient numbers. With primitive peck-order types at the top of the social order and (therefore) a perennially starved and psychically stunted mass at the bottom, it is only natural that as much hysteria and as many frightful deeds can be provoked by crying "heresy" as in later times are unloosed by crying "Communist" or "capitalist bandit." And even the most horrible torture and butchery committed in the name of our Lord in times past can scarcely equal the systematic degradation of human beings, the creative cruelty and destruction and murder, practiced by the Germans once they had been "liberated" from their ancestral faith.[40]

Modern nationalism is, in other words, merely a later, and for most civilizations a final, form of the retribution just described. Whereas in religious eras persecutions or wars of faith may break out, there is perhaps a certain element of chance in those misfortunes. Parts of the culture—for instance, England, in the Western world—are often spared the worst of them. With the beginning of modernity—that is, with the ap-

---

systems. Propelled as we are by such fears, how can we hope finally to avert their consequences?

40. A possibility which Heine, a man himself of some ferocity, clearly foresaw and warned the world against. See also *The Ciano Diaries,* Count Galeazzo Ciano (Doubleday, 1946), p. 490: "Sorrentino on his return from Russia, gives his impressions and makes forecasts. . . . The brutality of the Germans, which has now reached the proportions of a continuing crime, stands out from his words so vividly and so movingly as to make one sceptical of his truthfulness. Massacres of entire populations, raping, killing of children—all this is a matter of daily occurrence." This entry is dated May 27, 1942. There is little reason to doubt its truth or to suppose that all this carnage and cruelty was the work of specialists of the SS.

pearance of an increasingly restless and psychically formless majority and of an ethic of pure success at all social levels—the situation changes in that nationalism and potential revolution become general, and war, always likely, is now virtually certain. Either it arises as a direct continuation of revolution, as in Napoleonic France, or it becomes the habitual condition of the state and as such a permanent substitute for revolution, draining off, on an external foe, impulses to revenge and destruction and armed plunder which would otherwise expend themselves at home, putting great strain on the machinery of law and order, which is all, finally, that controls us. No sooner had Hitler consolidated his position as Chancellor of the Reich than he began to prepare for war, basically, perhaps, for the reason I have just given. It was not merely that he had promised national aggrandizement, or even that such aggrandizement was really necessary to Germany by 1933, and so worth the risk. The more important fact was that Germany was profoundly revolutionary, as witnessed by the size of its Communist party; and as an inspired intuitive, Hitler probably quite well understood that to hesitate would, for him, be disaster. In such an event others would soon rise to do what he had more reasonably decided against. For the "dynamism" of totalitarian states is rooted, so to speak, in the deepest statistical reality of the day: in a certain psychological majority and in a related general outlook or *Geist*. Once the doors admitting the mass men and their leaders to control of the state have been burst open, the only choice is between permanent stasis and permanent instability on the South American plan or permanent expansionism and war on the Hitlerian, the essential reason being that the men who thenceforth control events are of such psychic crudity that they can neither bootstrap themselves back up to the "human" state nor see any need or way to do so. All they *can* see is the danger of others' doing so: the threat to the state of the really good man— that is, the man free enough of the Id to be able to think clearly and to act not always from predictably selfish motives. It was this type, both in the flesh and in the realm of ideas, that Hitler set out with particular ferocity to get rid of. Much more underlies this phenomenon than mere practicality, the elimination of dissidents or potential rebels; and such persecutions accordingly go to lengths which seem at first glance senseless. They are not, but spring rather from what may be the profoundest envy man is capable of: envy of the *being* of another. By the burning of the books, by murder and torture of the cultivated, the man of the Id, rising at the end of history, tries to wipe out everything that once stood superior to him—and not merely socially superior. For in rising he has gotten what he once envied and respected: power. But that is not the whole prize, nor does it repay the worst of those sufferings which made him revolutionary to begin with. It is what he can *not* have—the fully grown psychic self, the soul—which he hates and sets out to punish wherever it shows itself. It is only incidental that men of soul are a threat to him, are more moral and nonsenseproof than most. Of all his enemies they are the least immediately dangerous because also the least inclined by nature to conspiracy and violence. He hates them, Camus would say, for a metaphysical reason: because they are better than he in a way no amount of success can ever change.[41] They have transcendence of a kind and by that fact become reminders as bitter as handsomeness is to the ugly; bitterer, for looks are only the surface of life, whereas to be robbed of one's soul is to go to one's grave without really having lived, to have suffered torments of anxiety and strain and effort for nothing.

Modern Germany's insane persecution of the Jews, which probably cost millions more as a form of industrialized murder than it ever earned as a form of robbery and enslavement, may have had one of its deeper roots in this sort of envy. Spengler mentions that medieval anti-Semitism seems to have been due to the suspicion with which the simple men of that day regarded the ability of the Jews to make calculations and manage money. In a sense, that is simply the same phenomenon, expressed in terms of religious superstition. Those who think too well, who have achieved a way of being, inside of their heads, which is far beyond your own, must be witches.[42] While there are certainly other factors which

41. "The hostility of the common man toward Intellect is of all times and places. . . . Socrates was a victim of the same spontaneous resentment which makes the majority at school gang up on the bookish boy. . . . It is enough that intellectual work enforces sedentary habits. . . . But animal energy is only one threat. Intellect is also hated because it is envied . . . as a sign or pretense of social superiority." Jacques Barzun, *The House of Intellect* (Harper, 1959), p. 8. In fact, I believe the truth goes beyond this hackneyed explanation. While usually a mark of caste, intellect, unlike some others, represents a gulf nothing can bridge, a sort of freedom which the psychically underprivileged correctly sense they will never enjoy.

42. The monk Gerbert, who later became Pope Sylvester II, was suspected of sorcery and reported to have been seen flying home from Spain, where he studied geography and mathematics under the Moors in the tenth century. See Brooks Adams, *The Law of Civilization and Decay* (Knopf, 1943), p. 122.

have contributed to anti-Semitism—among them, simply a primal xeno-phobia which we share with the rats[43]—the crucial offense, for the modern German Jew, the characteristic which he may have regarded as his surest claim to decent acceptance, was his intellectuality. More than the competition he represented in business and law and medicine, more than all talk of "sharp practice," all real or fancied differences in mores between the Jewish and Christian communities, it may have been the imputation of the Jew's superiority in mind, dating back to medieval times and, as it were, vindicating itself anew in Freud and Einstein and the Vienna Circle, that doomed him in Hitler's Reich.[44]

It may sound strange to say so, but the same envy of intangible su-periority—of the mind or self of others—and with it the same sort of virulent anti-Semitism[45] are widespread in this country. Traditionally,

43. See Lorenz, *On Aggression,* pp. 157 ff. Two other factors which have con-tributed to anti-Semitism are the connection between the Jews and the Cruci-fixion and the peculiar statelessness of the Jews since the modern Diaspora which brought them as an enclave society into Russia and Europe. On this point, see the *Dialogues of Alfred North Whitehead,* by Lucien Price (Little, Brown, 1954), p. 262. The Jew's detachment or lack of true nationality, added to his intellec-tuality, made him peculiarly hateful to the type of Germanic mass man, ferocious yet slavishly obedient (and slavishly open to glorious myths or nationalistic "ideals"), who comprised the Nazi rank and file. The irony was that by the time German persecutions of them began, many Jews had become *echt Deutsch* in everything but the unfortunate fact of ancestry. In this they were like our own nisei of World War II, but fared much worse—a fact which didn't prevent numbers of them from returning to Germany after the war.

An additional irony is that the Jews' cosmopolitanism and their specialization in usury were, to a considerable extent, forced on them by their overlords in medieval Europe. They were forbidden to own land, to serve as soldiers, to belong to gilds and so on.

44. "Nothing interested [Hitler] except power. Racial theories bit more deeply into his mind than 'geopolitics'; and he explained everything, from the disunity of Germany to British policy, by the influence of the Jews. Yet this, too, was claptrap. What he hated in the Jews was civilisation—the virtues of com-promise and conciliation." (A. J. P. Taylor, in the Manchester *Guardian Weekly,* June 25, 1953).

45. A recent study, based on two thousand interviews of seventy-five minutes each, representing a "national cross-section of the population", showed that about one American in three is antisemitic (has a "negative image" of Jews), the other two-thirds being equally divided between indifference and pro-Jewish feeling. (*The New York Times,* Sunday, April 20, 1969, p. 41) These figures recall White-head's appraisal of us (one-third first rate, one-third second rate, one-third crim-inal) in reverse order. See *Dialogues of Alfred North Whitehead,* Lucien Price (Little, Brown, 1954), p. 316.

our egalitarianism is supposed to represent a reaction against entrenched privilege. In debased form, it is simply an excuse for rancor directed toward the more fortunate or successful. However, in practice, it is often subtler than these descriptions suggest. For what the egalitarian hates and envies, even more than material advantage itself, is the differences in psychological caste, in the very texture and quality of men's being that often go with it. He senses and rebels against what is, in fact, the supreme injustice:[46] that differences in material fortune eventually become differences of race as well. The men at the top, or their educated descendants, are psychically of another species. So long as the man who has that advantage—who is of the upper psychic caste or "race" —takes care to hide the fact, we do not begrudge him many other forms of real (and often unjust) privilege. Let him be exclusive in his social life or carry on in public and show off his money and his women like a movie star. So what? We can still pretend he is not *really* different from us, just different in outward circumstances, which anybody, with luck, can take on the way one puts on a new suit. The other difference—the difference in real freedom, in inner dimensions or the soul—is lifelong and irremediable.[47] Partly a matter of inheritance, like good looks or a talent for drawing, partly of early and fortunate nurture, it is in any case unforgivable.

By a further irony, the egalitarian is often disillusioned to discover that many who *seem* to be his real psychic superiors turn out, in fact, to be only more efficiently adaptive than he. This, indeed, is his traditional position: that since we are all basically pretty much the same, differences in power and status must be 90 per cent unfair. From that it follows that circumstantial advantage, like the view of human behavior which derives from biology, is a standing argument against the reality or validity of our older moral notions. Democratic politics therefore proceed from a kind of paradox. While the pressure of mass discontent offers opportunities to parties of the opposition and so leads to a slow redress of social ills—a change particularly accelerated in the hard times of the 1930's —the public that demands such essentially moral improvements, and by degrees gets them, is itself increasingly cynical, seeing only the workings

46. See Chapter IX, p. 207, the quotation from James Agee.
47. And in eras like the present, in which the "soul" in millions is dwindling, the gulf between the psychically privileged and deprived becomes continually greater. Hence, in part, the increasingly virulent anti-intellectualism in such eras.

of power everywhere in life and little dreaming how precarious its own power is. It is for this reason that organized labor, which never really existed as an estate in America before Franklin Roosevelt and may again be reduced to insignificance at some not distant time with the help of a dummy leadership, now tends to push its advantage with the same bald cynicism that big business did back in the days of the robber barons. Similarly, there is a curious lack of public morals or of any sense of responsibility to the community, which leads many ordinary people to foul the parks in our cities, to litter the countryside with garbage on their outings, or to take advantage of public welfare by drawing unemployment insurance while in fact holding a job or while being well provided for by other members of the family. What this paradox means is that even as some of the social improvements implicit in Christian morality are finally coming into being in the shape of Medicare, Social Security, and the like, those who most benefit from them are regressing to a primitive adaptive way of thinking, which makes them increasingly unable to understand or to react appropriately to their own good fortune and may, in time, cause them to forfeit it.

The other sort of egalitarianism—the sort that impels us to deny the more intangible, more profound inequalities among men—combines with our envy of others' circumstances to produce a complex of attitudes and behavioral conventions which the world has come to regard as typically American. Goethe said: "The only way in which we can come to terms with the great superiority of another person is love. But we can also come to terms with superiority, with true Excellence, by denying that such a thing as Excellence can exist; and in doing so we help to destroy it and ourselves."[48]

It is worth repeating the point that this aversion to the (really) superior had apparently begun growing up in us in de Tocqueville's time, or the 1830's, the same era in which the emotional timbre of Western culture as a whole was starting to change, Wordsworthian reflection and love giving way to an increasing wildness and embitterment, à la Poe and Rimbaud, and finally to the virulent, almost subliterate literature of the present *avant-garde*. It is as though the capacity to "come to terms with" the superiority of others through love, and the capacity to think or write clearly about them—to grasp anything at last but the seamier

48. Randall Jarrell, *Poetry and the Age* (Vintage, 1953), p. 23.

animal side of life—had gradually declined together. From the principles of physiological psychology proposed here, it follows that they would be likely to do so, being aspects of the same phenomenon.

The gist of everything said to this point is that we may be drifting into a phase of expansion and empire, neither aware of the profound forces in ourselves which are bringing that change about nor even disposed to see that it is occurring. In the long run, it might be far better for this nation to try to save what is left of its culture—which is to say, of itself—by concentrating on internal problems while taking a softer line toward its enemies, that is by being less warlike and accepting the risk of attack, which such a policy might well entail. There seems to be little likelihood of our doing so, partly because many believe our economy would suffer, but more, perhaps, because our fear and hatred of communism has always transcended the practical. Our first Red scares and anti-communist literature[49] appeared when the Communists abroad were still weak. And ironically, it was Hitler's "crusade" against Russia, and the combined assaults of Japan and Chiang Kai-Shek on Mao, which created the infinitely more powerful Communist bloc confronting us today. Nor is it that those nations differ so radically from us. They do; but it is the features we share with communism which may have produced our almost metaphysical aversion to it. The communist world perhaps early became a "projection" of our fears for ourselves—our secret awareness of what we were becoming. In its declared (instead of covert) atheism, its overtly (instead of covertly) enforced conformism, its bald belief in *things* as not merely the sign but the substance of civilization,[50] and its fierce amorphous masses that brought this whole "philosophy" into political being, the communist ideology was simply a *reductio ad absurdum* of our own. By the testimony of its own organizers, it has never gotten much of a foothold here.[51]

In the same way that our being more middle-class than mass inclines

49. Witness the Red scares of the early 1920's, or works like *The Communist Shakes his Fist* (Bruce Reynolds, Sully & Co., 1931).

50. I remember the shock with which, in 1946, we read, or heard at first hand, that a number of G.I.'s preferred the Germans to the French because the former were cleaner, had more facilities at home, more of an American conception of how life should be organized.

51. See George Soule, in H. E. Stearns, ed., *America Now* (Scribner's, 1938), p. 258. Note also that the period referred to was the Great Depression, when there was far more reason to doubt our form of social system than there is now, when few seem to have a good word to say for it.

us to hate communism as the caricature of our own way of life, so our lack of a distinct or accepted aristocracy of the morally and intellectually excellent obviates the sort of revolution which occurred in Germany. It was not merely that Hitler and his party felt impelled from personal motives to destroy the older culture at a blow; it was also, in a sense, necessary, though not perhaps on such a scale. In our case the whole process set in so long ago and has gained momentum so gradually that today there is no need for us to burn books or persecute the learned. We have so largely turned culture into something else that it would be silly now to attack it. Common sense tells us that to do so would merely be to dry up the fountains of know-how. So long as science continues to supply industry and the military with know-how and does not get too many Ideas (as the late Professor Einstein did or Linus Pauling still tends to do), by all means support it and let it be. The same goes for literature and even for peace movements. Secure in an ultimate consensus and in certain techniques which, far more effectively than crude force, guarantee it, we can afford to indulge our "oddballs."

> Fetters and headsmen were the coarse instruments which tyranny formerly employed. . . . Monarchs had so to speak, materialized oppression: the democratic republics of the present day have [made it] entirely an affair of the mind. . . . The master no longer says "You shall think as I do, or you shall die"; he says, "You are free to think differently from me, and to retain your life, your property and all that you possess; but you are henceforth a stranger among your people. . . . You will remain among men, but you will be deprived of the rights of mankind. Your fellow-creatures will shun you like an impure being; and even those who believe in your innocence will abandon you, lest they should be shunned in their turn. Go in peace! I have given you your life, but it is an existence worse than death."[52]

This passage, which may have sounded more rhetorical than literally true when de Tocqueville wrote it, came to be true enough for many who were victims of our Communist hunts in the 1950's. To some degree it has been true since Melville's time for a number of our writers and intellectuals who, though not dissidents outright, had the misfortune to run counter to current opinion.[53]

52. De Tocqueville, *Democracy in America*, I, 338.
53. It is rather striking, as Van Wyck Brooks noted in *The Flowering of New England* (Dutton, 1936), that some of the best writers of that time—

Today, as result of the pressure of this sort of thought control on a population perhaps less and less equipped mentally to resist it, intellect and goodness—even creative individualism—are disappearing into movements and committees. The young rebel in search of "identity" joins an army of pathetic bohemians indistinguishable from himself; the writer meshes in with some existing group, whose style and attitudes are soon his own; the reformist becomes an organizer and parliamentarian, the scientist a "worker." No *one* stands out. In the profoundest sense—not merely by the force of current opinion, but more effectively by the example and explicit training we are given in our youth—distinction (as opposed to *status*) is discouraged among us. And the general blurring of our older standards, which in many cases have been discredited without being replaced or radically improved, extends not only to morals but even to our language in which, as Dwight MacDonald has pointed out,[54] important distinctions or shadings of meaning are, with

notably Melville, in *Pierre,* and Hawthorne after his return from abroad—succumbed to what we would probably call crises of alienation: a profound uncertainty, a sense of the pointlessness of their own lives. Vernon Parrington said of Melville: "Lifelong he was lacerated by the coldly moral in his environment and harassed by the crudely practical. . . . The white gleams of mysticism that now and then lighted up his path died out and left him in darkness. Life could not meet the demands he laid on it, certainly not life in American in the eighteen fifties; the malady lay deeper than Greeley thought; it lay in the futility of life itself. . . . Cooper was a critic whom America could understand. . . . Melville it could not understand, and it turned away and ignored him. . . . He was troubled about life, and not about things. . . . Perhaps it was well enough that his generation . . . called him mad . . . this maligner of all tribal fetishes." *Main Currents in American Thought* (Harcourt, Brace, and World, 1954), II, 249 ff.

54. See, for instance, his review of the Revised Standard Version of the Bible, in the *New Yorker,* November 14, 1953, or his more recent and more devastating review of Webster's Third International Dictionary, in the same magazine. Both pieces are included in MacDonald's *Against the American Grain* (Random House, 1962).

See also George Steiner, *Language and Silence* (Atheneum, 1967), who suggests a parallel between the decay of language in this century and the loss, in modern music, of "a certain grammar or articulation in time" (*ibid.,* p. 23). He describes Hemingway roughly as I have done here, contrasting his sparse, mannered style with Joyce's: ". . . The treasures which Joyce brought back to language . . . remain piled glitteringly around his own labors. They have not passed into currency. They have caused none of that general quickening of the spirit of speech which follows on Spenser and Marlowe. . . Joyce's performance is a monument rather than a living force."

This phenomenon shows quite clearly the power of the *Geist.* Spenser and Marlowe came at a time when the "I" of western man was expanding. Joyce occurs on

official acquiescence, being lost. These are preconditions of revolution in the modern sense, creating a vacuum in which the power of the Executive expands of itself. By such criteria, America may be the most revolutionary of Western nations.

Unlike Germany, we are revolutionary not from the bottom up but simultaneously at almost all social levels, as the result of a slow shift in consensus in the direction of "modernity"—which is to say, toward an ethic of success or nihilistic self-help and a greatly diminished imaginative self or "consciousness." While that shift has caused some strain within classes and tends to divide us more along age lines than caste lines, it also acts, true to Anglo-Saxon tradition, to preclude any sudden *bouleversement* of the existing order. It is these features of our present national life which give it its air of general perturbation, but also reduce activist groups like the Birchites to insignificance. Joseph McCarthy, even communism in the worst of the Great Depression, failed here for the same essential reason, as did Huey Long, who, for all the alarm he caused, was never more than a parish bad boy.

It would be a mistake however to conclude from such facts that what occurred in Germany cannot occur here. Our revolution differs greatly from the European in form and tempo; but in principle and in its ultimate consequences, it may be identical. Both are simply an end result of psychological changes which, since the end of the eighteenth century, have been taking place throughout the Western world.

Since the 1930's America has passed from a state of unarmed isolation into one of permanent "preparedness," if not of nearly permanent war. In this, we strikingly resemble the ancient Romans, who came to the period of the Punic Wars as a relatively simple upstanding people, whose very virtues, added to a certain crudity of mind, may peculiarly have suited them to become the last great power of classical times. With them, what had been a culture became a civilization; and what had been a diversity of city-states became one world, dominated by a few colossi. In a passage comparing Russia and America, de Tocqueville[55] foresaw something of the kind for the world of the twentieth century. It is hard

---

the downslope of the same curve of inner development. He has consequently been without real issue—"a monument"—whereas Spenser and Marlowe led on, quite naturally, almost inevitably, to the brilliant literary culture which Trevelyan describes in 17th century England. (See above p. 77.)

55. De Tocqueville, *Democracy in America,* I, 558.

to escape the conclusion that what he and the historiographers, in their different ways, anticipated is today coming true. Like the Romans, from sheer force of circumstance, if not from quite similar specific causes, we may now be entering a phase of expansionism whose momentum we neither understand nor are prepared to resist.[56]

To rephrase Santayana's remark, quoted at the end of the previous chapter: It is not because we have forgotten the past that we may be about to repeat it. The meaning of the past has never been clear to us. It is possible that some of the reasons for the "cyclical" form of history are to be found in the principles of psychic structure and of mind-brain relations which I have given in rough outline here. One may still wonder if understanding of this sort, coming so late and confronting so immense a phenomenon, will be of any real use. The irony of Western civilization is that it has become more informed and more technically capable—and therefore, one would suppose, more in control of its own future—than any human society has ever been. But in the same era in which we were reaching that level of collective virtuosity, the price paid in attrition of the individual may have been too high. As a consequence the moral and intellectual resources which we might have brought to bear on our situation may now be too dispersed, too little the property of any *one,* to result in the new sort of self-understanding and the new consensus which are needed. In short, the time when self-understanding might have taken effect may for us already have gone by. The remaining question is whether, given man's nature as it seems to be, there was ever such a time or is ever likely to be one.

56. The recent public outcry against the war in Viet Nam suggests that the victory of the New Order in this country will not come without a struggle. Unfortunately it is perhaps as much the fact that we failed to win in Viet Nam, as the fact of the war itself, which has aroused public sentiment. Few protested our interventions in Guatemala or the Dominican Republic.

*Chapter IX*

---

CONCLUSION

SOME years ago, Kurt Lewin conducted an experiment involving two task groups of school children, one organized on "liberal" lines and the other on "totalitarian." Two of his findings are pertinent here. One was that the liberal group turned out to be the more productive of the two. The second was that it proved more difficult to switch the totalitarian group to a liberal regime than to turn the liberals into totalitarians. Essentially what this experiment may tell us is something about the relative strengths of the two major subdivisions of the Id. That part related to sex, ferocity, and the milder emotions of parenthood—presumably favored in the liberals—is more related to productiveness, here perhaps conducing to a "spontaneous" willingness in the individual which rises to occasions involving the group.[1] By contrast, that part of the Id mediating fear and self-protective action impairs the productive and spontaneous in us. Given an external imperative, it *drives* us to co-operate, but also kills our drive to do so when such imperatives are lacking.[2] And it is apparently harder to unseat once it has become established as the controlling division of the instinctive self (that is, dominant more or most of the time, as it may have been in the totalitarians). These differences in a rough way parallel those between liberal and totalitarian nations. They also illustrate the principle according to which the rule of fear and dog-

1. A study of "gifted" university students showed them to be, among other things, less "authoritarian" than the average. *Science,* Vol. 133 (1961), pp. 1981 ff.
2. That is, in the case of anxiety, edginess (and related feelings such as intense competitiveness, or intense awe of the tribe), which may for various reasons have become habitual. People of this psychic type comprise the large minority of "compulsives" in our society, their outstanding attribute being not merely a tendency to overwork at what they feel *must* be done (for their own security) but a proportioned inability to do, or give themselves to, the casual and the unexpected. The physiology of emergency reactions, which I have gone into at length in my first book, quite plausibly accounts for these traits.

matism has greater inertia or social viability than does the rule of the milder emotions and reason. Hence, as we have long known, tyrannies of the South American type tend to be endlessly self-renewing, whereas representative government has been rare in history and in all cases short-lived.

One difficulty, of course, is that the distinction between liberal and totalitarian societies is far from sharp. In democracies there has always been a considerable majority in reality nearly powerless and controlled by fear (of unemployment, the police, and so on)—hence "totalitarian-ized"—whereas in absolutist states there have often been favored classes, like the scholars and scientists of prerevolutionary Germany who in varying degrees escaped authoritarian rule and its psychic consequences and were hence "liberal."

In contrast to autocracies,[3] which tend to be well organized against attack, if not themselves inclined to it, democracies, by their nature, are obliged to live in double jeopardy. Being inclined to peaceableness and trade (and accordingly prosperous), they invite attack. And because given to a businesslike practicality of mind, they succumb perhaps even more readily than do some autocracies to an "enlightenment" which destroys their earlier ideals and moral convictions and so, in the psychic sense meant here, proletarianizes all classes. Particularly when attacked in this latter stage they may, through the very efforts required of them in self-defense, emerge not only victorious but remade in the image of their attackers. If the conclusion from Lewin's experiment is to be trusted, it follows that that might be the case: that having defended themselves successfully, the liberal nations might find it difficult or impossible to return to their prior condition, and that not from practical causes only. In fact, of the three which survived World War II, France has since reverted to a qualified absolutism in the person of de Gaulle, while the United States has emerged as not only the most heavily armed but also (in foreign eyes) the most stubbornly warlike of the Western powers.

For us, the question is what is to prevent that process from going to its logical conclusion. Given a world almost wholly totalitarian—technologically minded and profoundly competitive as we ourselves are, and already in limited possession of the Bomb—the problem is no

---

3. Like that of Frederick the Great of Prussia, or of the Kaiser in 1914.

longer that of the desirability of empire. Now that intense nationalism has become nearly universal (witness that of even the tiny new African nations), it may be that empire is not really possible for anyone; whereas the blind attempt at it may very well result in a holocaust. Worst of all is the fact that the attempt, when made, *will* be blind, because almost no one in power, East or West, is disposed to look honestly at or try to change the psychological realities out of which modern revolution and its subsequent imperial phases spring. The result is that all are driven forward with the same momentum, and a major collision seems inevitable. This situation is as much due to ourselves—*vide* our recent undertakings in Viet Nam, the Dominican Republic, Guatemala,[4] Iran, Spain, and Germany—as it is to communist-bloc powers, with theirs in Cuba, middle Europe, the Near East, Egypt, and Southeast Asia. If the problems underlying this development were realistic ones—if it were purely a question of *Lebensraum* and of adjusting certain gross inequalities in distribution of the world's goods—there might be more chance of striking a reasonable compromise and so of maintaining peace by old-fashioned balance-of-power politics. A number of men of good will in this country still try to see the situation in that light. And indeed, as some recent evidence suggests, the Russian revolution, if left to itself, might move in the direction of a more moderate, more liberal system of government with foreign policy to match. For in Russia, which seems historically to be a "pseudomorph,"[5] there may

---

4. Few people in this country seem to be aware that in the early 1950's the Eisenhower administration engineered a *Putsch* in Guatemala, ousting the remains of Arbenz liberalism and establishing a regime of the more familiar malleable type. Anyone reading our own press at the time and not, say, the Manchester *Guardian* could easily have fallen into that error. See the Manchester *Guardian Weekly,* June 24, 1954, p. 3, and August 19, 1954, p. 12, from which the following is quoted:

"We must call a spade a spade. The Guatemala War was an American intervention. . . . There are still to be seen in the airport of Las Mercedes some Thunderbolt fighters that had been sent for the . . . war. This intervention constitutes a grave setback for America's 'good neighbor' policy. *And it has given the Soviet Union a moral victory that country could not have won for itself so quickly"* (italics mine)—one which may have helped in the Soviets' political conquest of Cuba. Johnson has characteristically continued this brilliant policy with his intervention in the Dominican Republic. It still comes as a genuine surprise to many Americans that we are regarded abroad as an aggressive power, and one usually in alliance with the most corrupt and repressive elements in the countries unfortunate enough to become our "clients."

5. A pseudomorph is, roughly, a young or relatively new culture which falls

still exist a considerable well of the old faith and the old idealism, of the sort which sustained the men of our own Middle Ages through centuries of misgovernment. In the easing of state intolerance and thought control which has occurred in Russia since the regimes of Stalin and Khrushchev, that spirit may be reasserting itself and may in turn have contributed to the rift which has opened beween Russia and the still militant Chinese.

Past differences notwithstanding, our own most logical ally, in this era, is probably the Russians.[6] Our spheres of influence are on the whole geographically remote from each other. We are not yet strong competitors for particular segments of the world market. (For example, our biggest competitor in cameras and electronic equipment is the Japanese, whom we have licked by partially joining.) And provided Russia and the United States were solidly united, they would act as a formidable check both on Chinese expansionism and on any recrudescence of German power in Europe. Johnson's decision to expand the war in Viet Nam shows clearly how far we are from adopting any such policy or indeed from understanding our position at all. In the long run, to keep that corner of Asia from governing itself as it likes, which probably means by a revolutionary committee rule similar to the Chinese, will be impossible except at the perpetual risk of world war. If the object is to insure a permanent base of operations aimed at

under the influence of an older, more powerful neighbor to the point of dressing itself up, as it were, in foreign disguises. The same can, of course, happen to tribal societies or fossil civilizations such as the Chinese. Japan is a quite successful pseudomorph of the latter type; Russia, of the former. The Russian pseudomorphosis began with Peter the Great and was long resisted by pan-Slavs like Dostoevski, who should not be regarded as nationalist in the modern Western sense.

6. The presumption here being that international relations will continue indefinitely to be based on a would-be realism or, as an English Prime Minister of the last century put it, on the proposition that nations do not have friends, they only have interests. The *volte-face* in policy suggested might however be less easily accomplished in this country than in Russia, for the reason that manipulated public opinion in democracies has a real and lasting effect, via the ballot box, on their conduct of foreign affairs. The result is often to give policies which are no longer workable a dangerous longevity. Totalitarian states, by contrast, enjoy the greatest freedom since in them public opinion has no direct influence on government except under extraordinary circumstances. Even then (as happened during Stalin's tenure) it may be punished by massacre rather than deferred to as a legitimate political force.

China, the advantage of such a base may be canceled in advance by the fact that we may well force Russia back into the Chinese camp by our attempt to establish it—making it likely that at such time as we do come to grips with the Chinese, we will have lost an ally and added an adversary we can ill afford. And if the 1966-67 Viet Nam campaign has been merely an attempt to save face—first the nation's, then the President's—it becomes an absurdity outright. A rich country of nearly two hundred millions, spending over a quarter of its annual budget to support an army approaching half a million men and a formidable naval and air force, has proved itself unable to suppress an ill-equipped colonial nation not one-sixth its size—and done so in full awareness that this enterprise was likely at any time to erupt into a general war capable of wiping out half of mankind.

The object of this brief review is to illustrate the sort of "realism" to which men of action are prone. It argues, I think, that an ability to rise in the peck-order—that is, Darwinian superiority—is not to be confused with intelligence. Quite apart from the thick-skinned cruelty of actions such as we have recently carried out in Viet Nam, it is doubtful if they have any practical value or even partially repay the damage done to the people required to prosecute them, to say nothing of those upon whom they are visited. It is a truism that wars—modern ones in particular—seldom earn anything over their cost. If anything, the contrary. Their cost, even to the victor, is astronomical and far more than economic. The fact that we continue to fight them illustrates two points: that instinct, especially survival instinct, does not necessarily produce behavior which is really adaptive; and that those "practical" men who habitually control human affairs are for the most part definable as men of instinct, whose acts are apt to be as blindly destructive as those whom they rule will permit. If it demonstrates nothing else, nine-tenths of history supports the truth of these truisms. The question for us is what effect decades of this kind of "realism" are likely to have on us, even should we escape the retribution of nuclear war.

It is obvious that many of our young people, and among them some of the best, are bitterly opposed to what we are now doing. They are repelled not only by Johnsonian *Realpolitik* but by much else in our national life, apparently including business.[7] One senses in them an

7. According to the *Wall Street Journal*, November 10, 1964, p. 1: "At college after college, an increasing percentage of graduates is shunning business

inchoate conviction that life can be better—must be made so, before it is too late—and their impulse is clearly to condemn and wash their hands of the whole adult world. There is reason for hope in their rebellious-ness. Nothing quite like it seems to have occurred in late Roman times (or even in Germany, just prior to Hitler). For all that our "modern-ity" has cost us, there have also perhaps been what experimental psy-chologists would call "savings" (or idealists, Progress). In the new "humanism" of the young, there is, though most of them would heat-edly deny it, a remainder of the idealism which once made our culture great. At peace demonstrations and sit-ins, in the half-illiterate "pro-test" songs and the pathetic posters reading Love, one hears a faint echo of the Christian belief in salvation through goodness to which the saints and reformers of our past clung with such tenacity. Nor can it be said, as it now often is, that that tenacity was wholly without result. For modern liberalism, "the noblest cry that has ever resounded on this planet," is its direct descendant. And despite the cheap abuse which it too has lately attracted and the perversion it has undergone, liberalism is the foundation stone of our society: the source of such institution-alized decency and political freedom as, for the moment, we still enjoy. The humanism of our children may be one of its last manifestations.

For the same young people who protest against the Viet Nam War or, as whites, march in protest against segregation, who try to be less "phony" than we have been and less cold, are also sadly shapeless and compromised. Their intellectual leadership is absurd—self-consciously so (as in the Theater of the Absurd). And without the mental resources really to understand themselves or their predicament, they easily slip into a cultism which invites, not coherent reform or rebellion, but tem-porary relief through indulgence of the Id. To see cruelty as "honest" or "just" (as one of them recently described it to me), to seek God in LSD, is neither promising nor new. It is simply a short cut: instant help for the frustrated and diminished. The hippies (like the earlier

careers in favor of such fields as teaching, scientific research, law and public service. Amherst College says 48 per cent of its alumni are businessmen, but fewer than 20 per cent of recent graduates have been entering business. Only 14 per cent of last spring's Harvard graduates plan business careers, down from 39 per cent five years ago. . . . The situation is . . . serious enough to worry the business community—one reason being that the decline of interest in business appears to be most marked at . . . private institutions noted in the past for contributing more than their share of talent to top executive suites."

hipsterism in the jazz world) represent, in this sense, an underground religion of the new Rome. One feels that the indignation and residual idealism of our young are almost fated to drain themselves away in a licentious revivalism, because our own impoverishment, which they so detest, has nonetheless been taken a stage further in them.[8] As a result, they produce no saints or prophets, no clear program to oppose to ours, but are merely feared and misunderstood and in some degree baited into the very excesses for which we blame them.[9] They are, in a part of themselves, struggling *not* to become the frightened mob which Mommsen describes in the time of the Marian and Sullan revolutions (page 110). "Perplexed as to their very selves" and beguiled by joke philosophers like Marshall McLuhan and Timothy Leary, who make the breakdown of reason and the release of the ancient phantoms of the Id appear novel and healing,[10] they have a little more to turn to than the Roman mob did, but not much.

8. Jazz, which we still speak of as a popular art and which, for a time (between 1935 and 1960), had a considerable following among white young people, has since lost out to rock 'n roll. One reason may be that in its astonishingly rapid evolution, jazz simply outgrew the musical intelligence of its public.

The most significant feature of rock 'n roll, next to its wooden rhythms and extreme poverty of lines and chord structure, is its lack of improvisation. As in life—even in lives supposedly dedicated to rebellion and the identity principle—no *one* stands out. The music is full of calculated effects—weird costumes, borrowings from Eastern music, gimmicks of lighting, electronic sound oddities—everything but the real individuals and real excellence which are still to be found in the dwindling world of jazz. As such, rock 'n roll is a sort of tonal McLuhanism—a too-faithful representative of the New Mentality.

9. In the teen-age disturbances which developed on Hollywood's Sunset Strip in 1966, a precipitating factor, according to some reports, was the hostility of middle-aged bystanders, a number of whom apparently came to jeer or to gape with obvious dislike at the crowds of young people.

10. George Steiner, in *Language and Silence* (Atheneum, 1967), pp. 251 ff., makes these points about McLuhan: "The McLuhan cult is characteristic of those confidence tricks of 'high journalism' which, perhaps more than any other force, deafen and cheapen the life of ideas." Steiner then speaks of the "nervous cheapness of McLuhan's prose," going on to say: "Many of the irritants, many of the crudities [of his prose] . . . are strategic. . . . It is precisely part of McLuhan's achievement that we should be irked and affronted by the strangeness or inadequacy of his resources. . . . He . . . is one of those shapers of the present mood who seem to mark a transition from the classic forms of Cartesian order to a new, as yet very difficult to define . . . syntax of experience."

So far as I know, no one has pointed out the fact that McLuhan's notion of the "mosaic," or instant total perception, as a substitute for old-fashioned serial appraisal (as in reading or listening to music or scanning a picture), is physiological

If their revolt fails, as it may do, what then? What will *their* children be like? Where, morally and intellectually, can we expect our civilization to go next? Supposing that in a gross sense we survive the wars we find ourselves inwardly as well as outwardly driven to wage, will we, a few decades hence, have anything like the society we once knew or would have wanted? Are there any now, among the millions of self-absorbed specialized intelligences which make up our republic, disposed to consider these questions seriously or able to bring to them the perspective and the determination to act which they require? These, for us, are the fundamental issues, the point upon which the whole of the discussion in this book converges.

The basic question is not "Can we survive?" Physically we may. The question is whether man, in sufficient numbers, can be improved to the point that we are no longer forced to think habitually and primarily in terms of brute survival and therefore of force and advantage. Man's problem is once and for all to break the grip which instinct, in the shape of survival behavior, has always had on his politics and so on his history, forcing him, with each successive rise from animality, back into animality again—into interminable eras of tyranny and pseudo culture and self-repetition, that black interregnum of the spirit which centuries ago closed over the classical world and China and Islam and may even now be closing over us.

Whether man in general is improvable, specifically in the direction of the Christian-Wordsworthian ideal of rationality and mildness,

---

nonsense. Both the central mechanism of attention and the peripheral mechanisms of sense, which depend heavily on "lateral inhibition," make serial perception almost unavoidable. Given that there are very stringent limits on the number of items we can take in at a time in one or more sense modalities, it would seem to follow that the "mosaic" is something that emerges after the fact: a serially elaborated mental construct, but not a possible alternative mode of apprehending the world directly. A series of psychophysical experiments could settle this point, if anyone seriously feels it needs settling.

My own view of McLuhan is that he has elaborated a mystique which justifies to the age its increasing incapacity to understand or to continue the rational literate tradition it has inherited. He is a book burner whose appeal is to those millions like himself who would have done, once and for all, with forms of conscious order which they find meaningless and oppressive. It is thus quite significant that McLuhan himself writes a debased, repetitive, contradictory English and uses a technique of deliberate irresponsibility reminiscent of the style of argument which Sartre describes in the anti-Semite (see above, Chapter VII, footnote 16).

comes down to a question of how his mental and instinctive functions are organized—which in turn reduces to the way in which these functions may be "represented" in the brain. C. J. Herrick, perhaps the greatest of our earlier neuroanatomists, wrote:

> Our mode of life has been achieved through eons of evolutionary change, during which the conservative and relatively stable organization of the brain stem has been supplemented and amplified by the addition of cortical apparatus with more labile patterns of action, resulting in greater freedom of adjustment to the exigencies of life. In all behavior there is a substrate of patterns of great antiquity.[11]

Much of the work done in ethology and physiological psychology since Herrick wrote that passage confirms what he said. There can also be no doubt as to the fact that, in standard biological terms, man has been a huge success. All other species, and many millions of his own kind, have bowed to him because of the superiority of his "cortical apparatus" as the servant of adaptation. The paradox now is that that same apparatus, having produced the Bomb, may be insufficient to prevent him from using it and so, in a last Wagnerian burst of "survival" behavior, wiping himself out. What this paradox means essentially is that *the* adaptive problem for man is no longer external—the "exigencies of life," in the sense Herrick meant—but internal. Can the same cortical apparatus which has worked prodigies of conquest and organization in the outside world turn its powers inward and control or radically reshape the now *un*adaptive Id? Can human intelligence have a significant effect on that "substrate of patterns of great antiquity" to which we owe our present peril?[12]

In earlier chapters of this book I suggested certain basic principles according to which mind, in parallel with the neocortex, might gain varying degrees of control over the (subcortical) Id. Even supposing those principles may have been stated correctly, we still have no way of deciding whether it might take special endowment—that is, a better than average native intelligence and possibly a feebler than average "survival" system—to become radically free in mind and proportionately "human." So far as the salvation of mankind is concerned, this

11. C. J. Herrick, *The Brain of the Tiger Salamander* (University of Chicago Press, 1948), p. 122.

12. And not from the bomb only, but from Eros, who, to rephrase Freud, is "putting forth his strength" in the shape of millions too many babies.

question—to which conservatives and liberals, both, have always known the answer[13]—is crucial. It is really the question addressed in Snow's discussion of the Two Cultures. Is the ideal of Universal Man simply too much for all but a tiny minority? Can it not possibly be realized, even in principle, by large numbers? Can a man, for instance, gifted with no ear for music or eye for painting or head for figures, also develop no modicum of understanding of the arts or finance, no tolerance or respect for those who practice them, as offsets to his natural antipathy or indifference to what is beyond him? Common sense says that such a conclusion, which was not Snow's, goes too far. It entirely depends on the man, and then not on his general intelligence so much as on his basic "set" or attitude: what we sometimes call his character. There is many an ungifted average man who is generous in his feelings toward those with abilities he himself lacks and receptive to what they may have to tell him. Conversely, there is many a highly gifted and intelligent man who is overweening and jealous or coldly indifferent in the face of abilities equal to or greater than his own. In short, the ideal of Universal Man comes down not to a drive for intellectual power, but rather to a hope of many-sided understanding without prejudice; and this in turn springs not from native intelligence as such nor from practical ambition, but from a moral and emotional position deliberately adopted—the position of the man determined to see the world as clearly as may be in the light of his own receptive good will, which is to say, the world undistorted by "interest" in the more usual creature sense. He seeks to free himself from the narrow vision and the destructiveness which almost inevitably go with "interests" and competition—that is, with survival behavior, or dominance of the primal emergency system. All of Christian morality aims

13. A survey of scientists disclosed that in youth they tended to be Democrats and environmentalists, while from forty-five on they are predominantly Republicans and hereditarians. In this country there is a type of liberalism—really a covert anti-racism—which almost refuses to accept genetics as applied to man. This extreme environmentalism was the subject of a heated correspondence in *Science* several years ago, one writer alleging that facts had been suppresed or misrepresented in a UNESCO report so as to support the "liberal" biological position. Hereditarians, for their part, have always known human nature was past improving, being fixed in the genes; although of course it can be damaged by the admixture of inferior strains or by "coddling" of the unfit. The evidence for either of these extreme views is by no means clear, which hardly matters, since they were not arrived at by reason in the first place.

essentially a re-equilibrating man's instinctive life so as to shift it away from the competitive and toward the affectionate, the aspiration to "universality" being only one of the consequences of that shift. As such, it requires that man be in-formed, certainly, but a high degree of special intelligence (and, as Snow points out, most higher intelligence is also somewhat special) is *not* required. On the contrary, the more gifted one is in certain ways, the more, ideally, one should guard against being carried away by one's talents—the traditional Christian would say into a state of "sin"[14] or "error" (pride, narrowness, vainglory, jealousy of others, egoism, misuse of one's gifts in the interests of success, and so on).

In fact, there may be a clear physiological basis for these notions. For the man who endeavors to admit as much of the world as he can to disinterested awareness is, to the degree that he succeeds, in-forming himself as few ordinary men do. Given certain starting principles by which to interpret what he sees, he may then go on, by his deliberate generosity of spirit, to take in much more and thus complete himself: achieve "centrality." In physiological terms, he is constructing an edifice of abstract memories whose logic is not *only* that of diverse island domains—his field or special interests—but ultimately reflects or "unifies" nearly all that he perceives. Whatever his native intelligence may have been to start with, it, and his control over the Id, are apt to be enormously enlarged by the process I have just described. That process is what is meant by integration—becoming "integrated"—or, in older terms, becoming wise.[15] By the same argument, be he never so able, the specialist who washes his hands of much of reality, who encourages in himself, as many moderns do, a coldness and dislike toward the "outside" world, a fear of the alien and of useless intrusions upon his time, may be crippling himself far more than he knows. Beginning

14. "Poverty in itself mattered nothing; what [St.] Francis wanted was poverty of pride. . . . Against riches or against all external and visible vanity, rules and laws could be easily enforced . . . but against spiritual pride the soul is defenceless, and of all its forms the subtlest and the meanest is the pride of intellect." (Henry Adams, *Mont St. Michel and Chartres* [Houghton Mifflin, 1933], p. 330.) That same pride, rampant today in the special worlds of science and scholarship, if not in the worlds of business and state, is bringing an ironic retribution; namely, liquidation of intellect itself.

15. How many of us, including scholars and scientists, could be called wise? How often do we even use the words *wise* or *wisdom* except in an empty old-fashioned sort of tribute?

as a tree with all but a few limbs pruned back, he continues the pruning and becomes a grotesque, often a fragile, one, mysteriously at the mercy of hurricanes arising in the "unconscious." It is not merely the conventional specialist, but modern man in general, who is apt to be self-destroyed in this sense,[16] and that by a kind of privacy, a dedicated

16. A point which I have not so far gone into is that man, in failing to develop as he should in mind, may also show some stunting of his instinctive self. The reason is that the "higher" one looks in mammalian evolution, the greater seems to be the role played by learning or memory in the organization of instinctive behavior. For example, cats emerging from kittenhood have a number of (apparently innate) bits of motor behavior which they use, in no particular sequence, in their play. At this stage, a cat will harmlessly frolic with a mouse, chase it, seize it gently by the neck, possibly even groom it. Somewhat later, the combination of physical maturation and slowly acquired learning will cause many of these same motor mechanisms suddenly to knit up into a unit: the cat's method of pursuing and seizing its prey.

There are in the literature other experimental reports illustrating the sporadic, disorganized, almost accidental nature of sexual behavior in immature primates. Experience, even in forms "lower" than primates, is evidently important to later sexuality, as shown by the fact that cats which have mated before castration tend to show mating behavior afterward, whereas those which were virginal before tend to remain so afterward. (Hormonal factors cannot be ruled out here; however, they might also be regarded as forming a physiological unit with related learning processes, in that learning stimulates hormonal development and conversely.)

The process just described amounts to a functional differentiation of the instinctive self, in the course of which sexuality and ferocity come to be clearly separate, the male animal seldom or never attacking a female of the same species. The courting displays of birds, while quite similar to their threat displays (to other males of the same species), become distinct from them in that they do not lead to accidental attacks on the female by the male.

The differentiation of human sexuality, or its divorce from the brutal and ferocious in us, reaches a peak in eras in which the differentiation of intellect and imagination are also approaching an apogee. It is not accidental that the troubadours' ideal of love appears at a time when the intellectual and artistic growth of the West is gathering great momentum (soon manifest in such figures as Petrarch or the remarkable Ramón Lull, who anticipated Leibniz' notions of a universal logical calculus and modern ideas of a universal computer or general problem solver).

A reverse trend, in sexual mores as well as in art or intellect, seems to have developed in the twentieth century, sex in modern mass man reverting to a relatively undifferentiated function, closely fused with ferocity or a brutal "taking advantage." Much of the present psychopathology of sex may be explainable on this basis; for instance, many rape killings or homosexual murders and many sexual eccentricities, including oral sexual practices, representing the persistence of a very early Freudian stage (the "oral") into supposed maturity (or the "genital" stage). If, as I believe, sexuality, ferocity, and alimentary functions comprise subdivisions of

stick-to-business attitude, which he regards as protective and cultivates as a virtue.

By contrast, the striking thing about the few really good people one has known is not so much that they are intelligent. Some are not, in fact, extraordinarily so. What strikes one is that their powers are *available* to them in a way often not true of the more gifted, many of whom, in our era, are felled by unaccountable inner forces and go sterile before their time.[17]

If the foregoing is a reasonably accurate summary of the mechanics of individual salvation, there would seem to be at least a hope that to achieve it we may not require a higher average of native intelligence than we now have. *En bloc* we may not *necessarily* be condemned to live in submission to that "substrate of [behavioral] patterns of great antiquity" which Herrick speaks of.

What is more to the point—if not fully as serious as any innate limitation might be—is that we carry into the present an immense majority of the psychically stunted or unreclaimed. Neglected since the beginning of history, and today, at best, poorly and superficially educated, this majority has recently suffered a loss of religious faith which is in no way compensated by the special attitudes and competences which a few (or, in America, quite large numbers) have developed, as it were, in place of the older beliefs. This last is the essence of the

a main division of the instincts (emergency functions comprising the other main division) the psychic regression of modern man involves first a progressive failure of the I to develop, a similar failure of the subdivisions of "normal survival" instinct to differentiate properly at maturity, and last a primacy of emergency instinctive functions, as it were, by default. The result is Man the Anxious Amorph, whose sexual behavior is frequently impaired by his persistent fears and frequently an odd fusion of the brutal (or "sadomasochistic") and the alimentary (that is, excessively "oral"—whence the vulgar expression for fellatio: "eating it").

17. Just as, I believe, it could be shown that a century ago in the sciences the same fundamental progress we are making today was being made by a far smaller number of people on infinitesimal budgets, so now we require an enormous literature of the mediocre to produce a Sinclair Lewis or a Hemingway. And even the best of our writers, having exhausted their childhood recollections or run through their stock of dominant ideas tend to go dry after their first few books, though not, unfortunately, to stop writing. Both Lewis and Hemingway seem in middle age to have led rather haunted lives and to have written themselves out relatively early. One thinks of similar casualties in other fields; for instance, painting and mathematics. These are, of course, only impressions. What is needed, and what someone will surely come up with, is a statistical technique for comparing past and present creative efficiency.

transition from the state of culture to that of civilization, described earlier. And just as the culture was never really the property of more than a few, civilization, whether widely shared, as it is in this country, or narrowly, as it was in Germany, completes by its very virtues the destruction of the earlier culture at all social levels. As an example, the real object of education—which is at bottom not only a practical but also a *moral* process, an effort to raise children in a certain ideal of unity and clarity of mind—is becoming totally incomprehensible to us. Most of our teachers are as practical, as specialized, and as much careerists as the rest of us. Besides getting children already ill- or under-prepared by early parental example, they do not then set them a materially different one, but simply complete the work Mommy and Daddy began.

It is because we no longer understand the ideal which underlay the study of classical languages that these are now being abandoned. And because many other items still in our curricula—for instance, courses in great poetry or other humanities—represent the same ideal, much of the literature and history that earlier generations seemed to absorb and retain with ease makes a hardly detectable imprint on the minds of our young today—is barely mastered in school or college and 90 per cent forgotten ten years later. The underlying reason, I suspect, is this:

Children are notoriously sensitive to what their parents and other exemplars really believe or take seriously and what they do not. Much of the in-forming, official or incidental, which takes place in the critical learning periods of childhood may be subject to this sort of sincerity-testing. There tends to be a seeding of young minds with those principles, concepts, and so on, which they perceive to be "real" (effective, treated with respect by their elders) and, equally important, an exclusion of those precepts perceived to be just words (not respected, honored in the breach). Much that once constituted our tradition now falls under the latter head, and is discarded by the young, almost before they or we know it, as "unreal." The psychological consequence for them is that in mind or "consciousness" large tracts—larger perhaps with each generation—are left fallow in the critical formative epochs of youth, while only certain tracts become well seeded and so capable of further cultivation later on.[18] In physiological terms, the failure early

---

18. Hence, as I mentioned earlier, our "mechanical-mindedness," which is not

in life of the "seeding" process—the formation, in outline, of an adequately "rounded" or inclusive abstract memory system—results later in adolescents or young adults who are in many directions ineducable. Quite literally they cannot "see" the value of ideas and activities traditionally considered important and are hence not "motivated," as we say, to study or truly assimilate much that their forebears regarded as staples of the educated life. This defect shows signs of extending to more practical matters, such as awareness of current events[19] or mastery of the rudiments of English grammar (let alone style). It is quite remarkable, particularly in view of the class from which these boys probably came, that college freshmen, in this era of supposedly higher educational standards, could write:

"A change from the optimastic view of the individual man as put forth in transcendentic philosophy to the pessimistic view of man, frought with invalid morals living a superficial life with no direction such as T. S. Eliot flitting buy-eyed from Antwerp to Brussels to London."

---

a *native* ability suddenly sprung up in Americans, but the result of certain aptitudes enormously expanded by default, at the sacrifice of others.

19. A number of surveys have shown that not only the Man in the Street but many high-school and college graduates are astonishingly ignorant of foreign affairs and even of the personnel and major departments of our own government. See, for instance, George Gallup's book *The Miracle Ahead* (Harper and Row, 1964). Nor is the situation necessarily much better among those with the highest of Higher Education. Some years ago H. J. Fuller, Professor of Plant Physiology at the University of Illinois, tested fifteen graduate students (working in the fields of horticulture, agronomy, botany, and zoology) for their general cultural knowledge. Of the fifteen, only six gave an adequate answer when asked to define or identify the Renaissance; only five had clear ideas about the Reformation or knew who Voltaire was; seven had heard of Plato, but only one, of the Medicis; two were up on Magna Carta and on the Monroe Doctrine. Only the Koran and the Treaty of Versailles were correctly identified by more than half (ten; eleven). *Scientific American* (December, 1954).

A much larger study, involving twenty questions concerning art and twenty concerning science and covering 3,000 professors and students, was conducted by Kenneth Richmond of Glasgow University. The *highest* averages for any subgroup were 7.3 in the arts and 10 (correct answers out of 20) in science; the lowest (made by students at a women's training college for teachers) was 3.2 in the arts and 3.7 in the sciences.

According to *Science,* Vol. 134 (1961), p. 1393, "those who do well in science are on the average more one-sided than those who do well in the arts; and few do well in both fields. . . . It is not clear," the editorialist continues "whether the pattern of one-sidedness and the attitudes that accompany it are set so early that broader education could not correct the imbalance."

Or: "When Twain was writing *Huckleberry Finn* he decided to implement the voyage as a cohesive catalyst. Twain used a general local. Faulkner has a restrictive local, and Thoreau wrote for everybody in the universal."[20] (One wonders what Thoreau,[21] never blindly optimastic, might have felt on seeing this little summary of his work.)

Professor Thorp, who collected these and other dreadful examples of "No-English," goes on to give samples of the sort of jargon to which his English students are subjected in their science courses, with the strong implication that science and practical idioms such as ad-writing have undermined their literary intelligence. In a sense that is true. In a deeper sense, freshmen, scientists, and ad-writers are all simply variations of the same phenomenon—namely, of the erosion of our stock of principles or abstract memories to the point that mind itself is becoming seriously hampered, not only in the special fields still open to it[22] but in that of everyday communication.[23] The parallel of this condition, in our emotional lives, as I have mentioned several times, is an

20. From Willard Thorp, The Well of English Defiled, or Why Johnny Can't Write, *Princeton Alumni Weekly*, September 26, 1958, pp. 6–9.

21. In Chapter IX, footnote 28, I quoted a passage from Thoreau, a part of which is apropos here: "There is in this town (Concord) . . . no taste for the best of for very good books, even in English literature, *whose words all can read and spell*" (italics mine). Elsewhere in the same essay, he begs us to sacrifice building one real bridge and instead "throw one arch at least over the darker gulf of ignorance that surrounds us." The task still stands.

22. As a further example, I have on file a sizable correspondence with a young physiological psychologist in California who has done good experimental work and has what I think are some promising theoretical ideas. He is, however, all but incoherent in print, to the degree that an influential psychologist whom I know refuses to read his work. At this point, command of language ceases to be a question of "frills" and becomes one of professional survival.

23. One can find almost anywhere the sort of writing Professor Thorp objects to. "While intensifying the loyalty of students, faculty and alumni to the common purpose, new sparks were lighted." This pawky nonsense was the work, not of an undergraduate, but of Yale's President Kingman Brewster, in his report of 1963–64. A former President of Yale, Whitney Griswold, said in his report of 1952–1953: "Before me as I write is the annual report of the dean of one of our professional schools which complains of 'widespread illiteracy among college graduates . . . want of competence effectively to read, write, and spell the English language, and even more to read, spell, or write any foreign language . . . accordingly . . . want of capacity to acquire and apply intelligence.' Beside it is a letter from a professor of economics, the distinguished graduate of European universities . . . who has taught at both Yale and Harvard, expressing dismay at the 'near-illiteracy' of his graduate students in both institutions." So the language difficulties which Oliver La Farge reports are not confined to the hinterland (see Chapter VIII, footnote 19).

increasing vulnerability to anxiety, that is, to the primal emergency system which is released or becomes dominant in proportion as mind (or neocortex) fails to reach proper functional maturity. Thus, to a greater degree perhaps than a people like the English, we are a prey to fear of the alien—which means in politics today principally a fear of communism. And our fear is exactly proportioned to the degree of ignorance and mental incoherence we bring to this or other problems of strangeness. Finally, fear whose biological function is to prepare the organism for direct violent action, acts as a wound spring in us, forever threatening to release, either on those at home who disagree with us or on those abroad who fill us with dread, a tremendous outpouring of aggression, a kind of ferocity by rebound.[24] This is our fundamental psychological situation: the "set" which will determine much that we

24. As is clear by now, this account of man's present predicament is somewhat different from Konrad Lorenz' in *On Aggression* (Harcourt, Brace, and World, 1966; see especially p. 236 ff.).

Lorenz' main point is that human ferocity, once useful and bred up by intraspecific selection, has now become unadaptive and creates in moderns a relentless pressure of aggression. He cites Margolin's study of the Ute Indians as an extreme example and sees the "death wish," manifested in their very high auto accident rate, as a kind of hostility turned against the self. In my view, the situation may be more complex. How much of the Utes' aggression (or of our own) is primary and how much arises as a rebound, or *contrecoup,* from chronic anxiety—the anxiety in turn arising from an inability to grasp or intellectually master the world in which they (and we) find ourselves? To be conclusive, Margolin's study should include physiological measures (for example, of the galvanic skin reflex and of resting-state skin resistance and circulatory catecholamine levels) which would permit strong inference as to the emotions habitually dominant in these people. The fact that better-educated Utes seem equally disturbed may merely mean that, like modern slum children, they come to their education too late for it to have real effect.

This is not to deny Lorenz' basic proposition. Unquestionably there has been strong selection pressure, breeding up the "warrior virtues," particularly in certain peoples. However, if sex and ferocity (and parental affection) comprise a subcortical "instinctive" system which, unlike the emergency system, is a natural ally of mind (or neocortex), it follows that the most ferocious peoples may also be those most apt, through the agency of great religions, to become highly civilized and rationally in command of themselves. The Europeans are perhaps evidence for that proposition, having once been the most savage of barbarians. What we are seeing today, in other words, is not a simple direct consequence of intraspecific selection; otherwise how do we explain the relatively tranquil civilized epochs of recent centuries? What may be happening, rather, is a return of primal ferocity, and more especially of primal fear, as mind deteriorates and the reclamation of parts of the Id through alliance with mind ceases.

do in the immediate future and on which any attempt at general improvement must intrude. How might any such intrusion begin? Granted a consensus could be found to permit such an attempt, what effect could it hope to have?

For if much of what I have said is correct, it follows that this book is addressed to a largely nonexistent public. It is unpleasant enough to be told, with some basis in evidence, that our whole way of life is founded upon certain grave mistakes which may be leading us into political calamity. It is harder still to accept that we may all, in some measure, have been deprived of our most essential selves.

> Or to say it another way: I believe that every human being is potentially capable, within his "limits," of fully "realizing" his potentialities; that this, his being cheated of it, is infinitely the ghastliest, commonest and most inclusive of all crimes of which the human world can accuse itself; and that the discovery and use of "consciousness" which has always been and is our deadliest enemy and deceiver, is also the source and guide of all hope and cure, and the only one.[25]

As against the minority, however, which may see itself mirrored in these pages, there is a majority which will never do so and not a few who, with or without reading them, will dismiss them as nonsense. By the time the truth of some of the principles I have suggested has been supported in the laboratory, if it is, we may be decades beyond the point at which sensible action might still have been possible. It may not in fact be possible now. By that I mean two things. The first has already been made clear: that since we are far along in "specialism"

---

25. James Agee, in *Let Us Now Praise Famous Men* (Houghton Mifflin, 1960), p. 307. It might be noted that as the servant of the Id, "consciousness" is indeed our "deadliest enemy and deceiver," which may be one reason why men, in eras in which it is becoming fit only for that role, become disenchanted with intellect and through their disdain of it complete its ruin. Hence the paradox of the modern anti-intellectual writer, of whom Hemingway was one. Far more is involved than a mere "sellout." Benda's "treason of the clerks" has its roots in a kind of devastating introspection, an awareness of mind's inadequacy, not in the world at large, but in oneself. For as an instrument of the Id—which is to say, an organ of adaptation or tribal behavior—mind's "inadequacy" consists in large part in its overpowering tendency to sacrifice truth telling to rationalization. This position, which begins to be taken with the intellectual "discovery" that there *is* no truth (as in logical positivism), ends up as that of Dr. Goebbels: the position that propaganda can make men believe anything, since lying to himself is man's natural way.

and find that mode of being both congenial and in a practical way indispensable to us, we are not likely to understand or welcome any challenge to it. The second is more fundamental and relates to the way in which, in general, consensus is arrived at in human affairs.

What history seems to say, and ethology to second, is that nothing men collectively do is ever done for purely logical reasons. One can amass overwhelming evidence that smoking conduces to lung cancer or war to extermination of all human life, but we continue in the majority to smoke and to fight. Only when the signs of cancer appear in *us,* or when *we* find ourselves in the front lines, do our convictions about smoking and war really come clear to us. In short, most of us are "response" types[26]—men whose fears, when keen enough, may propel them into a kind of clarity on the rebound and thence into action, but who lack the power to reach the same intensity of conviction through thought and imagination alone. We need "deadlines" or other clear immediate imperatives to drive us. Mind lacking the necessary momentum, we cannot bootstrap ourselves into true rationality, or a life of actions determined more by reason than by the combined effect of external circumstance and primal motivation. That being the case, by what methods can man be improved? Is he improvable at all? The evidence suggests that he is; but what then are the practical mechanics of the process? Can such improvement be carried far enough in our time to prevent the next of those "homeostatic" returns of the Id which have slowed and finally turned back each of the successive waves of human progress, as though no great culture, no body of aspirations, were strong enough in the end not to break on this ancient reef?

The fundamental difficulty for man—for us here and now—resides in a paradox. The paradox is that to obtain a consensus, whether good or bad in itself, rational or irrational, requires a grip first of all on the

26. "As one advances in life, one realizes more and more that the majority of men . . . are incapable of any other effort than that strictly imposed on them as a reaction to external compulsion. . . . For that reason the few individuals we have come across who are capable of a spontaneous and joyous effort stand out . . . monumentalized so to speak, in our experience. These are the select men . . . the only ones who are active and not merely reactive, for whom life is a perpetual striving, an incessant course of training. Training equals *askesis.* These are the ascetics." They are also what remains, in our day, of the fifteenth-century ideal of being described by Burckhardt (see Chapter V, page 76 above). The quotation here is from José Ortega y Gasset, *The Revolt of the Masses* (Norton, 1932), p. 72.

Id, since the intellect is in most men next to powerless and next to blind. This means that the reign of reason cannot begin with appeals to reason itself, for the reason appealed to is false—is the one "Ulysses shares with the foxes," not that which "Plato shares with God"—is the reason which rationalizes and subserves the Id, but never truly gives rise to "thinking." While, as I have tried to show, that difficulty is perhaps not due to a defect of *intelligence,* it is nonetheless formidable, condemning men not merely to mental confusion but to a kind of reflex dishonesty which is a principal source of their confusion. If it is not in our private adaptive interest to see certain truths, we almost literally cannot[27]—can scarcely extricate ourselves from the passionate muddle aroused in us by our double vision, the mind seeing what objectively is or should be, while the Id drives mind to deny or repress or crudely misinterpret the selfsame facts.

The great religions perhaps owed their power over men to the fact that their first appeal was not to reason, but to the Id. Here we come back to the question of the two roots of religion, mentioned several chapters ago. The first and perhaps older root is in fear, or the emergency system; and the primary effort of many religions has been to deliver man from the dominion of fear by the promise of some form of (literal, bodily) salvation. It is by doing that, one might say, that religions earn the right—really, in physiological terms, the power—to begin teaching us other things which lie more on the side of positive aspiration. Through the Id they obtain the keys to our attention. It is not enough, in short, for men to come over from a violent nomadic life to a settled agricultural one to become truly civilized or capable of culture. Many terrors remain, including the certainty that we must die and the ominous mystery of what, if anything, lies beyond. It is religion's function to complete the emotional shift, or shift from dominance of the emergency system to that of the sexual, which begins with a more ordered agricultural life.

Having by promises of blessedness and ultimate deliverance established a kind of animal serenity in its flock, the church may then, by its more lucid moral teachings, encourage the appearance of men who have achieved real "centrality"; that is, a radically new power and independence of mind and a proportionately increased control over

27. As in the slang phrase for something we dislike: "I can't *see* that."

their instinctive selves. But such men, while they understand many things, usually do not understand their own psychological origins, the processes by which powers such as their own have at last come to fulfillment. What they *do* see is the fearful amount of nonsense the church teaches and the fearful things it does as simply one human institution, or pecking-order, among others. As a result, anticlericalism and agnosticism begin among the really enlightened, who can stand it, and presently spread to the mass of mankind who cannot—who are inundated by fear and a slow wrath of desperation. The church, no longer a bulwark against these ancestral emotional evils, becomes hated almost as a betrayer of the race.[28] The very universe becomes hated as a wilderness in which parental warmth has died and God the Father vanished.[29] With the return of fear, or dominance of the emergency system, the family, or domestic warmth, also begins to fail, even as men, in their panic, huddle together in what remains of sexual bliss, often abandoning their families in order to find it elsewhere, when desire has gone dead at home:

28. The Grand Inquisitor: "But Thou wouldst not deprive man of freedom, . . . thinking, what is that freedom worth if obedience is bought with bread? . . . Dost Thou know that the ages will pass, and humanity will proclaim by the lips of their sages that there is no crime, and therefore no sin; there is only hunger? 'Feed men and ask of them virtue!' that's what they'll write on the banner which they'll raise against Thee, and with which they will destroy Thy temple. Where [it] stood will rise a new building; the terrible Tower of Babel will be built again and though, like the one of old it will not be finished, yet Thou might have prevented that new tower and . . . cut short the sufferings of men for a thousand years; for they will come back to us. . . . They will seek us again, hidden underground in the catacombs, for we shall be persecuted and tortured. They will find us and cry to us 'Feed us, for those who have promised us fire from heaven haven't given it!'
"There will be [again] thousands of millions of happy babes. . . . Peacefully they will die . . . in Thy name, and beyond the grave they will find nothing but death. But we shall keep the secret. . . . It is prophesied that Thou wilt come again in victory . . . with Thy chosen . . . but we will say they have only saved themselves [while] we have saved all." Fëdor Dostoevski, *The Brothers Karamazov* (Modern Library), pp. 310, 318.

29. "In its critical aspect, the revolutionary movement of our times is primarily a violent denunciation of the formal hypocrisy which presides over bourgeois society. . . . After the French Revolution, the transcendence of the formal principles of reason or justice serves to justify a rule that is neither just nor reasonable. God is dead, but as Stirner predicted, *the morality of principles in which the memory of God is still preserved must also be killed. The hatred of formal virtue . . . has remained one of the principal themes of history today.*

We will build a world of our own
That no one else can share
Our sorrow we will leave behind us, there
No one can find us there
When we build a world of our own

says a sad popular song of this decade. ("Ah, love, let us be true/To
one another" for as long as the Id will allow.) The reality of our time,
as opposed to its yearning, is better expressed in Yeats' "Second Coming":

Turning and turning in a widening gyre
The falcon cannot hear the falconer;
Things fall apart; the centre cannot hold;
Mere anarchy is loosed upon the world,
The blood-dimmed tide is loosed, and everywhere
The ceremony of innocence is drowned;
The best lack all conviction while the worst
Are full of passionate intensity. . . .[30]

The poem ends with:

And what rough beast, its hour come round at last,
Slouches to Bethlehem to be born?

What humanist doctrine, arising now as the centuries-long cycle
completes itself and the rough beast slouches to Bethlehem (Pennsylvania?) to be born, can hope to do what Christianity in its distant
springtime did? It is useless to tell men, convinced that we have no
principle of transcendence built into us, that really we *do* have; that salvation *is* possible, maybe not for us here and now, but for our children

Nothing is pure; that is the cry which convulses our period. Impurity . . . is
going to become the rule, and the abandoned earth will be delivered to naked
force" (italics mine). Albert Camus, *The Rebel* (Vintage, 1956), pp. 135–136.

30. W. B. Yeats, *Collected Poems* (Macmillan, 1951), p. 184. This poem was
part of a collection first published in 1921 and is therefore roughly contempora-
neous with "The Wasteland." It anticipates some remarks made much later by
Dr. Robert Lindner (New York *Times*, April 17, 1955), who "declared that if
society continued on its present course 'we will unquestionably enter another
dark age, with blackouts on opinion, checks and restraints on freedom of expression, and what is most important, inaccessibility of knowledge. . . . We are
entering an era that will be dominated by primitive emotional appeals, rather
than reason.' "

if only we will make certain difficult and subtle sacrifices, will force ourselves to believe in ideas and principles long since abandoned as meaningless. To the man of the Id, which most of us are, what kind of a bargain is that? Our most pressing problems *are* here and now: to survive, to fight off the horror of existence as we really see it, to ease the uncertainty and pain and fear of day-to-day life as best we may, and to discharge, if we are lucky, some of the tension or blind "activation" generated in us by our relentlessly overactive emergency systems on an officially sanctioned competitor or victim or enemy. What is wanted is a doctrine with immediacy—some form of political or religious revivalism, a Cause permitting the release of much pent-up feeling at the smallest possible cost in thought; or failing these, the pleasures of material ambition satisfied; status, physical comfort, and various other forms of anesthesia ("We will build a world of our own") —all fragile solutions, admittedly, but *direct* and in a sense proven; incredibly ancient. By contrast, the ideal of Universal Man, of the rational I—powerful and free to the point that one becomes rationally good and disinterestedly interested in all things—seems a pale sort of alternative, if not a dream. Even the rare man we meet who appears to have achieved grace of that sort is not really welcome among us— is more an accusation and an object of dislike or suspicion than a model for anything we ourselves might hope to become. Once ideals have died, they cannot, it would seem, be willed back to life—given renewed emotional authority simply because reason sees the need.

Possibly at the bottom of this phenomenon there lies another, touched upon several chapters ago. The stock of ideas which comes to comprise a people's tradition may be quite large, as ours is, and quite mutable; but it is for all that finite and perhaps limited in another way, in that it represents a repertoire of transforms of a certain fundamental logic—a set of basic theorems, overlaid by a multitude of later elaborations, in themselves without real novelty.

Something of the fundamental logic of various traditions may be reflected in the grammatical structure of their corresponding languages, although that implies no necessarily fixed limitation. We have lately become aware of some of the logical restrictions, or presuppositions, concealed in our own language and taken steps to get round them. Spengler's notion of the culture "soul" implies a hypothesis of the basic fixity of traditions, such that once a certain number of variations on its fundamental themes have been run, the tradition and its accompanying culture are exhausted. From the great flexibility which modern systems of thought such as mathematics have shown, I am inclined to believe that that hypothesis may be wrong. It is true, probably, that a given man, having reached middle age, will, no matter how intellectually gifted or free, have developed a *certain* organization of his working principles (or in his neocortex, of abstract memories) which he will thereafter find it increasingly difficult to change in any major way. Nonetheless, given a community of men properly developed in mind, the pace of change between generations becomes, as we have seen in mathematics, extremely rapid, and the unpredictability of the *course* of change seems to increase with the pace itself. If Spengler's fundamental supposition were correct, it is doubtful if the foregoing would be so. Indeed, according to his timetable, we should have ceased making this sort of progress some while ago.

It might be more correct to say that traditions do not logically exhaust themselves and so fail: rather, they become increasingly useless, because increasingly incomprehensible, to those who inherit them. In turn, this phenomenon may be due to the processes I have described by which mind, in late skeptical eras, unwittingly liquidates itself. While those processes involve certain profound errors—essentially defects in self-understanding—they are not attributable to errors or limitations of the tradition as such (witness the fact that men's traditions have varied greatly in their root ideas and in the arts and intellectual works they have produced, whereas all the great cultures appear to have had approximately the same life span and to have ended in a similar emotional and political climate). However, with the contraction of mind—statistically a per capita decrease in the number of "whole" men, with all that that implies in loss of both rational perspective and moral force—traditions may come to have a massive inertia, standing at last between men and reality as an impenetrable screen of stock thoughts, half meaningless and totally incapable of further development, but preserved from long habit and used in the futile "explanation" of everything. Like our spoken clichés or the spinning of prayer wheels in the Orient, they "stand for" motions of the mind which no one is really making any longer.[31] The same armamentarium

31. That is, Man the New Barbarian can grasp the older forms, but cannot really respond to them or continue their evolution. At this stage traditions freeze

of mental heirlooms becomes the ground for an obstructive pride in peoples such as the Moslems or prerevolutionary Chinese, who feel they *have* culture once and for all, the rest of the world being merely the barbaric periphery. Such complacency is forced to overlook much that is embarrassing in the present; but late civilized man is nothing if not a rationalizer.[32] There is something of the same serene assurance in our own scientific community, which is little disposed to wonder or open-mindedness in certain directions and all too prone to make light of or simply ignore problems beyond its competence of the moment. These are perhaps vices of empiricism in its late middle age—the complacency which comes of having in one's pocket keys which will infallibly open certain little doors.

What then are we left with? Suppose that in a few years time physiological psychologists show beyond a doubt that the ideal of "centrality" or Universal Man, about which I have said so much, is in fact a realizable one and does in fact depend on principles of brain organi-

---

into an immobility which may last for millenniums, and the language, except where preserved by a mandarin class, regresses because many distinctions and subtleties once thought important and arrived at with much effort simply drop out of use.

"Words grow longer and more ambiguous. Instead of style there is rhetoric. Instead of precise common usage there is jargon. . . . All these technical failures accumulate to the essential failure: the language no longer sharpens thought but blurs it. . . . In short the language is no longer lived; it is merely spoken."

(George Steiner; in Language and Silence, p. 96. He is speaking of the changes in German since Bismarck's time, but the description applies equally to modern English.)

In parallel with this change, the content not only of the popular arts but of *avant garde* works begins to evaporate and what is left is simply ferocious spectacle, a malignant triumph of the Id as in Pinter's Homecoming, the film Breathless, or the play of a few years ago in which the hero, a middle aged homosexual, is beaten to death by his boy friends of the evening. A similar nakedness, devoid of meaning or insight, seems to have been a feature of the drama in late classical times:

"Human immolation also assumed *recherché* dramatic forms. The Colosseum was the scene of theatrical performances in which the murders were not fictitious but real. Under Domitian the public was able to see plays in which one criminal plunged his right hand into a fire, and another prisoner was crucified. Such spectacles in the amphitheater outdid the Circus Games and in the end cleared the theaters. . ."

(Michael Grant, The World of Rome, World Pub. Co., 1960, p. 124)

32. On the simple principle that stupidity, either innate or as intellect *manqué,* is a natural wellspring of self-deception.

zation roughly like those I have stated here. Will such a discovery, with the full authority of science behind it, really be able to change the tenor of our parental care and our formal education—not to say our customs and public morality? Will we, in a decade, say, or over a generation or two, be persuaded to bring about such radical and apparently unrealistic reforms in our own outlook—and do so with no supernaturalist sops to throw to the Id, no heaven or hell to console us or harden our resolve? I rather doubt it.

The problem is the inertia, not of traditions, but of living men. What of the millions of pupils and teachers and parents, all cut from the same psychological cloth—in this country, unbelievably uniform —who can only view with dismay and incomprehension ideas so alien, can only be made uncertain and resentful by any such odd program which logic and scientific fact between them might seem to dictate? Already, perhaps, the past stands too massively between us and what might be our rational salvation. Like the Chinese, we have the Way, are hypnotized by successes not really our own, and proportionately inaccessible to those very powers of reason and imagining which laid the foundations of our present grandeur.

Whether science proves me right or wrong, whether other psychological theories better and more persuasive than this one arise to tell us what should be done, my guess is that we will do nothing—will shut our eyes which already see so little and follow the course we have set out on to its end. The time when that decisive leap forward in self-understanding might most naturally occur, bringing not a handful but large numbers of mankind to the condition we like to regard as human, lies, if anywhere, in the more distant future—in the springtime of a religion of which Christianity will be seen to have been but a primitive precursor. We are left, in meantime, with very little.

I should have liked to close on a more splendid note. Toward the end of *The Decline of the West,* Spengler wrote:

> With the formed state, high history lays itself down weary to sleep. Man becomes a plant again, adhering to the soil, dumb and enduring. The timeless village and the "eternal" peasant reappear, begetting children and burying seed in the Mother Earth—a busy . . . swarm over which the tempest of soldier-emperors passingly blows. In the midst of the land lie the old world-cities, empty receptacles of an extinguished soul, in which a historyless mankind slowly nests itself. Men live from

hand to mouth, with petty thrifts and petty fortunes, and endure. Masses are trampled on in the conflicts of the conquerors who contend for power and the spoil of this world, but the survivors fill up the gaps with a primitive fertility and suffer on. . . . It is a drama noble in its aimlessness . . . as the course of the stars. . . . We may marvel at it or we may lament it —but it is there.[33]

To the prosaic mind of an Anglo-Saxon this spectacle, which overpopulation may make infinitely more horrible, is quite devoid of grandeur. It also, I think, lacks the qualities of the fated and the mysterious with which Spengler invested it. Genuine tragedy, in life perhaps as well as in plays or novels, seems to appear chiefly at the zenith of cultures, when men of the stature to *be* tragic are produced in the greatest number. There is little one could call tragic in the aftermath Spengler describes, any more than there is in the world of the present. Both are characterized by the brutal inadequacy of victor and victim alike, by sufferings not deeply enough felt or clearly enough understood to eventuate in anything but more of the same—a deepening of the horrors Camus has so thoroughly anatomized. In contrast to real tragedy, these events are in no understandable human sense *necessary*. Despite the scale on which they are occurring, there is about them an emptiness and perverse stupidity which make them almost trivial. The German massacres of the 1930's and 1940's, the incredible slaughters in postwar India, the decades of official cruelty and murder in China, the recent blood bath in Indonesia, the Russian obliteration of the Hungarian freedom movement, the American dismemberment of Viet Nam —all have had a kind of blind almost mechanical impetus, have been so disproportioned to any sane or definable purpose as to seem the reflex actions of animals. That, in fact, is what they are. What we are witnessing, if my analysis to this point has been correct, is yet another of those periodic victories of instinct which reduce history to a battle as senseless as a melee of sharks. Whereas religions are part truth and part nonsense, "modern" ideologies are nonsense pure—the purer the better, to accommodate the shrunken intelligence of the faithful. The concept of *propaganda* could only arise in eras like this one, since at bottom it is both cynical and anti-intellectual. The propagandist does

33. Oswald Spengler, *The Decline of the West* (Knopf, 1932), II, 435.

not distort the truth; he treats it as a total irrelevance, as nonexistent. No Shakespeare has arisen to ennoble our age, because it cannot be ennobled. One simply waits, hoping that the Darwinian tics of those in power will not cause the very worst to happen and trying to control one's shame and disgust at being a member of this dreadful species.

Some may find consolation in Toynbee's view:

> By A.D. 4047 the distinction—which looms large today—between the Western civilization as an aggressor, and the other civilizations as its victims, will probably seem unimportant [or will long since have been turned around]. . . . What will stand out will be a single great experience, common to the whole of mankind: the experience of having one's parochial social heritage battered to bits by collision with the parochial heritages of other civilizations, and then finding . . . a new common life springing up out of the wreckage. . . . The historians of 5047 A.D. will say, I fancy, that the importance of this social unification of mankind was not to be found in the field of technics and economics . . . not in the field of war and politics, but in the field of religion.[34]

As an empiricist, however, I cannot but wonder what may go wrong in the meantime, not merely through overpopulation, but as a consequence of those mutilations of our genes and those massive and enduring mutilations of the earth itself which are likely to result from nuclear war. The problem is no longer simply the philosophic one of understanding history, but the practical one of controlling it. If our techniques and our population were those of half a millennium ago, we might have afforded yet another "interregnum of the spirit"—have lapsed into a new Dark Age and emerged finally into the daybreak of a more lucid faith. But that is not our situation. Returning this time, the Id finds itself in possession of fearful instruments and of a world ripe by sheer numbers for famine and degradation on an undreamt-of scale. We are trapped, as Freud might have said, between Eros and Thanatos. That being so, we must bootstrap ourselves out of our animality in new ways, and quickly, or face better than even odds of becoming an evolutionary casualty—victims of biological "virtues" indispensable in Neolithic times but suicidal now.

What I have tried to show are some of the psychic principles and

---

34. Arnold Toynbee, *Civilization on Trial* (Oxford, 1948), p. 215.

processes which have brought us to that predicament. I have tried to "explain" the kind of man described by Ortega y Gasset: the man whose prevalence throughout human society today *is* our predicament.

> The average type of European at present possesses a soul healthier and stronger, it is true, than those of the last century *but much more simple.* *Hence at times he leaves the impression of a primitive man suddenly risen in the midst of a very old civilization* [italics mine]. In the schools which were such a source of pride to the last century it has been impossible to do more than instruct the masses in the technique of modern life; it has been found impossible to educate them. They have been given the tools for an intenser form of existence but no feeling for their . . . historic duties. They have been hurriedly inoculated with the pride and power of modern instruments, but not with their spirit. . . . They will have nothing to do with their spirit. . . . The new generations are getting ready to take over command of the world as if [it] were a paradise without trace of former footsteps.[35]

In the not distant future, it may be almost literally that—and better so perhaps than the world foreseen by Khrushchev, in which the living will have come to envy the dead. It is sad, indeed a monstrous absurdity, that the long and not wholly blind effort represented by man's history should end by confronting him with such possibilities. But that, in fact, is how the matter stands.

---

35. Ortega y Gasset, *The Revolt of the Masses* p. 55.

Just recently, writing in *The Yale Alumni Magazine,* (January 1969) Robert Jay Lifton said: "I have become convinced that contemporary psychological patterns are creating a new kind of man—a 'protean man.' "

This type might be described as Man the Amorph desperately in search of himself, experimenting with new identities, trying one *persona* after another.

"While he is by no means without yearning for the absolute, he finds fragmentary images more acceptable than the complete ideologies of the past."

Often feeling himself an orphan, which in the deepest sense he is, being cut off from the past by his own psychic diminution, he "responds with diffuse fear and anger. But he can neither find a good cause for the former nor a consistent target for the latter. . . . His difficulty is that focused indignation is as hard for him to sustain as any single identification or conviction."

Not only have religious notions of immortality lost their hold on him; the Bomb, by its very existence, threatens what Lifton calls "symbolic immortality" as well. Of what value were the masterpieces of scientific reason if they led to this grotesque impasse? Why think at all, if thinking in the end only sharpens the claws of instinct? Why not give up and simply *be* an animal?

## EPILOGUE

In making what I felt to be my major points, I am aware of having omitted or grossly simplified much. At that, the several earlier chapters dealing with mind-brain relations may ask a great deal of readers belonging to the nonscientific wing of C. P. Snow's double culture. For that reason I have avoided anatomizing the psyche further — have said next to nothing about the components of the "unconscious," about the central nervous mechanisms possibly involved in "repression," about "temporary" versus "permanent" memory or the processes of "consolidation"; about dream symbolism or the "analogical reflex"; or about many other things. I have discussed almost none of the profound psychic changes that occur during adolescence and have cited but the scantiest evidence relating to the way in which mind or the self-aware self may begin to take shape in childhood.

Some of the foregoing are considered in detail in my earlier publications (see Bibliography); and others I hope to take up shortly. The psychological "system" that I have outlined is similar in some respects to Freud's, although quite differently arrived at. It also differs from Freud's in major ways, especially on the question of sublimation and in the role assigned to the rational I. In his distrust of the powers of the I or ego and in the almost unqualified dominion he grants the unconscious (really nonconscious) Id, Freud was perhaps less the scientific visionary and more a spokesman for the prejudices of his age than we, his near contemporaries, are likely to see. He nonetheless arrived at much that was new, although the therapy evolved by Freud himself and practised by a generation of psychiatrists since may have been premature and without real result.[1] In the case of the psyche, because of the unique subtlety of its workings and the virtually irreversible effects of early experience,

---

1. The clinical failure of psychoanalysis has been discussed by a number of writers, including Eysenck, Sargant, Allen Wheelis (who gives a most discouraging insider's view in *The Quest for Identity* [Norton, 1958], pp. 124 ff), and Percival Bailey. See, for instance, Bailey in *Perspectives in Biology and Medicine*, Vol. 4, No. 2 (1961), p. 239.

there may be no such thing as curative medicine, only preventive. My belief is that the really reliable evidence we have both from the clinic and from animal experimentation supports that idea. For this reason and for others, I think that we can expect little help from psychiatry in our present emergency. Simply as treatment, let alone as the source of a *Weltanschauung,* the counseling or analysis that a few patients can afford, the "tranquilizers" that calm the Id by a literal numbing of its higher centers of representation, or the more drastic procedures such as electroshock or resection of brain tissue that grossly deform or blunt the mentally ill in the interests of their salvation, are all sadly inadequate and in future may seem as "medieval" as confession and bloodletting and the flogging of the insane now seem to us. Nor has the explanatory power of psychoanalytic doctrine, applied to history, proved very great. It neither accounts, in a clear, consistent way, for large clusters of fact nor really explains how the few men in history who achieved "wholeness" may have managed to do so.

The theorem underlying the view of human nature outlined in this book is, so far as I know, a new one. It says that man, because of the absolute extent of his neocortex, is unique among animals in being the only one that cannot come to full efficiency, or even to full creature contentment, through a life of pure adaptation. The reason he cannot is that that mode of existence leaves an important part of his central nervous system in a state of functional underdevelopment[2] and the whole consequently in a state of nearly chronic imbalance. As the organ par excellence both of reason and of "character" or rational self-mastery, the human neocortex, I believe, requires a system of abstract memories (equivalent to a general "retrieval" system or unifier of cerebral function) embodying principles more objectively valid than any that men are likely to arrive at merely through their herd behavior and the pursuit of creature rewards. Like it or not, man's task is then to bootstrap himself out of his perennially uneasy animality: to become not just what he genetically is, but what he humanly might be.

2. It has been shown, in rats, that those raised in an environment "enriched" with toys, stimuli to exploration, and so on, have at maturity significantly thicker and better-structured cortices than do litter-mates fed the same diet, raised in the same sort of cage, but starved of such "extras." Hence in the brain, as in the skeletal muscles, function can, within limits, greatly alter structure. See M. C. Diamond *et al.,* in *Journal of Comparative Neurology,* Vol. 128 (1966), pp. 117–125.

From this theorem, there follows a set of conclusions that will seem paradoxical to many but may nonetheless account, as other theories have not done, for certain facts of history. The first is that man's greatest intellectual, artistic, and political advances may necessarily have come in the wake of his higher religions (or more accurately, his higher religiousness). The second is that scepticism — understood as a worldly practicality, with or without the supposed sanction of science[3] — may of necessity be self-liquidating, resulting in periods such as the late Roman or our own, in which the inner development of man and finally even his material progress go into reverse. The third and perhaps most paradoxical conclusion of all is that even man's creature self and his creature pleasures may tend to remain stunted when his "higher" self is denied realization.[4] The reason this may be so is that in the course of evolution instinctive behavior has evidently become less and less a matter of "total patterns" and more and more a process whereby innate mechanisms, the bits and pieces of instinctive behavior, come to be synthesized into working wholes through the action of experience and consequent learning. It is this trend that has given higher mammalian forms their superior adaptability or the freedom to mold their behavior to the oddities of circumstance. In proportion as mind, in man, approaches full development, it may, by that fact, become able to reach down into the Id and further the processes of functional differentiation there. As a result, sexuality and ferocity, which are physiologically closely related,[5] may tend in men of high cultures to become clearly distinct from each other, whereas in psychic primitives or the regressed they remain more or less fused.[6]

In human history this differentiation of the instinctive self might

3. In ancient Rome, China, or Egypt, largely without.

4. From Margaret Mead's *Coming of Age in Samoa* (Morrow, 1928) and numerous studies of American Indian life, one gets the impression not only that tribal man is not very clearly aware of his own or his fellows' identity, but also that tribal life including art and love-making is haunted by a certain flatness or perennial depression. How much this depression is due to the alien presence, represented by the observer, is difficult to say.

5. C. M. Fair, *The Physical Foundations of the Psyche* (Wesleyan, 1963), pp. 21–22.

6. Hence rape, or gang attacks on women, occur chiefly among slum primitives or men primitivized by war. The connection between love-making and assault, in the common mind, is shown by the use of "fuck" or "screw" to mean victimize.

therefore be expected to run in parallel with the emergence of intellect and imagination, since physiologically these two sets of events are complementary. The ideal love of which the troubadours and knight-poets[7] of the Middle Ages sang may thus have been not merely a lovely fancy but the natural counterpart, and in a sense the prophecy, of unrelated forms of great accomplishment just then beginning.

Finally if my analysis of the human (psychological) condition is close to the truth, it follows that man is unique among creatures in being condemned from the outset to long millenniums of turbulence and discontent, even under the best of external circumstances, or when his adaptive success has minimized the more obvious causes of his distress. Properly understood, the "sense of sin" is perhaps the beginning of his awareness of his own psychic predicament, a discrepancy gauge which tells him the fearful distance that lies between the self as it is and as it might be. The quest for happiness then becomes really a quest for "grace." And if sin is taken to mean not this or that specific offense, but the cardinal offense of trying to live simply as a supremely proud, supremely crafty animal, the "darkness of sin" may for vast numbers be a literal reality — a state of torment and inner blindness that are natural features of the I half-formed. Sin in the more sophisticated sense is the refusal to admit that there may be anything wrong with this program, even though a distant voice, the uneasiness of the aborted soul, tells us otherwise. This stubbornness in the face of one's own misery, as it acts in fact to perpetuate and even to worsen the conditions that produced it, is the essence of what the older moralists called the state of damnation. We have given it other names (neurosis, alienation) without, I think, really understanding it.

Following the overt destruction of Victorian standards (long ago covertly destroyed by the Victorians themselves), we have entered an era of libertinism the results of which, in the light of our realistic *idées fixes,* are puzzling. The lifting of sexual repressions, the easing of conflict which Freud and others evidently expected to come when men stopped taking extreme idealist positions and began to "accept" themselves, should by now have eventuated in a more relaxed, more humane and

---

7. For instance, Thibaut of Champagne who is said to have covered the walls in his chateau with verse, none of which, unfortunately, survived. Those of his love-poems (on paper) that have come down to us are fine examples of the *genre.*

permissive way of life. In fact we have become somewhat more humane and permissive, for instance, in the treatment of children or of rebellious minorities at home, but that may be mostly due to the lingering influence of the Christian past. The ease of spirit and the improved psychological health for which we hoped, have *not* come, even with the unprecedented affluence of the past two decades. Our crime rates continue to rise,[8] and in our sex lives we appear to be bedeviled by odd abnormalities and a widespread jadedness.

The resort to promiscuity or in the extreme to orgiastic sex games, which is a feature of modern life, although one not easy to document statistically, has I think, a definite meaning. It is not simply that we are indulging ourselves sexually as never before; we are also in the process depersonalizing an act that our highest tradition had made intensely personal and private. Essentially, perhaps, we are submerging ourselves, using drugs or alcohol or free-wheeling sex to overwhelm what is left of the I, drowning the self that discriminates and chooses in the Id, which is no respecter of persons, oneself included. Better no "me" at all than the shapeless, doubt-ridden, anxiety-vexed one that most of us as adults find ourselves to be. Better the Dionysian abandon of the romantics than the grey vacancy of the conscious life as we are obliged to live it. This, fundamentally, is the ground of our anti-intellectualism. Like the Germans of three decades ago, we are turning against mind, because the further promises of rationality have not been fulfilled; because as the I dies, all that was once clear and beautiful to it becomes opaque and ugly.[9] And yet we know that there are others for whom even now that

8. In an interview on NBC television on July 2, 1968, Attorney-General Ramsay Clark reported that the ten-to-eighteen-year-old group accounts for 13 per cent of our population, but approximately 50 per cent of all "property" crimes. He added that juveniles were not a comparable problem in England.

The most recent F.B.I. report (*New York Times* August 27, 1968) showed "serious crime" up by 18 per cent in the preceding year. The news account cited included an interview with a Harvard Law School criminologist, L. E. Ohlin, who had formerly been critical of F.B.I. statistics. Apropos of the present report, he was quoted as saying, "Although I'm pretty good at explaining crime increases, I simply do not have an explanation for this." New York City's rate per 100,000 of violent crimes was approximately double the national average.

9. It is all the easier to despise intellectuals too when so many have become the *reductio ad absurdum* of their species. But these are simply used as a stick to beat the real enemy, a way of destroying a once noble ideal by associating it with the effete and niggling and mean-spirited. Those who use this technique, how-

is not so; indeed, we know that it was such men who made much of the present world possible; and because the difference between ourselves and them is irreparable, it can never be forgiven. In the end it will be punished. The same civilization that becomes orgiastic in its old age is apt eventually to kill those who will not join the party. This is the point that, I believe, we are now approaching.

In physiological terms, the neocortex has begun to fall far short of that minimum of functional development necessary to its own dominance and is ceding control to its ancient masters accordingly. Nor is this process confined to certain social classes, as was more the case formerly. The parallel in our social life is a progressive collapse of rational restraint, not only on our sexual behavior, but on violence or other forms of primitive self-seeking. The age of sexual freedom also becomes that of the riot, with or without good ostensible causes (Lauderdale, Berkeley, Columbia), and that of the crime of pure perversity (see above, p. 134, footnote 27). And it is the younger generations who most clearly act out this inner change, not simply from the greater energy of youth but also because in them the psychic diminishment that I have described may be reaching a critical phase in which both identity and the capacity for compromise or a reasoned tolerance are decisively breaking down.

Dr. Robert Lindner, the author of *Rebel Without a Cause,* told a Los Angeles audience:

> "The brute fact of today is that our youth is no longer in rebellion but in a condition of downright active . . . mutiny. Within the memory of every living adult, a profound and terrifying change has overtaken adolescence." Dr. Lindner isolated two main aspects of this change. One is the tendency of today's youth to "act out . . . his inner turmoil, in direct contrast to the suffering out of the same . . . turmoil by adolescents of yesteryear." The other peculiar trait of the modern adolescent is, according to Dr. Lindner, "the abandonment of that solitude which was at once the trademark of adolescence and the source of its deepest despairs [and] ecstasies. . . . Frequently this solitude was creative. From it sometimes came the dreams, the hopes and the soaring aims that charged life thenceforward with meaning and [gave] us our poets, artists, and scientists. . . . But youth today has abandoned solitude in favor of pack-running,

ever, are rarely interested in such distinctions or much concerned with the honesty of their own methods.

of predatory assembly, of collectivities that bury if they do not destroy, individuality . . . In the . . . herd or gang, it is a mass mind that operates — a mind without subtlety, without compassion."[10]

The abandonment of solitude,[11] the immersion of oneself in some sort of collectivity (often not a destructive one, sometimes merely the Establishment) follow naturally, perhaps, from the fact that mind is no longer up to the anguish of "finding itself" because there is not now enough to find (and too little patience to look). The group does not destroy identity; it supplies one for men of this psychic type; and as I have tried to show, this development has been longer in coming than we sometimes think. Writing in 1896, Le Bon said:

> The divine right of masses is about to replace the divine right of kings. The writers who enjoy the favor of our middle classes . . . display profound alarm at this new power which they see growing. . . . They talk to us of the bankruptcy of science. . . . There has been no bankruptcy of science; and science has had no share in the present intellectual anarchy. . . . Certainly it is possible that the advent to power of the masses marks one of the last stages of Western civilisation.[12]

I believe that it does, and for reasons far deeper and more complex than the "laws," if any, that govern the behavior of crowds.

What I have tried to show in this book are the principles according to which "the masses" came into being in their present form, or more accurately the psychic "laws" that make for the appearance, and disappearance again, of human identity on the stage of history. An interesting feature of that account is that it not only plausibly relates these "laws" to the physiology of the nervous system, but also leads to conclusions the reverse of those reached by logical positivism or American pragmatists such as John Dewey.[13] Much of modern thought has tended toward

10. In Dwight MacDonald's "A Caste A Culture A Market," *The New Yorker,* November 29, 1958.

11. A classmate of mine at our old boarding school stayed on to become a master after our graduation in 1936. Years later he told me that during World War II and just afterwards the boys suddenly and for no clear reason gave up the optional activites of hut-building and roaming in the woods, which were the cherished privilege of loners in my day. In the same period, the spontaneous discussion groups or daily teas at masters' houses ceased for want of attendance. "They want everything organized now," my friend said.

12. Gustave Le Bon, *The Crowd,* Benn, Ernest (London, 1952), pp. 16–17.

13. Of whom Santayana said: "In Dewey, as in current science, there is a

the view that there is no real basis for preferring one system of morality over others. In effect, that view has reduced morals to ethics and idealism to an enlightened practicality. The good is what, on the whole, works and can be enforced. Good and bad are better defined as the adaptive and the unadaptive; and adaptiveness itself is defined from the standpoint of the collectivity or tribe. What is good for the tribe becomes the summit of adaptiveness (hence the sense of absolute *rightness* that sustains everyone's nationalism; hence our present almost global impasse).

If my account of the way in which the self arises out of the brain is approximately correct, it becomes clear that there *is* a real basis for preferring one morality over another; and the type of morality deserving preference is a perfectly definable one. As Ortega y Gasset said of liberalism,[14] it may be "a discipline too difficult and complex to take firm root on earth"; but, on the other hand, if something like it does not do so, we may be, in quite a literal sense, doomed — absurdly enough by our dedication to ideas of the good that we believe to be corroborated by science and the height of common sense.

... tendency to dissolve the individual into his social functions, as well as everything substantial and actual into something relative and transitional." By substituting "inquiry" for truth, Dewey lets mind out of difficulties of synthesis now perhaps becoming too much for it and in so doing involves himself in certain logical absurdities. For an analysis of some of these, see Bertrand Russell, *A History of Western Philosophy* (Simon & Schuster, 1945), pp. 819 ff.

14. And might better have said of its parent, Christianity.

# INDEX